Circle of Triumph
The Bobby Allison Story

Circle of Triumph

The Bobby Allison Story

By Ben White

Edited by Steve Waid

Produced by
GRIGGS PUBLISHING CO. INC.
Concord, N.C.

For Eva and Aaron

Cover photo by Elmer Kappell
Cover design by Carolyn Hemingway
Book design by Zelly Drye

Manufactured and Printed in the USA

Library of Congress Catalog Card Number: 92-082984

White, Ben
   Circle of Triumph, The Bobby Allison Story

This book is dedicated to the memories
of

Edmond Jacob "Pop" Allison

and

Clifford Lawrence Allison

Edmond Jacob "Pop" Allison
1905 - 1992

Clifford Lawrence Allison
1964 - 1992

ACKNOWLEDGEMENTS

It is very difficult to express in words the depth of gratitude felt toward those who have played such an instrumental part in the completion of this book. Without them, it would not have become reality.

To my wife, Eva, who gave total support to this project from the minute it was first discussed as a possibility. She always offered positive comments and at times, kept my spirits up when faced with many hours of work. My deepest love and appreciation goes out to her for being so considerate of the need to write.

To my 16-month old son, Aaron, who contributed to the effort at times when Dad needed a smile or a hug. His timing was always perfect and his occasionally coming into my office with a children's book to read would always be a welcome and needed interruption. There's no way to express the amount of joy I've gotten from him in the short amount of time with us.

To motorsports historian Greg Fielden, who played an instrumental role by providing facts and figures for this project through his "Forty Years In Stock Car Racing" series. There were also many consultations in an effort to insure total accuracy.

To John McMullin, executive producer of MRN Radio, for allowing some broadcast dialogue from the Miller Genuine Draft 500 NASCAR Winston Cup race held on June 19, 1988 to be included.

To Robert and Betty Griggs, for allowing the use of the publications Winston Cup Scene, Winston Cup Illustrated and American Racing Classics as reference materials. Selected quotes and information from the past have come from those publications.

To Becky and Donna Brown, for working diligently transcribing countless tapes of interviews with various people who played key roles in Bobby Allison's career. Their exhaustive efforts are most appreciated.

To Steve Waid, for his meticulous editing of the book simply to make it more enjoyable for the reader.

To Zelly Drye, for her production expertise, Carolyn Hemingway for creative designs of the cover and center-spread and proofreaders Kim Nash, Helen Rodgers, Pat Hite, Jennifer Arbogast and Elaine Helton. Each has played a significant role in the production of this book.

Then, there are those who have helped indirectly: Donnie Johnson; Ed Gossage; Tom Roberts; Carolyn Carrier; Gary McCredie; Deb Williams; Al Thomy; Jim Fluharty; Frank Vehorn; Elmer Kappell; Paul Brooks; Jimmy Fennig, Donna Cox and Zeta Smith. Their advice or assistance has been most helpful.

To the entire Allison family, who also gave of its time. Even though all are obviously not directly recognizable within these pages, each has contributed heavily to the story with information retrieved from family letters as well as childhood recollections.

And then, there are Bobby and Judy Allison. Each have given of their time freely and patiently on countless occasions and made me feel welcome within their family. Through extensive interviews and conversations, both have helped immensely to reconstruct the story in as much detail as possible. Bobby's present day thoughts are reflected in italics.

And finally, to the children, Davey, Bonnie, Carrie and the late Clifford Allison. Each were very helpful and expressed their excitement that a book was finally being done about their father.

Throughout this project, a stronger friendship has emerged and is something that will continue to flourish long after the book is put in its place on the shelf.

I thank you all.

Note: Much of the dialogue contained within these pages has been reconstructed to the best recollection of those involved. No harm whatsoever is intended in any way toward anyone mentioned, living or deceased.

TABLE OF CONTENTS

CHAPTER ONE
A Dark Day
At Pocono

This day, June 19, 1988, dawned with no reason to suspect anything out of the ordinary.

Lives continued on . . . quietly . . . routinely . . . as if it were the day before or the day after.

So it seemed for Robert Arthur Allison.

From an early age, young "Bobby" had been introduced to stock car racing and quickly found his direction in life.

As the morning dawned, he was in the midst of a stellar NASCAR Winston Cup driving career that spanned three decades. During that time he had logged 716 starts and 86 victories, even though two of them did not officially show in the record book.

As light peeked through the curtains of his hotel room, Bobby could not have known the success he had enjoyed on so many occasions since coming into prominence in the early 1970s would suddenly come to a halt. No one would have thought that his 717th start would be his final one.

He was about to compete in the last race of his career.

The Miller Genuine Draft 500 Winston Cup race at Pocono International Raceway was only hours away.

After a breakfast of eggs, fried potatoes, juice and coffee, Bobby set out to begin another Sunday. Sunday was always the most important day of his week for the majority of his 50 years.

Since the early days, big-league stock car races have traditionally found their place on Sunday, mostly to give the common working man some recreation on his only day off from the plant or the fields.

For Bobby, driving stock cars was his only real form of liveli-
hood since his days as a teenager.

At the time of his 7:30 a.m. breakfast, there was no reason to
think he would begin the toughest race of his long career just five
hours later. It would be a race for time, a precious commodity as his
life hung in the balance. Later in the day, every heartbeat threatened
to be his last.

A Catholic, Bobby would usually attend an early morning Mass,
no matter where in the United States the Winston Cup schedule took
him. This particular morning, he and his wife, Judy, attended the
gathering at Lady of the Lakes Catholic Church and later attended the
service held at the Pocono track.

Once at the garage area entrance, Bobby exited his rental car to
the cheers of a dozen or so fans who greeted him. He raised his right
hand slightly and produced a wave as a smile broke over his face. He
felt for the thick, felt-tipped pen in his shirt pocket, an instrument
perfect for signing autographs on programs, photos, and even T-
shirts. One right after another, he signed his name with personal
acknowledgments to each fan.

"Thank you, Bobby," one fan said.

"Go get 'em, today, Bobby. We're pullin' for ya," said another.

"How's the car running, Bobby?" asked a young man in his mid-
20s.

"Not bad at all," Bobby replied, flashing his trademark "OK" sign
with his right hand. "We've got to tinker with a thing or two, but come
race time, we'll be in good shape."

Soon, all of the autographs had been signed. Bobby turned to
leave, but waved once more. The same scenario had taken place on
countless occasions throughout his career.

The morning passed as a busy one. There were special digni-
taries to greet, especially those from Miller Brewing Co., sponsor of
the event as well as the Buick Bobby drove on the 29-race schedule
for Stavola Brothers Racing, headquartered in Harrisburg, N.C. He
soon met with Jimmy Fennig, his crew chief, over concerns about race
strategy. The start of the 500-mile race was three hours away.

At 9:50 a.m., Bobby reluctantly broke away from some friends in
the garage area to attend the mandatory 10 a.m. pre-race drivers'
meeting conducted each week by NASCAR Winston Cup Director,
Dick Beaty.

After the roll call to check the attendance of the driver and crew
chief of each race team, Beaty discussed a few procedures to be fol-

lowed during the race and then asked if there were questions.

"Yeah, Dick, I've got a question," Bobby said. "I want to know what you think a person should do if some asshole spins him out during the race?"

Bobby had encountered such a problem the previous week at Riverside, Calif.

Before Beaty could address the question, Michael Waltrip stood and said, "I'm not the asshole, I'm just his brother!", a reference to veteran driver Darrell Waltrip, who was Bobby's Riverside antagonist. At that point, there came a mighty laugh from the crowd of participants, public relations representatives and media in attendance. It would prove to be one of the lighter moments of a very bleak day.

Beaty offered a suggestion or two as to how the problem should be handled within the realm of the NASCAR rules. If Bobby were unhappy with the general procedure for handling such items, he could see Beaty when the meeting concluded.

The traditional prayer was spoken and Bobby soon returned to the transporter to change into his gold-and-white driver's uniform and fire-retardant shoes.

Before leaving the compartment, however, he removed a new cap from the box of sponsor hats located in one of the cabinets above his head in the small plush office built into the rear of the transporter and adjusted the band to fit his head. As soon as the cap was secure, he carefully stepped down the stairs which led to a walkway between walls of brown wood, stained cabinets full of extra parts and a spare engine or two. He lowered his head, so as not to strike the spare second car that sat waxed and shiny on the top rack. In the event that the number one car was crashed too badly to be repaired, the spare could easily be placed into service with some chassis adjustments.

As Bobby stepped out of the rolling shop, he spotted a close friend standing alongside of his own race car as final preparations were being made to it.

It was none other than Bobby's 27-year-old son, Davey.

In September of 1986, the younger Allison was given the break of his career when Harry Ranier, a wealthy Kentuckian and long-time team owner, offered him the opportunity to drive his Fords for the 1987 Winston Cup season. It was a good ride vacated by Cale Yarborough, who chose to start his own team that year. Allison won the "Rookie of the Year" honors and showed the critics he had learned a thing or two from his famous father.

There was little doubt Davey was already on the way to becoming a superstar in his own right.

"Mornin'," Davey said with a healthy smile underneath a black mustache as thin as his agile frame.

"How are you this morning?" asked Bobby.

"Ready!" Davey said, confident of his chances to win the race.

"That's good, 'cause you're gonna need to be ready," shot back the elder and wiser father.

A nearby photographer in search of an interesting subject decided to capitalize on the light-hearted conversation between the Allisons and made a common request.

"Hey, how about a photo of you two standing together?" he asked.

Davey was to the photographer's left and Bobby was to the right. Each put an arm around the other at the waist and smiled broadly for the camera. The shutter clicked once, then twice. Those smiles were genuine displays of affection and admiration for one another. Once out of the frame of the lens, they briefly exchanged glances. No words needed to be spoken at the time, even though circumstances would dictate the need otherwise later that day. The chance to communicate verbally with one another would be lost, at least for a time.

No one knew those black-and-white photos would be the last ever made of the two men as race car drivers.

Forty-five minutes before race time, Bobby continued his routine activities, which included a quick lunch from various cold cuts complemented by chips, cookies and bananas placed on a small cabinet below the microwave. In a cooler just down the way were a variety of cold soft drinks.

Ed Gossage, public relations representative for Miller Brewing Co., stopped by to wish Bobby a good race. Bobby acknowledged the comment with a wave while taking a bite of his ham sandwich.

Gossage chuckled to himself as he thought of the time the two of them had had the night before. It was a function for local Miller Brewing Co. representatives held at a lakefront hospitality room in a condominium complex near the speedway.

Bobby was in rare form, throwing stories across the table that put those within earshot rolling out of their seats. He had brought his briefcase telescopic fishing pole and was telling some questionable "fish" stories.

As Gossage recalled the evening in his mind, he found himself appreciating the many good times he had shared with the Allison family since taking the job as public relations representative five years earlier.

Often, Gossage would attempt to keep Bobby in line, especially in front of the press. But in typical fashion, the more Gossage crossed his finger over his throat from the back of the room in hopes of halting Bobby's comments, Bobby would speak louder, with words harsher than ones used five minutes earlier. At the sight of Gossage with head in hand at the back of the room, Bobby would smile widely and then console his bewildered P.R. man.

Gossage reached the press box and spotted Bobby getting into his race car on pit road, with the assistance of Fennig and some of the crew members.

Each driver readied himself for the command to fire his 650-horsepower engine. Sitting still, each looked like a quiet but colorful billboard for his or her given sponsor. Once the ignition switches were flipped, their real identities would surface.

Two days earlier, the student, Davey, had qualified better than the professor. His Ford sat in the sixth starting position, while Bobby's Buick rested in 28th.

After both men had been introduced to the many thousands of fans that had gathered in the grandstands, they stepped off the makeshift stage and searched out their respective rides from the cars that sat two by two on pit road.

Seat belts were tightened with a tug of each shoulder harness, while two-way radio communication from car to pit was checked and goggles lowered into place. No more preparation was needed. The test of physical and mechanical stamina would come once the 40-car field rolled off the line only minutes away, following the conclusion of the National Anthem.

At 1:02 p.m., the voice of the grand marshal blared out a familiar command over the public address system.

"Gentlemen, start your engines!"

With that, the sea of multi-colored machines roared in deep baritone sounds that sent a chill through the crowd. To expend their nervous energy, crew members rechecked air guns with loud whistles of the trigger, or positioned gas cans.

Pole position winner Alan Kulwicki and outside front row starter Ken Schrader slowly pulled off pit road and headed into turn one.

"Everything look OK, Bobby?" asked crew chief Fennig over the two-way radio.

"Everything looks great, Jimmy," Bobby replied. "All the gauges look to be pegging where they ought to be."

"10-4, Bobby. We've got two pace laps. Your starting lap will be the third time around. Have a great race."

Bobby acknowledged Fennig's words with a quick key of his microphone as a blurt of static sounded in the crew radios.

Tragedy was only minutes away.

The field completed the pace laps and was at full speed at the start-finish line as the green flag waved.

Bobby glanced at the passenger side of the race car after detecting a slight vibration seemingly coming from the rear. The race was beginning on a dismal note. It could cost laps to locate and correct the problem.

By now he had shifted into fourth gear, and the unsteadiness was becoming progressively worse. With his left hand, Bobby keyed the radio again from the button located at the nine o'clock position on the steering wheel.

"I think I've got a right rear tire goin' down," Bobby said to Fennig and the crew. "Get me one ready! I'm comin' in."

To the people listening to the conversation, the click of the microphone was loud and aggravating. Fennig jumped onto the pit road wall in hopes of catching a glance of Bobby as he limped by. At the sight of him, the crew sprang into action. The race was lost unless the car could be nursed to pit road quickly.

Little did anyone know that those words — "I think I've got a right rear tire goin' down!" — would be Bobby's last as a competitor.

Barney Hall, co-anchor for MRN Radio, producers of the national radio broadcasts for the majority of the 29-race schedule, made note Bobby was dropping off the pace, apparently with a problem in his car.

Like a wounded eagle, Bobby motored his Buick low around the sharp first turn of the 2.5-mile Pocono speedway. Even so, many felt his speed was a bit too fast for a car with a flat tire.

Gossage, now positioned in the press box, had seen Bobby drop off the pace. Through his binoculars, he noticed that even with a flat tire, Bobby's Buick was flying. It still had quite a distance to go to reach the backstretch of the speedway, triangular in shape and quite wide from turn to turn.

The problem at the rear of Bobby's Buick continued to worsen. Both of his hands were sawing the steering wheel back and forth in hopes of keeping the car stable.

NASCAR flagman Harold Kinder spotted Bobby's predicament and displayed the yellow caution flag to the field. But even with that, each car is required to race back to the start-finish line to be credited for completing the lap. If there was a deciding element of fate that day, many felt it was clearly that rule. The consequences could have been quite different had the field been required to slow when the caution flag was first displayed.

Bobby began his entrance into turn two, known as the "tunnel turn." There, the rear end of his car began to break loose in the direction of the high groove. With smoke bellowing out, contact was made with the boiler plate retaining wall.

As his head jostled firmly at the impact, Bobby regained his composure and turned his head left. There before him was every race car driver's worst fear.

Bobby's eyes danced wildly at the sight of a car coming right at him.

Front grille . . . gloved hands fighting the steering wheel . . . tire smoke . . . blunt impact!

Jocko Maggiacomo's Chevrolet hit Bobby's Buick hard in the driver's side door. Maggiacomo had attempted to race back to the yellow flag. With nowhere to go, his path was completely blocked.

Maggiacomo had been one of Bobby's friends throughout both of their respective careers. Sadly, now, and without malice, a terrible crash involving both of them had occurred.

A stillness settled over the race track as shock registered on the face of each person in attendance, including the entourage of newspaper reporters and public relations representatives stationed high atop the frontstretch grandstands.

Suddenly, no conversation was worth continuing.

Gossage knew from his vantage point it was a bad wreck and ran out of the press box to the underground pedestrian crossover tunnel located under the frontstretch.

"A crash has just occurred involving the No. 12 of Bobby Allison and the No. 63 of Jocko Maggiacomo," said Alan Bestwick, turn announcer for MRN Radio. "Allison, in the Stavola Brothers Buick, was nursing a flat right-rear tire and suddenly broke loose right into the path of Maggiacomo, whose Chevrolet was high on the track racing back to the start-finish line. We'll give you an update in just a moment."

With that, Hall was cued to speak.

"Hopefully, both drivers are OK over there," said Hall. "We'll check back very shortly."

Bestwick, whose delivery was shaky at best, tried to compose himself.

"Hey, I'm sorry guys," Bestwick said after going off the air during the commercial break. "That was the hardest hit in a race car I've ever seen in my life."

"That's OK, Alan," said Eli Gold, co-anchor with Hall. "We understand. No problem."

"Allison is not moving," Bestwick said, again off the air. "It looks pretty bad."

As Davey drove under the caution flag, he had a strong feeling his father was involved in something very serious.

"Robert, what's going on?," Davey asked his car owner Robert Yates, who had purchased Ranier's team. "Is Dad involved?"

"Davey, it is your dad, and I've got to tell you it doesn't look good," Yates answered.

Track rescue workers estimated 40 seconds passed before help first arrived to the drivers involved in the crash. Maggiacomo was dazed, but was loosening his shoulder harnesses and moving around inside of his Chevrolet when the medical team arrived at his side.

Bobby, however, sat slumped to his left, unconscious. Even though he was breathing, his physical appearance seemed to indicate the worst as he was ashen gray in color. Immediately, the situation appeared critical to those who began to administer to him.

Judy, his wife of 28 years, sat in the pits, listening to two-way radio conversations in hopes of finding out who was involved.

"The cars involved are the No. 12 (Allison) and the No. 63 (Maggiacomo)," came a voice over the scanner.

Her worst fears were confirmed.

"What's going on up there?" she asked a nearby NASCAR official, as she tried to keep her composure. "Is Bobby all right?"

"I'm sorry, ma'am," said the NASCAR official. "We don't have any information at this time. The rescue workers are there and are working with him very closely right now."

"But you must know something. You've got radios!"

"They haven't said anything to us," the official said. "Just as soon as they do, we'll let you know. For now, they've asked for you to come to the track hospital."

Judy left her tall folding director's chair and was two steps behind the official, who had busied himself with clearing her a path through the crowd of people that had gathered behind Bobby's pit stall.

As she walked, her mind began to race as she envisioned the

very worst. "Is he bleeding . . . ? Is he alive . . .? Why are they taking so long to get him out of the car . . .? Why haven't we heard anything. . . ?"

Suddenly, the path became wider and Judy felt her feet move at a faster pace. But she was in a state of fog and confusion, as if involved in a terrible dream from which she could not wake. As her eyes met those of the people around her, she could only see haunting looks of disbelief and shock. Some even whispered and pointed as they acknowledged to friends that she was Mrs. Bobby Allison.

She was then joined by a member of Bobby's crew who was close to the family.

A couple of minutes passed before she and the crew member arrived at the infield care center. But once at the gate separating pit road from the medical area, a security guard stopped her with his hands raised to his chest.

"I'm sorry, you can't come in here," the guard said forcefully. "We've got a couple of drivers out there that are hurt and they're going to be coming right through that entrance over there. I can't let anyone through."

"I'm very well aware of that," Judy said. "One of those drivers is Bobby Allison, and he's my husband."

Once past the guard and through the entrance of the care center, she was greeted by a group of physicians and nurses who were poised and ready for the victims of the crash. But neither of the two men had arrived. Information was Bobby had not yet been removed from his heavily damaged Buick, while Maggiacomo was en route. All Judy could do was pace the floor – and wait.

Davey slowed his Ford as he reached the crash site. But a rescue worker told him to get out of the way and drive on past. The second time around, the rescue worker became even more verbal, again wanting Davey to continue and not get in the way of those administering to his father. Finally, Davey got the attention of the worker the third trip by.

"Why do you keep stopping?" the worker said. "Can't you see we've got someone hurt over here?"

Davey, strapped in behind the wheel, reached through the area between the top post and window net and pulled the worker down to his level.

"Listen here," he said. "That's my dad in that car. By the time I get back around here I'd better have some information about his condition."

"I'm sorry," the track worker said. "I'll get it right now."

But what Davey saw through his dad's windshield was a nightmare.

The younger Allison strained to see through the passenger side opening and stared helplessly at the man who was his father, his hero and his friend. As his eyes threatened to tear, he though . . . "Where was the smile he was so accustomed to seeing . . .? Who was this man being cut out of this race car and where was his father . . .? Oh God, there's no way this can be happening."

Taking a hit in the driver's side door is always the biggest concern of those who race. Davey knew that from a very young age.

Davey momentarily placed his hand on the lever that would release all the safety belts that met at the junction buckle latch in his lap. Thoughts of parking his car and going to the aid of his father flashed through his mind. But he reasoned he would only hinder the efforts of those attending to him and thought better of it.

Davey shifted into first gear and released the clutch. As he did so, he keyed the two-way microphone with a forceful push.

"Robert, what's going on with Dad?" Davey asked of his car owner. "I'm asking, but they aren't telling me much. And what is this crap I keep hearing on the P.A. when I go by? Give me something."

"He's alive and they're working with him as best they can," Yates said. "They'll have him out of the car shortly. As soon as we know something, I'll let you know."

Meanwhile, the national radio broadcast continued with information concerning the crash. But throughout, the announcers carefully searched for the right words as the tense situation unfolded.

Hall and Gold delivered each periodic address from the broadcast booth, while Bestwick and pit road announcer and former driver Dick Brooks broke in from time to time with information. At one point, Brooks said Bobby was moving and not seriously hurt. But he could only report what was given him at the time and in no way attempted to give false information to those listening to the broadcast.

"To update you, we are working our first caution period of the day which occurred on lap one of this 200-lap Miller Genuine Draft 500," Hall said. "Bobby Allison, of Hueytown, Ala., is being administered to after being involved in a hard crash with driver Jocko Maggiacomo. The cars made contact in the second turn of this triangular shaped two-and-a-half-mile speedway — known as the 'tunnel turn' area here at Pocono International Raceway.

"Currently, Allison continues to sit inside of his Stavola Racing

Buick, as careful consideration is being given to him so not to complicate any injuries that he may have. We will keep you updated with information as we have it."

No one except the rescue workers on the scene knew the true gravity of the situation, but everyone suspected it. Bobby's injuries were indeed severe.

By this time, Judy had been joined at the hospital by an anxious gathering of family members, friends and associates, each with questions that could not readily be answered. Soon, everyone was cleared away by track security. Judy, however, was allowed to remain inside.

She thought to herself how thankful she was her husband had forgotten his shaving kit. She thought back on his phone call to her two days before and how trivial his request seemed then. At that moment, she said a silent prayer of thanks that God allowed her to be with him.

Suddenly, the door opened with mass confusion as a sea of orange rescue vests entered the room. Dr. Edward Spoll, chief physician at Pocono International Raceway, was given vital signs and other information by those who first administered to Bobby's needs in the field. Throughout the time Bobby was being administered to, radio contact was made on several occasions to the infield care center.

Maggiacomo was admitted first and treated for bruises and received 26 stitches to his chin to close the severe gash suffered in the crash.

"Mrs. Allison, I'm sorry, you'll have to leave," said a nurse stationed in the room.

"He is my husband. I've got to stay with him. Don't you understand . . .? I'm not moving! You'll have to physically throw me out of here!"

"Let her stay," said Dr. Spoll. "Just stay back a bit . . . say, right over there." He pointed to a tile in the floor about thirty feet away.

Several things seemed to go on at once, as six people worked feverishly over Bobby with great intensity. Dr. Spoll was in charge of the infield care center and gave other assistants direction. His background in race-related trauma cases included experience as Chief Physician for the U.S. Grand Prix at Watkins Glen (N.Y.) International, Assistant Chief Physician at Indianapolis Motor Speedway and Chief Physician of the Sports Car Club of America before heading the PIR medical team. He was also in family practice and was on staff at Lehigh Valley Medical Center in Allentown, Pa.

Dr. Spoll was assisted by Dr. Victor Dy, general surgeon with extensive trauma background, and Dr. David Cooper, a local orthopedic surgeon. Also in the room were four nurses and several medical personnel.

Before intravenous fluids were administered, it was determined Bobby's injuries included fractured ribs, a fracture of the left leg at three points, a fracture of the left shoulder blade and possible internal injuries which caused a dark-blue bruise from his left shoulder to just above the ankle. Also suffered was a cerebral concussion, which caused the most concern. A neck brace had been placed on Bobby before he had been removed from the car.

Several attempts were made to stabilize Bobby's heart rhythm, as it was unsteady due to a cardiac contusion or bruise to the heart. Treatment was administered in the form of medication. No electronic stimulation was considered necessary but it was readily available.

Dr. Spoll checked the intubation procedure, which consisted of a tube placed into Bobby's lungs to insure proper breathing; administered in the field after permission was given to the paramedics via radio transmission.

To the physicians in the room, the broken leg was a concern, but not of the same degree as the head injury. The bones were stabilized with mast trousers, a device used to stabilize the break as well as draw blood to the upper extremities of the body to enhance the victim's blood pressure.

After extensive care was taken to insure the heart rate was stable, Bobby was ready for the MediVac helicopter for the 11-minute trip to Lehigh Valley Medical Center located 45 miles away in Allentown. Fortunately, it was considered one of the finest trauma hospitals in the state of Pennsylvania.

Within the next 10 minutes, a helicopter arrived for Judy's use from Drs. Joseph and Rose Mattioli, chief executive officers and owners of the speedway. There was room only for patient and doctor in the MediVac helicopter.

Davey continued to race, even though his heart and soul were with his critically injured father. During each caution period, the public address system at the speedway continued to broadcast what information was available on Bobby's condition. But information was sketchy and those announcing simply had little to go on.

Each time Davey communicated with his pit, more information would be given to him, separating fact from fiction. Once the checkered flag fell, Davey found himself in fifth place, a miraculous finish considering the circumstances.

He was then given a police escort to the hospital after exiting his race car.

Judy had entered Lehigh Valley Medical Center in search of her husband when she encountered a Dr. Slaven. He had initially seen Bobby upon arrival but did not have extensive training to recognize cerebral injuries. Dr. Harry Stevens, a highly respected neurosurgeon, was there visiting another patient and quickly realized Bobby was in serious trouble.

Judy made camp in a small waiting room just across the hall from her husband's bed in one of the trauma units.

Bobby's first cousin Dave Demerest and his wife Millie soon appeared at the hospital to comfort Judy.

Stevens, with slightly bulging stomach usually covered with his folded arms, entered the room with information on Bobby's condition. With feet pointed slightly outward, he stood tall with unkempt brown-gray hair, half-lens spectacles and white jacket.

His gruff voice and hard demeanor caught everyone's attention.

"Mrs. Allison?," he asked.

"Yes," Judy replied as she sprang from her chair.

"I'm Dr. Harry Stevens and I'm one of the neurosurgeons here at Lehigh."

"Have you seen Bobby?"

"I have," he answered bluntly. "I must tell you that the situation looks very grave. Very grave, indeed. We must take extreme measures right away or we'll lose him."

CHAPTER TWO
The Early Years

The summer heat in Miami, Fla. always seemed so unforgiving. Usually, by nine o'clock in the morning, the temperature would reach a stifling 80 degrees. Even after years of residing there, most of the city's occupants could tolerate the humidity, but they never actually became accustomed to it. Light cotton clothing seemed to provide some relief.

On 19th Street, located on the north side of town, Edmond Jacob and Katherine Allison busied themselves with working hard and raising their children. They were married on Oct. 23, 1927. They had met at a dance. Ed had come to Katherine's rescue to try and open a stubborn old freezer, but spilled ice cream all over his shoes in the process.

But it did lead to marriage. Along the way came a total of 13 children — and the occasional best friend who stayed over from time to time.

Bobby was fifth in line behind sisters Dorothy, Claire and Patsy and brother Eddie. Next came Donnie, Tommy, Stanley, Mary Katherine, Margaret, Jeannie, Mary Agnes and Cindy.

Dorothy, Stanley and Mary Katherine were thought of often, as their parents had told them stories of their deceased sisters and brother. Unfortunately, each of their lives spanned over very short periods of time.

On Sunday mornings before breakfast, the family would head out for the 8 a.m. Mass in shifts. One of the children would always be involved in the service and was required to arrive earlier than the others. Some would pile into the old family station wagon while the others would come later with their grandfather. The same held true for those in need of the bathtub, as each of the children would stand in line for the privilege. Everything was conducted in shifts.

The Allison home was an old and large structure, bought with hard earned money to accommodate the large Allison family. It was not fancy but adequate with six bedrooms and two occupants to a bed. There were few luxuries, except for being together a great deal of the time — which to them seemed to be the best luxury in the world.

Upon returning from religious services before breakfast, a wholesale switch was made from dress clothing to their more casual trousers and T-shirts for the boys and sleeveless sun dresses for the girls.

Later, Katherine, a petite woman with dark hair that was graying slightly at her temples, stood at the kitchen sink peeling potatoes and preparing dinner. She was very insistent that Sunday dinner be the most elegant meal of the week and usually served roast beef or chicken, vegetables and a salad. And, of course, those famous mouthwatering apple pies.

Suddenly, there came the sound of children's feet running down the hallway, accompanied by the slam of a screen door leading to the porch at the rear of the house. Her son Eddie, 8, was just a step behind her son Donnie, 5, each hoping to be the first to get to the football lying on the back lawn.

"Boys, no running in this house," she replied without looking up from her work.

"Yes ma'am," said the two boys from outside, as their feet slowed dramatically. Eddie managed to grab Donnie by the back of the shirt collar and get the advantage a bit. Their mother was used to such behavior, for all her children were very competitive.

Their father, known simply as E.J., was tall and very muscular with a big chest and trim waistline. He was so strong he could wrap his bear-like arms around one of the gas pumps at his local service station installation business and move it without assistance from any of his helpers.

The gas tanks he placed underground did not have to be level according to any state laws on the books. But he could not sleep at night knowing a tank he placed in the ground was not up to his quality standards. He would scoop dirt with his bare hands for hours until the level gave a perfect reading.

And if painting or pouring concrete foundations was required, E.J. could handle the task at hand.

He worked constantly, day and night and on weekends. Due to

the need to support his large family, he was rarely home to tend to the children. But he did find time in his busy schedule to attend Mass every Sunday and take time for Sunday dinner.

There were many times when he and Katherine would be resourceful. Once, they both worked diligently to remove rocks from the backyard and used their harvest to build a rock wall and barbecue pit. Many times, E.J. and the boys would bring sand perch from their famous fishing trips and have fish frys on that old pit.

The Allisons were above poor, as their father made a respectable living, as he knew the value of a dollar and did not believe in credit. After all, with many children to support, he didn't need a college degree to realize the need for fiscal conservation.

But in those days, monetary status was not considered a measure of happiness by most. Enjoyment of life required small amounts of money and no one really acknowledged there was ever a lack of it in everyday life. While other families may have had more material possessions, the Allisons were rich through love and respect for one another.

When bad behavior dictated it, Katherine, better known as "Mom" Allison, was the disciplinarian. At times, the children would protest over one of her commands, but a stern look and the threat of a switching proved to be a great persuader. Compromises were readily made by the children with the threat their father would discover they had been bad. Nothing was worth the risk of explaining things to E.J.

But for the most part, home life was fun, especially Saturday nights, the only time of the week when hamburgers, potato chips and R.C. Cola was served. Other than at birthdays, the children were not allowed to have soft drinks.

Birthdays were special. Once it was his or her day, the child with the birthday was allowed to choose his favorite dinner, which often included having a favorite friend come over.

In most cases, the choice was steak (or shrimp if the birthday fell on Friday) and french fries. Steak in those days was rare and the potatoes were, too, if Bobby were home. Usually, a 10-pound bag would be gone in a flash.

But the most special treat during an Allison birthday party was the honor of sitting in the chair decorated with bows, marking that person as the guest of honor. There were gifts of socks or underwear wrapped nicely in pretty paper.

If there was ever a testimonial to hard work and tireless effort, it was "Mom" Allison. Many times her sons could not fudge on the time they returned from a date. She would usually be up until the early morning ironing, washing or mending. Only a few hours later, she would begin the day again just as the sun was beginning to peek through the windows.

There were always small requests, too. But they were just as important as the big ones.

As fast as her little feet could carry her, Cindy, the youngest of the children, approached her mother with an announcement.

"Mom, my doll has lost a button. Can you fix it for her?" she asked.

"Certainly dear," her mother replied. "Right after I finish making dinner. Put her in your room and I'll come by for her later."

Cindy was satisfied with her answer and returned to playing.

Then another small voice broke Katherine's attention.

"Mom, I have a picture to show you," Bobby said, seven years old and full of imagination.

She stopped her knife from peeling for a moment to look at her son's creation.

"This is a jeep that I can drive to school and when I get there, I can use it as my desk," Bobby said excitedly. He had already constructed a motorized scooter, so the Jeep idea didn't seem so impossible.

"That's wonderful, Bobby. Where do you get such ideas?" she asked.

He flashed his wide grin and went back to his room.

Unknown to her at the time, it would be Bobby's first flirtation with automobiles and his first expression of interest in them.

The Allison home was never calm, but rather, always full of life. Along with her own children, those from the neighborhood would drop by regularly to play. Over the years, there was an early childhood friend named Bobby Frazier who lived a half block and a half away, and another boy named David Hundley who everyone referred to as "Nick." And there was Tommy Chalk, who was one of Bobby's closest friends.

There were many trips to Matheson Hammock where all the children would sharpen their swimming skills and use their father's shoulders as a diving board during their first diving lessons. His strong hands and steadiness gave the children the confidence to try. The words "My turn! My turn!" would ring out loudly as Katherine would prepare plates of fried chicken and cole slaw for her children. They were never referred to as her "kids," as she thought the reference was disrespectful to them.

The newspapers would constantly contain headlines pertaining to their mother's famous relative, Gen. George Patton, and his exploits of World War II. Some considered her never-ending strength a trait from the Patton family.

Arthur Patton, Mrs. Allison's father, also lived with the family for a time. He was an accountant in his early sixties and his meticulous stature fit the part. Constantly behind a desk pushing a pencil, he rarely had time for a lot of physical activity. His 5' 11" frame proved the point well.

Prior to any meal, each child was called and, one by one, they took their assigned seats and pulled their chairs close to the table.

After grace was said, general talk filled the room. One had to be able to talk and spoon food from the bowls as they were passed around the table. "Mom" Allison's dishes usually disappeared as if by magic.

"Who's turn is it to go with you, Granddad?" asked Eddie.

"Let me see, I believe it's Bobby's turn, is it not?"

A smile broke over Bobby's face, for he knew he was going to have fun exploring something new.

Katherine's father possessed a great love in keeping current of sports events of any kind. On more than one occasion, he would ask one of his grandchildren to accompany him to watch sporting events being held in the area.

"How would you like to go to what they call a 'stock car race'?" he asked. There was no need to inquire a second time, for Bobby willingly accepted the invitation.

"Are you sure you two won't get hurt doing such a thing?" Bobby's mother asked.

"Oh, no, of course not. Why, it will be fun, right Bobby?" asked Granddad.

Bobby's smile grew even wider than before as he nodded in agreement.

Once there, with wide-eyed enthusiasm he held his grandfather's hand and tried to take in everything. He saw the early modified Fords, Hudsons, Plymouths and Nashes move through the turns of an old fairground dirt track and quickly decided the sport had a great hold on him. From that moment, there was no doubt as to which direction his life would take.

Once he returned home, Bobby laid in bed and thought of those fast cars and how they excited him. That night, his mind was flooded with thoughts of his day and he slept poorly.

The next few months passed and he found it was hard to get those racing jalopies out of his mind. He would constantly draw them on paper and dream he was driving them.

A few years passed and Bobby found himself becoming more and more interested in mechanical items, including the car owned by the priest at the Catholic school he attended.

During the summer after classes were completed at Archbishop Curley High School, Bobby found himself underneath the old car, working diligently to get the engine to start when he heard footsteps and a muffled voice from above.

"Well, have you got her to start, Master Allison?" the visitor asked.

"No," came Bobby's voice from underneath.

"I say, do you have her fixed yet, son?" came the voice once more.

"Hell, no!" came Bobby's voice in disgust.

Suddenly, dark dress shoes and slacks caught Bobby's eye and as he slowly followed the pant crease, he saw the face of the priest who stood there scowling in silence with his hands on his hips.

Bobby slid out from underneath the frame and quickly searched for composure.

"Oh, Father, I'm so sorry," Bobby replied. "I had no idea it was you standing there. I realize that I have some punishment coming which is OK. I'll wash dishes, I'll sweep, I'll do anything you ask to make it up to you."

"That's not necessary, young Mr. Allison," the priest said. "You must be aware, however, that whether addressing me or anyone else in the future, using profanity to make a point is not proper. You can speak and make your point without having to use such language."

Bobby was humbled by the priest's words and breathed a sigh of relief that no punishment was forthcoming.

During those teenage years, there were other items Bobby tinkered with; virtually anything in need of repair. He would buy and patch his vehicles and "trade up" for something of more value. One such deal included the trade of a motorcycle for a 1938 Chevy Coupe owned by a friend in the neighborhood. The front fenders were missing, but no matter. It had a license plate on the rear and could be driven on the streets.

By Bobby's senior year, Hialeah Speedway was firmly in place and had just created an amateur division for the 1955 racing season.

Having seen those early races with his grandfather, the desire to race had long been implanted.

But Bobby realized he was faced with a major obstacle. In order to be eligible to compete, anyone under the age of 21 was required to have written permission from a parent or legal guardian. The thought crossed Bobby's mind he would have to convince his mother to sign for him to drive. He could think of many easier tasks to confront.

Finally, he approached her with his idea, thinking she would be the least difficult of his parents to convince.

"Mom, please try to understand what I'm about to ask you," Bobby said to his mother.

"Why, I always do, dear. What's on your mind?" she asked.

"I'd like to drive a race car down at Hialeah Speedway but since I'm not 21, I've got to have written permission from you or Dad."

"Now, why would you want to do such a thing?" she asked. "Those people that race cars are hoodlums that never take a bath and stay greasy all the time. I don't think you should get mixed up in such nonsense. You know you were brought up better than that."

"But mom," Bobby pleaded, "it's not that way at all. Granddad took me to a race a few years ago and he saw how it was. This really is a good thing."

"Still, I don't know," she replied. "And what about school? To get into college, your marks have to be real good."

"If you'll just sign it this one time, I'll make good marks and I'll help Dad out at the business all that I can."

After a few days of gentle persuasion, Bobby reemphasized his promise and finally, his persistence paid off. His mother signed the release, thinking her son's desire to race cars would pass with adolescence. Once the paper was in his hands with her signature in blue ink at the bottom, Bobby said to himself, "This ought to be good until I'm at least a hundred years old, anyway."

He took the old '38 coupe he'd traded for and mopped the number "41" on its doors. As manager of the high school football team, he wore a jersey with that number while on the sidelines, so it seemed to be an appropriate choice.

Bobby had tried out for football that same year, even though he was lucky to weigh 110 pounds soaking wet. Once he took a hand-off from the quarterback in a practice game, he ran the distance of the field and scored a touchdown. But not far behind were several linemen, each twice his size with a plan to bury him in the dirt if they caught him.

Fortunately, Bobby crossed the line untouched.

The coach called him over with a look of worry painted over his face.

"I realize how much you'd like to play football," the coach said. "But the whole time you were running that ball, I was trying to figure out what I was going to tell your mother after those guys caught you and fell on you. If they'd have caught you, they would have killed you.

"Maybe you should look at some other sport to get into."

The advice from his coach simply fueled the fire to drive race cars. After all, one didn't have to be all that big to turn a steering wheel. The car did all the work.

Once at Hialeah Speedway, Bobby took the headlights and taillights off and strapped the door shut. All the parts taken off the car would be piled into a box for reassembling after the races had concluded.

Out of the 40 cars entered in the race at Hialeah, he brought the old '38 coupe home seventh. The next week, he finished seventh again in a 50-car field. And the third week, among the 60 cars entered, he was victorious in the 25-lap event. With such impressive outings, Bobby felt he had a future as a race car driver.

A short time after his graduation from high school, Bobby accepted a job with Mercury Outboard Motors, based in Wisconsin. His uncle had worked for many years with the company as national sales manager.

While testing a new race motor on a small runabout boat, Bobby hit some waves—hard. Upon impact, the nose of the boat rose dramatically, came down, and plowed into the next swell and sunk. His friends, all in individual boats of their own, had long since gone and had already crossed Lake Butte des Morts when the accident happened. When Bobby didn't catch up with them, it was assumed he just had gone back to the factory.

Because he was dressed in heavy clothing, Bobby struggled to tread water. But at the time, the air was estimated at 15 degrees, the water about 40, near the verge of freezing over.

Ice had formed on his hat and he realized he was in serious trouble.

Just at the moment he was ready to give up, his feet touched bottom which gave him renewed determination to try to make it ashore.

He made it to a house where inside lived a registered nurse, who immediately saw what had happened.

She put him in a tub of hot water as his eyes were turning white and his pulse was becoming almost nonexistent. He was shaking so violently the nurse was forced to feed him tea from a child's straw.

Due to the first snow storm of the season which had blanketed the area overnight, the ambulance crew felt it was too hazardous to come to his rescue.

A phone call was made to those running the boathouse and two of the men working there transported him by passenger car to the closest hospital, located in Oshkosh.

The nurse did a good job of thawing him out. So much so the attending physician in the emergency room, who was her husband, immediately recognized the patient and said, "I know you're the victim because you're wearing my clothes."

When temperatures became unbearable in the winter, the company traditionally would move its testing facilities and their personnel to Sarasota, Fla. That move provided Bobby an outlet to return to his home in Miami on weekends to see his family and attend stock car races at Hialeah Speedway on Saturday nights.

Bobby worked in the proofing grounds located there from December until April.

Carl Kiekhaefer owned Mercury Outboard Motors as well as the famous Chryslers that competed with phenomenal strength in the Grand National division. His drivers were some of the best, such as Tim Flock, Buck Baker, Speedy Thompson, Frank Mundy, and Herb Thomas, among others.

Some considered Kiekhaefer virtually impossible to work for, as he would constantly become enraged at the slightest complication. But he took an immediate liking to Bobby and didn't ride him as hard as he did some of the others.

One day as the crew, which included three other youngsters from Wisconsin, Jimmy Kubasta, Jim Wirch and Marlin "Mully" Felker, was preparing to return the testing efforts to Wisconsin, Kiekhaefer walked in.

Kiekhaefer was known to walk into any of the his plants unannounced and draft help for his race car shop in Charlotte.

"Go and get your suitcase," Kiekhaefer said to Bobby. "I want you to get my car (a 1956 Mercedes 190SL) and go to the race shop in Charlotte.

Bobby readily agreed and was soon en route.

Once there, Ray Fox , a noted NASCAR Grand National mechanic, greeted him and the two immediately became friends. Bobby had already known of Fox's mechanical wizardry on the beach race course in Daytona Beach, Fla.

But like many, Bobby's employment with Kiekhaefer ended after only a couple of months. The personnel turnover was incredible and Bobby began to realize he had no future there. When three of his co-workers were fired during one of Kiekhaefer's displays of his temper, Bobby quit along with them.

From there, he returned to Miami to concentrate on his first love — racing. But his age, or the lack of it, was still a problem.

To ask his mother to sign more release forms for him was shy of all logic. He knew her feelings about those involved with stock car racing and remembered her hesitance to sign before. She wanted him to concentrate on more important ventures, such as something suitable for a steady income or possible enrollment into college.

"If you're going to live here, you won't be driving race cars," Bobby's mother said.

There was only one answer. Without written permission, Bobby would need to borrow a NASCAR license.

He knew exactly where to get one.

CHAPTER THREE
Constant Success

Bobby reasoned to himself his plan wasn't harmful to anyone, even though it wasn't exactly truthful. To him, he saw no difference in using his name to race stock cars or someone else's.

Bobby crawled behind the steering wheel of his battered '38 coupe, still with 41s shoe-polished on the doors, and paid a visit to a friend several blocks away. Bob Sundman was dating his older sister, Claire, at the time, but Bobby liked him more because he held a NASCAR license.

Sundman had worked with a gentleman named H.C. Wilcox, owner of a prominent commercial engine shop in Miami. The two had turned out a modified or two with some success at Hollywood Speedway in Opa Locka, Fla., by working nights and weekends. From time to time, Bobby's brother Eddie would turn wrenches on their cars when not working with their father at "E.J. Allison and Co.," supplier and installer of equipment to garages and service stations.

"How about letting me borrow your NASCAR license to sign in for the races at Holywood Speedway this Saturday night?" Bobby asked Sundman, taking somewhat of a chance that the news of his alias would get back to his parents through Claire.

"Sounds OK to me, Bobby," Sundman said. "But if you get caught by your parents, I don't know anything about it."

"Fair enough," Bobby said.

The chief steward at the track wasn't as blind as Bobby thought, but it didn't matter. He went along with the plan and even did Bobby one better. Thus, the alias of "Bob Sunderman" was created. The addition of the "er" in his name helped to make it sound a bit different in the newspaper, as the NASCAR pay-off was the source used for their stories on winners of the races.

For a few weeks, the papers were filled with headlines that read something like, "Sunderman Hot At Hollywood."

But "Pops" Allison wasn't born the day before and felt it was too much of a coincidence his daughter was dating a young man by the name of Sundman and this "Sunderman" character was suddenly running races and working on race cars and being noticed.

While turning wrenches on his old modified coupe, E.J. decided to ask a few questions and get to the bottom of the story.

"Look, Bobby," E.J. said to his son, "if you're going to race, you use your own name. I know what's going on, but you might give some people the wrong impression about you."

"What about Mom?" Bobby asked.

"Together, maybe we can convince her to let you race," E.J. said.

Finally, after some gentle persuasion, Bobby's mother agreed to let him race.

Upon reaching Montgomery, Ala., Bobby pulled the blue Chevrolet pickup into a gas station's driveway and met its proprietor, Bo Freeman.

Their new friend invited them in for a glass of iced tea and a look at Montgomery Speedway, located nearby.

The promoter came out and announced he didn't have a show for the evening but Dixie Speedway, just up the road in Birmingham, did. In order to save their money for race parts if needed, Bobby stopped along the way and bought a bushel basket of peaches for 50 cents. That would provide food for him and brother Donnie.

Bobby recorded a fifth place in the heat race, a fifth in the semi-feature and fifth in the feature.

Once the races concluded, Bobby walked up to the pay window and the attendant behind the counter counted out $135 in cash and handed it to him.

"Donnie, we just died and went to heaven," Bobby said. "Look at all this money. We don't have to sleep in the truck tonight. We can go down to that Miss Mary's drive-in that we saw coming in and we're going to have one of those $1.95 T-bones."

On the way back to Montgomery, the two "rich" businessmen checked into a motel where there were beds with clean sheets. It was the first such luxury in over three days.

The next night, Bobby was forced to stay up through the early morning hours to work on his race motor.

He arrived too late to qualify and was forced to start last in the field. But his position was academic, as his victory marked the first feature of his young career.

During the time Bobby's driving career was beginning to progress, so was a very special relationship. He had met a pretty young blonde, all of 15 years old at the time.

Allison had gone to the home of Ralph Stark to buy a tire and while there, met the sister of Stark's wife, Carolyn. Her name, he was told, was Judy Bjorkman.

One Saturday evening, Judy was asked by friends to go with them to Hollywood Speedway. But the request was rare, as she would often babysit on Saturday nights.

During the race a young man spun his car in the third turn, causing a fire. It was a white car with a large "1X" painted on the doors and top.

Judy knew who was in the car. She quickly stood and yelled, 'Bobby.'

But soon the fire was extinguished and there was no harm done.

After the races had concluded, Bobby's best friend, Bob Janelle, told him of Judy's outburst in the stands when the accident occurred.

Later in the evening, the group from the track moved over to a local hotspot called "Nevells Barbeque" in west Hollywood.

While there, Bobby and Judy continually made eye contact with one another from separate booths. But Bobby was with another girl at the time, but made sure she sat where the eye contact was possible. It was the first time Judy felt comfortable looking at someone in such a way.

As an excuse to see Judy, Bobby decided to see her brother-in-law again about a part. This time, however, he was not covered from head to toe in grease as he was during their first meeting.

"Is Ralph around?" Bobby asked.

"No, I think he's at the shop," Mrs. Stark said.

"Thank you," Bobby returned. "I'll check there."

In the hallway stood young Judy watching him leave.

As Bobby got to the end of the sidewalk, he turned and asked, "Would you like to go with me?"

Judy looked at her older sister for approval and was given a quick nod and half-smile.

The two were soon in Bobby's metallic blue Chevrolet truck. It was a vehicle known around town for its tiny caricatures painted on the doors.

Unknown to Bobby at the time, Judy went with him to get even with a boyfriend who had just started seeing someone else.

On the way, Bobby began to talk about all of his other girlfriends.

Judy didn't believe him at the time and wrote the conversation off as talk. She quickly formed an opinion of him.

Once back at the Stark's, Judy said goodbye and walked into the house.

"Well, how was your trip with your friend?" Carolyn asked.

"I think he's the most conceited guy I've ever met in my life," Judy said. "I don't want anything else to do with him ever again."

A couple of weeks later, Bobby took a car to West Pam Beach Speedway and through conversation with Stark, he discovered the cute little blonde was in the stands along with his friend's wife. Along with friend Gil Herne, Bobby searched through the stands and finally found her.

"How about letting me take you home after the race?" Bobby asked.

"I'm not sure," Judy said. "I've got to be home early because my mother and I are moving to Orlando tomorrow. I'll have to ask Ralph and Carolyn if it's OK."

"Fine, I'll be waiting in my blue truck for a while after the race."

Judy was a bit concerned over what her mother would say. After all, they were planning to be packed and on the road at 5:30 a.m.

At the time, Judy's father, Carl Bjorkman, recently died which played a major part in her having to move with her mother from Fort Lauderdale to Orlando. Her mother, Dorothy Bjorkman, had found work there as a beautician and needed the raise in pay.

Many times, Judy would join her boyfriend, along with the Starks, for catfish at a small fish camp after the races.

It was common for her boyfriend to ask her to join them. But this time, he saw her sitting on the passenger seat of Bobby's truck.

They sat in her mother's driveway for hours talking about their families, the good times and his interests — which mostly consisted of racing stock cars.

Suddenly, the porch light came on.

"Judy Bjorkman, do you know what time it is?" her mother asked angrily. "It's 5:30 a.m. and you've been out here all night."

"I've got to go," Judy said as she opened the door of the truck.

"Let me know where you're going and I'll come there to see you," Bobby said.

"OK. See you later," Judy answered.

But as his truck pulled away, she didn't think she would ever see him again.

Upon arrival in Orlando, Judy and her mother moved in with her other sister and her husband, Connie and Rocky Dwyer, as part of a temporary arrangement until they could find suitable accommodations.

Judy had scribbled her new address on a piece of paper retrieved from the glove compartment of Bobby's truck.

Two weeks later, Judy looked out the window one Sunday morning only to spot a metallic blue pickup sitting in front of the house.

A panic came over her, as she was clad in housecoat, curlers and wore no makeup.

Bobby came to the door, but she wouldn't let him in. The two talked through the door.

"Would you like to go to Mass with me this morning?" Bobby asked. "I'd really like for you to go."

"I'm surprised you came back," Judy said. "I didn't think you would."

"I told you I would," Bobby said. "Well, do you want to go to Mass with me? How long will it take you to get ready?"

"Give me ten minutes," Judy answered as she ran in the bathroom pulling curlers from her hair with each step.

Not long after their first date, they began to see each other every two weeks or so when Bobby would drive to get her so they could attend Mass together.

A month later, Judy's mother burned her hand terribly in an accident and was unable to continue her work as a beautician. With the bills mounting, Judy borrowed money from her sister Carolyn to attend cosmetology school to help lighten the financial burden.

Once her training was complete, she looked for a job for three months before finding one back in Fort Lauderdale. It was a small salon, but had great potential for the future.

Dressed in a sleeveless summer dress, Judy sat waiting for Bobby to arrive for their scheduled date.

He had asked her to join him for dinner to celebrate her graduating from beautician's school. She thought his gesture was very kind and excited her. Judy stood in front of a mirror brushing her hair, feeling proud of her accomplishment. Soon, there was a knock at the door.

"Can you come out on the front porch for a minute?" Bobby

asked.

"What is it, Bobby?" Judy asked.

"I just want you to come out here," he said, pulling slightly on her hand.

As she walked out, Bobby jogged back to the truck and got a small box off the seat.

He looked down at the ground for a second to gain his composure and then asked a bit sheepishly, "I'd like to know if you will marry me?"

Suddenly, Judy's eyes grew wide at the sight of the diamond ring encased inside the box. She had fallen in love with Bobby from the moment she met him, something she didn't want to admit it to anyone or herself. After all, this was the same conceited greasy race car driver with all the fictitious girlfriends.

But suddenly, everything felt right.

With that she said, "Yes . . . yes . . . of course I'll marry you!"

CHAPTER FOUR
A Wife And
A Family

On Feb. 20, 1960, the Allisons exchanged wedding vows during a morning service in a small Catholic church in Fort Lauderdale.

After their wedding, the newlyweds spent the next six days traveling through the South.

Bobby's racing schedule was gradually picking up, which required him to be away 10 days or so at a time. Racing in Alabama paid even more than before and Bobby was sure driving race cars would provide an adequate living.

In June, Judy informed her husband they were expecting their first child sometime in mid-to-late February of 1961.

In February of 1961, Ralph Stark had been working on a Chevrolet from the previous season for entry in the Daytona 500 at what was then called the Daytona International Speedway and asked Bobby if he'd like to drive it. It would mark his first Grand National speedway event of his career.

Stark had great confidence in his young brother-in-law's ability to drive, as Bobby had finished second in the national Modified standings behind Johnny Roberts and beat out such hot shoes as Red Farmer, Possum Jones and Bobby Johns in the process. Bobby was high in the point standings at Hollywood, Palmetto and Medley Speedways.

Before Daytona was built, only the Darlington Raceway in Darlington, S.C., the Atlanta International Raceway and Charlotte

Motor Speedway existed within the ranks of the larger speedways. But the new high banked speedway at Daytona offered something more—higher banked turns and faster speeds.

By the time his big chance came, two Daytona 500 winners — Lee Petty and Junior Johnson — had been crowned. It was now Bobby's turn to accomplish his dream of driving the mammoth 2.5-mile speedway for the first time in the 500 of 1961.

Out of 33 cars entered in one of two 100-mile qualifying races, Bobby wheeled Stark's Chevy to a 20th place finish and $50 in prize money. But it was a hard $50 to earn.

"As I remember it, we struggled with that old car to try to make it handle but never really got it right. We tried everything we could possibly think of and the leaders would still fly by me like I was sitting still.

"It was one of those deals where I had to just drive as hard as I could and hope for a respectable finish if some of the other cars fell out."

In that race, Lee Petty suffered a terrible crash.

His Plymouth locked bumpers with Johnny Beauchamp's Chevrolet and was sent over the guardrail in excess of 150 miles per hour.

The prognosis was grave for Petty, as he suffered a punctured lung, multiple fractures of the left chest, a fractured left thigh, broken collar bone and massive internal injuries.

Beauchamp suffered head injuries in the crash.

Just after the qualifying race was concluded, Bobby was notified by phone to return home. His wife was having a baby.

Bobby hopped into his red and white pickup and headed south to Hollywood, Fla., using some of his racing skills to beat the traffic in places along the way.

Once at the hospital after some three hours of driving, he discovered he was the father of a baby boy. Born Feb. 25, 1961, the couple chose the name David Carl Allison and would refer to him as "Davey."

Bobby stayed with his wife until the last possible minute before having to return to Daytona Beach for the 500. He drove into the night and made it back with hours to spare.

After a grueling 500-mile event with the car still not up to par with the other entries, 175 laps were completed and Bobby finished 31st in the 58-car field.

It was a good start. But Stark and his driver had a lot to learn about NASCAR Grand National racing.

With the big leagues set aside for a while, Bobby was racing from Wednesday to Sunday night. Before long, there were 33 feature victories which helped to spread his name around the southern states as a threat to win each week.

In 1962, Bobby won 41 features, the Modified-special championship and repeated the honor the following year.

During that time, Bobby's young son Davey showed he had a vivid imagination. His parents nicknamed him "the buffalo hunter" as he constantly talked of shooting buffalo with a bow and arrow with a small friend in the woods of the Indian reservation located close to their home in West Hollywood.

Later, young Davey also had the ability to predict when his father would return from a race or even tell his mother the events of a certain heat or feature event, only to have it confirmed when his father arrived. It was the beginning of a very close relationship between the two that seemed a bit eerie at times.

On occasion, Davey and Judy would accompany Bobby to the race track and while traveling late at night, Davey would keep his father awake by jabbering and making sounds of a race car before falling asleep in his mother's arms.

But by the end of the year, Dec. 4, 1962, Davey would have a sister named Bonnie Marie Allison.

Sadly, Bobby's sister, Margaret, died that year of complications created by Cystic Fibrosis.

Even though in great pain for much of her 16 years, she tried very hard to function normally, playing the piano and making the dean's list in school. But mostly, she brightened the lives of those around her. The loss was felt very deeply.

By 1963, Bobby finally left his native state of Florida and answered the call to go to Alabama. He found a suburb of Birmingham called Hueytown to call home. Also that year, another Modified-special title was added to his accomplishments.

Some eight years before, Bobby's old friend, Ray Fox, left the employ of Carl Kiekhaefer. The entrepreneur of German decent became disillusioned with Grand National racing after winning championships in 1955 and '56 under Fox's direction.

Fox returned to his automotive repair business in Daytona Beach but fielded Grand National cars of his own.

The crafty car owner was well-known around the Grand National cars, having employed the likes of such racing greats as David Pearson and Junior Johnson to drive his cars.

During the 1963 season, Johnson drove a Ray Fox prepared Chevrolet equipped with what was known as the "mystery" engine. In March of 1964, Bobby bought one of the "mystery" engines from Ray Fox to campaign on the Alabama Late Model Modified circuit.

The bug to compete in Grand National was stronger than ever and during the second week of that months, Fox called Bobby to come to Darlington, S.C., to attempt to qualify for the Rebel 300.

Once Bobby arrived, he found his longtime friend Fox and made himself available to drive.

"This place is pretty tricky," Fox said. "Do you think you can handle it?"

"I've driven a lot of races in Alabama and I think I can handle it pretty good," Bobby responded.

"OK, take it out and let's see how you do," Fox returned. "But take it easy. You can tear up a race car here in a hurry."

Bobby slipped behind the wheel of the number 03 Dodge, a 1964 model painted white with red numbers and trim.

Several laps were made, but the speeds did not reach those required to run the race.

Once Bobby returned to the pits, Lee Roy Yarbrough, also a Modified driver, stepped up and offered his thoughts.

"Looks like you need a driver for that car," Yarbrough said to Fox. "Let me have it and I can win with it. I won a Grand National race at Savannah last week."

After thinking the situation over, Fox took Yarbrough up on his offer and put him in the car. Since Yarbrough had a Grand National win to his credit, Fox really had no choice.

Fox flew Bobby back to Alabama in his private plane and turned the wheel over to Yarbrough. The next day, Yarbrough finished the 219-lap race in eighth, five laps down to winner Fred Lorenzen.

Bobby returned to the short-track Modifieds. Birmingham Speedway crowned a new track champion from Miami Springs, Fla., named Donnie Allison. Bobby was second in points and Red Farmer was third.

At Dixie Speedway, it was Farmer and Bobby, one and two, with Donnie, fifth. At Huntsville, the order was Donnie, Bobby and Red and at Montgomery, Red, Donnie and Bobby. The national standings awarded Bobby another Modified championship with Red fourth and Donnie fifth.

That year, Bobby used a 1961 Chevy with a 427 "mystery" engine and a 1955 Chevy with a 327 to win the title.

When the trio pulled their cars down the road together and drove through the gates of speedways at such places as Chattanooga, Tenn., or Atlanta , Ga., it was common to hear someone say, "Here comes that Alabama Gang." Early on, Bobby was dubbed the leader of the prestigious group.

On Oct. 20, 1964, Judy gave birth to a second son named Clifford Lawrence Allison.

The trip to Darlington earlier in the year simply fueled Bobby's urge to return to Grand National racing. With championships in other forms of racing under his belt, he felt he was ready for the challenge.

As Bobby entered the house late one fall evening, he discovered Judy had taken a telephone message for him while he was out.

"Bobby, someone called from Baton Rouge, La.," Judy said. "His name is Ed Grady. He wants to start a Grand National team next year and wants you to drive for him."

CHAPTER FIVE
A Second Try
At Grand
National Racing

It now seemed logical to make another attempt at Grand National racing. With Modified-special and Modified championships to his credit, at least Bobby had something in his resume' to bring with him when searching for a ride among the big league drivers.

Having won those championships in 1962, '63 and '64, respectively, Bobby's name had cropped up on the lists of various car owners for possible employment.

But, realistically speaking, using his local experience to gain a front-running race car seemed a bit far-fetched. These were the best drivers NASCAR had to offer and to get a ride in such a prestigious arena was not easy. That point was quickly proven to Bobby with Ray Fox in 1964.

Bobby felt the realistic avenue to gain knowledge and have a fighting chance at the big time, without the worry of being fired, was to field his own team. There were enough supporters of his racing efforts around Alabama and Georgia to realistically consider fielding a car in some of NASCAR's Grand National shows.

But money to race was scarce and a ride in someone else's car would certainly enable him to race more easily.

The 1964 Grand National season had produced electrifying

speeds, record attendance figures and the emergence of a popular points champion to represent the sport.

Due in part to those speeds, death seemed to come often. Some of the sport's greatest drivers, such as Joe Weatherly, Jimmy Pardue, Billy Wade and Fireball Roberts, lost their lives in crashes during races or tire tests.

As a result, some family members and friends felt Bobby's timing for such a venture in Grand National racing was questionable.

Speed was exciting to the fans but often very dangerous to the drivers. Superstars such as Buck Baker, Dick Hutcherson, Darel Dieringer and Richard Petty expressed to NASCAR officials their concerns for safety after their fellow drivers had been struck down. There was no question something had to be done.

Using carburetor restrictor plates and cutting cubic-inch sizes in the engines, NASCAR finally came up with ways of decreasing the speeds. But not all were happy with the rulings.

One noted driver, Richard Petty, became disgusted with the lopsided rules — the hemispherical combustion chamber engine utilized in his Chrysler-built Plymouths was outlawed — and elected to enter the drag racing ranks. Chrysler boycotted NASCAR.

It was then the call came from Grady to start the race team.

Ironically, he was part of the Teamsters Union and had turned state's evidence against Jimmy Hoffa during the 1961 Senate Committee hearings headed by U.S. Attorney General Robert F. Kennedy.

Around racing circles, he used the alias of Ed Grady, partly because of knowing what a dislike the sport's founder, Bill France Sr., felt toward unions, especially if he felt someone was trying to organize within the confines of his arena. In all actuality, his full name was Ed Grady Parton.

E.G. Parton had learned of stock car racing and Bobby's racing exploits over breakfast and coffee while reading the sports pages of the Baton Rouge, La., newspaper.

After Bobby returned his call, Parton informed him of his plan to put together a race team for that year. The race car already had been ordered from Holman-Moody in Charlotte, N.C.

Upon seeing the car, it was quickly learned it had been driven by Nelson Stacy on select dirt tracks around the south. It needed much work to make it raceable on asphalt, especially on a road course. The aspiring driver, car owner and a crew chief rented a flat bed truck and headed west to challenge NASCAR's elite. Allison, Parton and a young employee of Parton's named David Ashley set out for the Motor Trend 500 at Riverside International Raceway — a road course — scheduled for Jan. 17.

But once there two days later, their trip initially looked to be a waste of time, as the 1964 Ford was simply not ready to race. It required a great deal of work to pass NASCAR inspection and get into the field.

Norris Friel, Chief Technical Director for NASCAR, took one look at the car and began passing out adjectives.

"Well, what the hell is this?" Friel said, in one of his milder sentences. "You boys have so much work to do it will take you a week just to get through pre-race inspection."

Friel reached into his shirt pocket, which was often filled with note pads. Each page was usually full of thoughts and reminders to himself concerning the difficulties of keeping some of the world's most talented mechanics and drivers from cheating or killing themselves.

"Why don't I make you boys a list?" Friel said. "At least this way, I don't have to turn you away once you start through the inspection process. But I will if it's not right.

"You boys better get busy."

Bobby and Ashley worked feverishly to prepare the car to meet Friel's requirements and did not accomplish that until just before the start of the race.

Since it was Bobby's first trip to Riverside, less than an hour before race time, a NASCAR official drove him around the race track in one of the pace cars to allow him to see the configuration of the nine-turn course.

Once the 185-lap race began, Bobby found himself 41st in the 42-car field with a car that wasn't completely finished. It was allowed to start the event only because NASCAR did not have a full field of cars.

Allison finished 29th after suffering an overheating problem with the engine.

Parton also decided to enter the Feb. 14 Daytona 500. Once through the tunnel entrance in turn four and through the garage area gate of the 2.5-mile facility, Friel met Bobby and Ashley again with one hand in the air, as if to stop them before they went any further.

"Is that the same car you had at Riverside? " Friel asked.

"Well, yes, it is," Bobby responded.

"Then just turn that damn thing around and go back where you came from cause you're not running that car here."

"But Mr. Friel, we've done a lot of work to the car since you saw it last. Can you at least look at it?"

Friel crawled up on the side of the trailer and looked at the car closely — inside and out.

"You two are lying to me," Friel said. "This is not the same car you ran at Riverside. This can't be the same car."

"Oh, but it is," Ashley said. "We did everything you said and maybe a little more."

"Well, wherever you got it, you can run this one," Friel said. "This is the way you bring a car to a race track."

Friel walked away mumbling, "There's no way in hell that can be the same car."

Parton purchased an engine from John Holman especially for the Daytona 500 and spared no cost in doing so. At the time, a Grand National engine cost possibly $800. Parton, however, paid $1,500 for the powerplant in Bobby's Ford.

When the engine was fired for the first test session of Speed Weeks, water was discovered in one of the cylinders. Further investigation proved the water was in the oil, indicating a cracked cylinder head.

Parton, a strapping six-foot-three individual with wavy black hair and large bulging muscles, was not in the mood to be crossed. He walked into the Holman-Moody parts distribution shop located next to the garage area with the faulty cylinder head under one arm while Bobby carried the other.

"I want to see John Holman," Parton announced to no one in particular.

Holman, an overweight man with a flat top haircut and glasses, looked up from the paperwork he was reading. He was dressed in gray khaki trousers and a white short-sleeved shirt. Slowly, he rose from his seat and stepped up to the counter.

"What can I do for you?" Holman said with a bit of irritation in his voice.

"I think y'all need to give me another cylinder head," Parton said. "This one's cracked. It was on top of that $1,500 engine you sold me."

"Sure, I'll be glad to," Holman said. "Cylinder heads are $300. Just put your cash right here on the counter, big boy."

Parton quickly became angry and grabbed Holman by the shirt collar, pulled him across the counter close to him and looked him dead in the eye.

"Listen here, Porky Pig," Parton said. "I'm gonna go out the door and I'm coming back in 10 minutes. When I get back, I'd better have two cylinder heads laying right there on the counter, just in case there's something wrong with the other one. And if I don't have two cylinder heads sittin' right there, somebody is going to find you floating someplace."

Parton stared at Holman for a few more seconds and then released his shirt collar. Parton and Allison then turned and walked out of the room with the double door closing behind them.

Holman broke out in a nervous sweat and barked out some quick instructions. Lee Terry, an employee at H-M, was standing silently behind the counter in a bit of shock.

"Lee, get those heads off of that engine right there and get them up here on the counter," Holman said. "Hurry! That man's gonna kill me!"

When Parton returned, one could have heard a pin drop. As he retrieved the heads from the counter, his "Thank you" broke the silence. For several minutes, everyone stood and watched him leave, absolutely sure he meant what he had threatened to do. Only the rattle of the floor fan in the corner could be heard as each man looked at the other.

With the engine problems settled, one of the requirements for starting the 500 was to participate in one of two qualifying races on Thursday, Feb. 11. In that race, Bobby finished seventh in the 40-lap race behind winner Darel Dieringer.

In the 500, the race was shortened to 332.5 miles due to rain. When the race was red flagged on lap 133, Fred Lorenzen was out front in a Holman-Moody prepared Ford.

Bobby posted an 11th-place finish for his second attempt at the superspeedway trioval.

Many weeks passed before Bobby entered another Grand National event. He had plans to once again campaign his own cars in short track modified and sportsman events around the southern states and looked to be in line to repeat as a champion.

In an interview with radio personality Don O'Reilly, Bobby outlined his desires to race Grand National and having to juggle a busy schedule.

April 6, 1965:

O'Reilly: "Welcome to another broadcast of 'Inside Auto Racing.' Today, we have with us Bobby Allison, three-time NASCAR modified champion. Well, Bobby what are your plans for the 1965 season?"

Bobby: "Well, Don, at present our plans are a little unsettled. But we're going to run some Grand National, including Bristol (Tenn.), North Wilkesboro (N.C.), and I hope later on this summer to take a trip up north and race on the road courses of New York and so on up there. But, of course, I'll be filling in with some modified in the meantime. I don't know how much modified I will be running."

O'Reilly: "That northern swing in New York and those road courses you mentioned could be quite interesting. Have you ever driven a stock car on a road course before?"

Bobby: "Don, the first time I ever did was this past January out in Riverside and I really enjoyed it."

O'Reilly: "How did you get around that Riverside course?"

Bobby: "Well, at first I kind of had to hunt my way. But once I got used to the track I liked it. I improved my position real well until I had a head gasket failure."

O'Reilly: "Do you have to set up a car much differently for a road course than you do for an oval track?"

Bobby: "Yes, quite a bit. In fact, most of the turns on the road course are to the right rather than to the left. So we just about had to reverse the whole suspension. We had to put the heavy coils (springs) on the left side rather than the right and also had to add leafs to the left rear spring and take them out of the right rear spring."

O'Reilly: "Over in Birmingham, they're getting ready for the 1965 season on the short tracks. How much racing are you going to do around that area?"

Bobby: "Well, I don't know. It looks like during the week, they are going to have Thursday night steady and Friday night steady, and naturally, Saturday night, which has always been the thing at Montgomery. And, of course, every Sunday at Birmingham. If I run much Grand National, I'll have to at least miss some of the Sunday shows, which, of course, that will be giving up my favorite track over there. But I have to think of the future and if I'm going to advance any I'll have to go Grand National."

O'Reilly: "Well, lots of luck to you Bobby Allison. I'll be back after this message."

As O'Reilly pushed the button to stop the recording process on his portable reel-to-reel tape recorder, the two men discussed several topics of interest and unknown to them at the time, the relationship would remain strong decades later.

On April 11, Bobby was back to compete at Atlanta International Raceway, again in Parton's Southern Racing 1964 Ford. There, many of the sport's established team owners kept an eye on him and were impressed with a seventh-place finish in the 44-car field.

From there, it was back to the Alabama short tracks until more finances could be raised to campaign on the Grand National circuit.

But when the Grand Nationals came to Birmingham on June 6, Bobby was in the lineup in the Robert Harper Ford.

After becoming disillusioned with Grand National racing, Parton returned to Baton Rouge, selling the equipment to Harper. The new team campaigned No. 09 and dropped No. 12.

Having been so familiar with the half-mile oval, many felt Bobby could score a victory under the right circumstances. But again, there was a seventh-place finish.

Back at Atlanta on June 13, Bobby fell to 38th in the 42-car field after an engine expired on lap 69 of 267 laps.

Heating problems took Bobby out of the July 4 Firecracker 400 at Daytona International Speedway. After several pit stops to correct the problem, Bobby finished a dismal 25th.

At Bristol, Tenn., July 25th, Bobby again suffered heating problems and was forced to finish 32nd.

After eight Grand National events, Bobby's best showings were three seventh-place finishes. He did, however, manage to win his fourth National Modified Championship with 14 victories in 66 starts.

Even though highly successful on the local short tracks around Alabama, Bobby's mind was clearly on the Grand National circuit. That is where he felt his talents could be recognized most.

But his first taste of Grand National racing found him 34th in the season-ending point standings behind champion Ned Jarrett.

Harper was also running out of money and was beginning to have second thoughts about stock car racing. He hinted he would not be back in 1966.

Being one to look toward the positive instead of negative, Bobby knew someone would want him to drive their cars.

He knew his phone would ring again soon.

CHAPTER SIX
The First Full Season

Bobby found himself glad a new season was at hand, as the previous one had been a bit controversial and confusing where rules were concerned.

As the 1965 NASCAR Grand National season drew to a close, the sanctioning body found itself nursing a few wounds. The Chrysler boycott caused a box office disaster at each of the tracks on the circuit.

But on Dec. 13 of that year, Bill France stood watching the Detroit automaker pull Hemi engines off the assembly line one right after the other. To his delight, Chrysler was back into the fold of stock car racing and the Hemi engine was approved for use since it had become a production item.

Under the 1966 rules, however, the 426-cubic-inch engine would be used in intermediate and full-size cars on the short tracks and the road courses.

But the problem of equality among car makes seemed far from being settled. At the same time France watched the production of the Chrysler powerplant, Ford Motor Co. made an announcement of its own. NASCAR Ford teams would utilize a single overhead cam engine which would be out in force to defend their accomplishments of 1965. All of France's efforts seemed to be crumbling.

It was standard practice for automakers to get approval of a certain part or parts of a race car from NASCAR before they would announce such a decision. But in this case, the cart had clearly been placed ahead of the horse.

"I asked Ford officials if someone could order 50 OHC engines," France said. "The man told me they weren't available. If Ford is sincere about the OHC becoming a production engine, they will still make it available to the public without being able to use it racing."

In a countermove, Ford's Lee C. Beebe said they would not be able to field factory-backed cars for Riverside or Daytona, as preparing sponsored factory cars using different engines at such short notice was impossible.

Fearing another walkout, France discussed the situation with Ford officials and on Christmas Day, NASCAR and USAC said that Ford had agreed to continue it's support of stock car racing without interruption. The agreement called for the OHC engine to be looked upon as an experimental engine for the 1966 season, leaving the door open for Ford to produce their product and thus permit it to be eligible in 1967.

Still, many drivers and car owners felt what Ford had to offer wouldn't last three laps in competition. But in the end, most Ford drivers remained loyal.

Even though the engine controversy continued, Bobby was able to land a ride for the 1966 season with car owner Betty Lilly, whose husband was a wealthy entrepreneur from Valdosta, Ga.

Sam McQuagg, Bobby's longtime close friend from the modified ranks, wheeled her Fords to the 1965 Rookie of the Year title on a total of $25,000 in sponsorship money. When McQuagg was offered a job with car owner Ray Nichels, he moved on to the powerful Chrysler effort, leaving the ride open for the next year.

The budget given to Bobby was not a lucrative one, but adequate enough to enter some races with a degree of satisfaction.

Allison by-passed the 300-lap event at Augusta, Ga., on Nov. 14, 1965. At that time, some races at the end of a calendar year were considered the first events of a Grand National schedule for the upcoming season.

On January 23, 1966, Bobby wheeled Lilly's Ford to a 12th-place finish at Riverside, Calif., behind race winner Dan Gurney, who scored his fourth straight Riverside victory. That kept Ford on top, despite the question of adequate engines.

At Daytona on Feb. 25, Bobby's Ford fell silent after only 16 laps in the 40-lap qualifying race, which dictated a 44th-place start in the Daytona 500 two days later.

In that race, another engine expired, but not before Bobby was able to complete 143 of 200 laps for a 20th-place finish.

Rivals Richard Petty and Cale Yarborough battled fiercely, but rain cut the race short by two laps and Petty went on to score his second Daytona 500 victory.

Even though 12 laps down at North Carolina Motor Speedway on March 13, "the rookie from Alabama" was the talk of the garage area after the race.

At Bristol, Tenn., on March 20, Bobby once again was sidelined with a faulty engine. Of the 32 cars that made up the field, he managed a 28th-place finish.

Having underfinanced race cars in a scenario which required the best equipment possible, Bobby considered himself somewhat fortunate just to start and finish any of the events.

The Atlanta 500 on March 27 provided a 10th-place finish behind eventual winner Jim Hurtubise. But the budget dictated the need to sit out the next three races until the 200-lap event at Bowman Gray Stadium in Winston-Salem, N.C., on April 11 where Bobby finished fourth behind David Pearson, Tom Pistone, and Petty.

There was a 26th at North Wilkesboro, N.C. on April 17, a seventh at Martinsville, Va., and a 16th due to a faulty wheel bearing at Darlington, S.C., on April 30.

The next outing on May 10 gave Bobby a third-place finish at Macon, Ga., to the tune of $400 in prize money. Again, he finished behind Petty and Pistone.

But it would be the last race for Betty Lilly's operation, as the blown engines had taken their toll on the budget. Later, the operation would resurface with Tiny Lund as the team's driver.

With the turn of events, Bobby replaced Curtis Turner in the Smokey Yunick Chevrolet for the May 22 World 600 at Charlotte Motor Speedway. But only three laps were completed before the engine erupted. Poor horsepower had been Turner's complaint throughout the year.

To Bobby's disappointment, the arrangement turned out to be a one-race deal and with no other prospects waiting in the shadows, he had no choice but to build his own car — a Chevelle — out of a two-car cement block garage located behind his house on Cresent Drive in Hueytown.

With exhaustive assistance from brothers Eddie and Donnie, as well as Chuck Looney, an employee and close friend, the car was completed just prior to the 200-lap event at Beltsville, Md., on June 15. Bobby's run was impressive but ended with a 15th-place run, due to a faulty rear axle suffered after 174 of 400 laps.

The surprising performance of the car drew the interest of Bill France Sr., who called Bobby and offered a 427 cubic inch engine that Junior Johnson had been experimenting with. The offer from France would provide Bobby the engine to use in the Firecracker 400 at Daytona on July 4 in an attempt to build a competitive Chevrolet. A lot of hard work went on there, but the performance was somewhat disappointing. Bobby found himself 14th in the 40-car field, 11 laps behind Sam McQuagg.

Three days later, Bobby entered the 400-lap event at Manasses, Va. where he scored his first career pole position. Ultimately, he finished 15th after being sidelined with a broken carburetor fuel log.

Getting ready for the 52-lap event at Bridgehampton, N.Y., a great deal of engine trouble kept the crew working constantly.

The Chevelle suffered another engine failure after only 11 laps, forcing a 23rd-place finish.

But Bobby's luck changed quickly.

With the engine supply depleted, Bobby was forced to purchase an engine en route to Oxford, Maine. He stopped at a Chevrolet dealership in Boston where a high performance engine block assembly was found on their pile of rejected parts.

Once in Oxford, Bobby was offered space to work in the garage at a dealership located across the highway from the speedway. Working through the night with the help of Chuck and Bob Latford (a public relations representative), they rebuilt the engine and installed it in the car.

The next evening, July 12, Bobby dominated the 300-lap event at the .333-mile Oxford Plains Speedway and logged his first-ever NASCAR Grand National victory.

Equipped with the small block 327 cubic engine, Allison started from the pole position and led the majority of the event, except for a few laps led by Tiny Lund.

It was the first Grand National win for a Chevrolet since Dec. 1, 1963 when Wendell Scott won at Jacksonville, Fla.

"I think a new wrinkle has started," Bobby said. "We're pleased in two ways. It handled well right off the trailer. And secondly, it blew right by all the hot dogs."

Bobby averaged 56.782 mph en route to the victory.

Two days later, Bobby severely damaged his Chevrolet in a crash at Fonda, N.Y., on lap 32 of the 200-lap event.

Feeling dejected, Bobby found himself far from home with a

badly damaged race car that had been shortened nearly three feet in the front end and rear end.

Bobby placed a phone call to his cousin, Dave Demerest, a paint and body specialist with extensive experience in automotive frame work.

While Bobby traveled, Demerest busied himself gathering fenders, a front end and various suspension parts that had been destroyed when the car hit hard into a mass pile-up of badly damaged race cars.

A total of 18 hours was spent rebuilding the car with the help of James Hylton, a fellow driver, and J.D. Roberts, Hylton's mechanic. After the reconstruction effort was complete, the red and white Chevelle wasn't pretty, but it was raceable.

On July 16, Bobby went to Islip, N.Y., and as he entered the gate to sign his car into the race, John Bruner, Sr., the NASCAR chief official, said, "I told them in Daytona Beach we wouldn't ever see this car again."

Bobby smiled widely and said, "Well, it doesn't look all that great, but we're here."

The Chevelle was placed into contention for the win at Islip when Hylton's Bud Hartje-owned Dodge ran out of gas with only seven laps remaining. Hylton's misfortune meant the second Grand National win of Bobby's career.

Bobby's average speed en route to the victory was 47.285 mph and was good enough for ninth place in the NASCAR point standings.

Even though 10 laps down at Bristol on July 24, Bobby managed to finish in fifth place and repeated the effort at Maryville, Tenn., on July 28. He was also third at Nashville on July 30.

The rule book was seemingly tossed out once the Grand National circuit got to Atlanta International Raceway on Aug. 7, as there were a couple of cars present which had undergone questionable modifications.

Junior Johnson's yellow Ford, nicknamed the "Yellow Banana," "Junior's Joke" and "Magnifluxed Monster," was clearly not in accordance with the rule book. The front end sloped downward, the roofline was lowered, the windows were narrowed and the front windshield was placed in a very aerodynamic position. Also, the rear deck lifted up in the air considerably.

Smokey Yunick's car was similarly different from what the automakers in Detroit had intended. The front of his car was neatly handcrafted, there was a raised lip at the rear of the roofline and the wheels were positioned in the body cutaways.

On the other hand, the cars of David Pearson, Lee Roy Yarbrough and Ned Jarrett were not approved by NASCAR Technical Director Norris Friel.

Johnson's Ford, driven by Fred Lorenzen, emerged 23rd in the 42-car field after a crash on lap 139 of the 267-lap event.

As Lorenzen took the long walk back to the garage area from the third turn, a member of the media said jokingly, "It's pretty hard to drive a banana at 145 mph."

Yunick's Chevrolet with Curtis Turner on board finished 24th after suffering a faulty distributor on lap 130.

Bobby's legal Chevrolet took 10th, nearly 20 laps down to race winner Richard Petty.

At Columbia, S.C. on Aug. 18, Bobby posted an 11th-place finish as well as an eighth at Asheville-Weaverville Speedway two days later.

At Beltsville, Md., Bobby took the lead from Petty when the Petty Enterprises engine expired on lap 30 of the 200-lap event. As a result, Bobby went on to score his third win of the season.

With valve springs and rods scattering across the racing surface, he held a lap lead over Elmo Langley when the checkered flag fell.

Three days later, Bobby found himself in a fierce battle with the older, crusty Turner and engaged in a car smashing confrontation that kept the crowd on its feet throughout half of the 250-lap race at Bowman Gray Stadium in Winston Salem, N.C.

Pearson got the lead in the 219th lap and went on to hold off Petty to secure the victory.

But the crowd, 15,000 strong, was more concerned with the Allison-Turner fight that saw both drivers continually ram one another with reckless abandon.

The storyline was set early into the event when Turner hooked Bobby's rear bumper, spinning the Alabama driver out on the eighth lap on the flat quarter-mile oval. As a result, Bobby lost a lap to the leaders, but he quickly began to regain the lost ground.

Turner was doing a masterful job of blocking the track and holding his rivals behind him. But when Tom Pistone attempted to take the lead, Bobby dropped low and caused a three-wide fracas coming out of the third turn. Pistone hit the retaining wall as Turner and Bobby touched and spun. With that, Petty shot into the lead on lap 106.

Turner returned to the track and was moving slowly, waiting on

Bobby's Chevrolet. But Bobby sensed an ambush and decided not to give Turner the satisfaction. He cut back and hit Turner in the rear.

Most of the confrontation occurred under the caution flag thrown for Pistone's spin. Surprisingly, neither of the drivers were warned by NASCAR officials. Reportedly, when an official in the press box prepared to send both drivers out of the race, a higher official touched his assistant's arm and told him to let the two settle the misunderstanding at the pleasure of the fans.

Turner spun Bobby; Bobby returned and spun Turner, who once again waited on Bobby and rammed him. In retaliation, Bobby put his limp race car into the front end of Turner's car. At that point, the NASCAR officials had seen enough and ejected both from the race. But that fact didn't matter since both cars were so badly destroyed. Neither car went another foot further.

The battered cars came to a halt on the backstretch and both drivers held a hard stare at one another. Turner emerged first and was en route over to the driver's side of Bobby's Chevrolet.

All the while, several of the fans had jumped the fence and were on the race track. Police officers quickly came on the scene and kept both drivers in separate corners and cleared the crowd that had gathered around them.

Turner's car owner, Junior Johnson, was openly disturbed over the incident and warned the Virginia driver he could fix the car out of his own pocket the next time something like that happened.

Bobby, however, reacted calmly to the situation. But a few days later, fines were placed on both drivers by NASCAR.

"It was necessary to warn and fine us," he said. "We know better than anyone the consequences of rough driving at high speeds. The thing between Turner and myself began and ended at Bowman Gray Stadium."

"It was a situation where I was fairly new to the sport and Turner had been around a while and was the old veteran. Anyway, as it turned out, I'm not all the way sure he was completely sober at the time.

"I hit him and he came back and hit me. This goes on a while and finally our cars sat in the infield damaged so badly we neither one could move them.

"I felt like I had just as much right to be on that race track as the new driver as he did as the veteran."

On Sept. 5, the tour moved to Darlington, S.C., for the Southern 500. There, the hype billed a second round of the Allison-Turner bout.

But both fell out of contention due to mechanical failure.

In the race, the lead changed hands 28 times with Petty and Darel Dieringer leading most of the way. In the end, Petty suffered a leaking tire, allowing Dieringer to take the victory.

Bobby looked impressive in the early going of the 364-lap event but fell victim to a blown engine on lap 71.

On lap 189, Petty tapped the rear of Earl Balmer's Dodge and sent it flying for several hundred yards along the top of the first-turn guardrail, where it threatened to wipe out the open-air press box located there.

The 100 to 125 press members were sitting just 15 feet above the track's surface and scrambled when they saw Balmer coming.

"We were diving for cover like soldiers seeking the sanctuary of a fox hole," said Tom Higgins, motorsports reporter for The Charlotte Observer, minutes after the accident occurred.

Balmer stood wiping his hands on a red shop rag trying to calm his nerves when some press members stationed in the infield cornered him about the incident.

"I don't know what happened," Balmer said while in the garage area after the incident. "My car hadn't handled well for several laps. I didn't see Petty at all. I thought sure as hell I was going into that press box. All I could think of was 'Oh, those poor people up there'."

From there, the tour moved to a series of short track events.

On Sept. 9, Bobby was seventh behind Pearson at Hickory, N.C., after a strong run. Prior to the race, Johnson came out of retirement and replaced Turner in his own Fords for the 250-lap event. Johnson finished 11th after calling on Dick Hutcherson for relief.

At Richmond, Va., on Sept. 11, a broken drive shaft put Bobby on the sidelines and caused a 20th-place finish. But he improved dramatically with a third-place finish at Martinsville, Va., on Sept. 25 after having an engine blow with six laps remaining.

Lorenzen won Martinsville by going a lot of extra laps without having to stop for fuel. However, NASCAR would not listen to Bobby's gripes about checking the size of the fuel tank.

Bobby lost yet another engine at North Wilkesboro, N.C., on Oct. 2 and that left him with a 30th-place finish in a 35-car field. It proved to be costly, as only two engines were available for the next race, one blowing in practice. Bobby ran well in the consolation race but blew the other engine and could not start the Oct. 16 National 500 at Charlotte Motor Speedway.

In a flurry of protests in the season finale at North Carolina

Motor Speedway on Oct. 30, Lorenzen was protested for a large fuel tank. But all of the first five finishers were eventually declared legal.

Bobby fell victim to another engine failure at NCMS and was 41st among 44 cars.

The season saw the retirement of both Ned Jarrett, the reigning NASCAR Grand National champion, and Junior Johnson, who hung up his helmet for good.

Pearson took the 1966 NASCAR Grand National championship in a Cotton Owens Dodge with 42 starts, 15 victories, 26 top-fives and 33 top-10s.

Even though there were several engine failures, Bobby managed to finish 10th in points with 34 starts, three wins, 10 top-fives and 15 top-10s.

But there was also a much bigger accomplishment. Bobby had gained the respect of drivers and fans alike with victories on the Northern Tour with his self-owned Chevelle. And then there was the incident with Curtis Turner at Bowman Gray Stadium. Both proved he could not be intimidated by the factory-backed teams or the veterans who drove for them.

There was no question among the other drivers that another young aggressive driver was on the scene to stay.

"I knew how well the car was running and I felt I had a solid chance at winning the race at night. We made just very few changes and that made me feel like we could at least give a good effort if we didn't end up winning the race.

"That Chevelle was one of the best race cars of my entire career. It was pretty much a stock body and a stock frame.

"About all I ever did to the body and chassis was to take the rubber biscuits out from under the body mounts which lowered it an inch or so."

CHAPTER SEVEN
Labeled A Ride Jumper

Thanks to Betty Lilly, Bobby's quest to be a regular on the prestigious NASCAR Grand National circuit had become more and more of a reality.

Car owner Bud Moore was impressed with some of Bobby's performances in Lilly's cars as well as those in his own machine and offered him a job on a part-time basis for the 1967 season.

It was a good arrangement, for when he was not behind the wheel of Moore's Fords, he could drive his own Chevelle or any other cars offered to him.

Bobby took the Chevelle to Riverside on January 22 but rain halted activities until the following week.

On January 29, Bobby started the 185-lap event in 20th position but fell off the pace after only 92 circuits with a faulty transmission. He ultimately logged a 24th-place finish.

Moore had a Ford prepared for him in Daytona a month later where he finished 15th in the 100-mile qualifying race, but posted a 40th place finish by suffering an oil leak after 34 laps of the Daytona 500 two days later.

Bobby competed in short track events at Weaverville, N.C., Greenville, S.C., and Bristol, Tenn., and won a 200-lap event at Winston Salem, N.C., on March 27. He returned to Moore's Ford in Atlanta the following week where he finished ninth.

At Martinsville, Va., on April 23, involvement in a crash on lap 264 of 500 laps saw Bobby park Moore's Ford for the final time.

Even with the high number of mechanical failures and a crash, there was no discord between car owner and driver. Bobby was given an offer too good to refuse a few days after the Martinsville race.

"Bud, as you know, we're only running a select schedule of races," Bobby said. "But I've been offered a full-time ride and I'm seriously considering it."

"Well, that sounds good," Moore said. "Who's it with?"

"Cotton Owens," Bobby said. "David Pearson quit the other day and he called and offered me the ride. He said we'd go to all the races and get appearance money and if so, we'd split it. The best part is we'll have the best of the factory stuff to go racing with."

"All I can say is you have my best wishes and I think you should take it," Moore said in his long South Carolina drawl. "I can't offer you a deal anywhere near as good."

"Thank you, Bud. I appreciate your support on this very much."

Bobby won a 100-mile event at Savannah, Ga., on April 28 in his Chevelle and began his employment with Owens just two days later at Richmond, Va., where he finished second to Richard Petty. He struggled to post such an impressive finish, as he spun the Dodge twice, the second time losing the lead to Petty. But he regained second place from Dick Hutcherson just before crossing the start-finish line to end the race.

Upon returning home, he was greeted by a newborn daughter, Caralene Allison, who is fondly called "Carrie."

Once his thoughts returned to the race cars, Bobby knew immediately there was a problem with what he considered to be outdated and non-competitive machines. Feeling open and friendly with Owens, he made an offer in the best interest of the race team.

"Cotton, the car was really loose at Richmond but I really think I can fix it, that is if you'll let me," Allison said. "I think the car needs some extensive chassis work."

"OK, fine," Owens said. "But you'll not get any help or any salary. I will pay for your brother Eddie to help do whatever you want to do, but that's all."

Bobby accepted the offer and within weeks made Owens' Dodges very competitive. The team's first win of the season came on June 10 at Birmingham, Ala.

Soon after, however, Owens began to break his promise to run all the races. Slowly, Bobby was becoming more of a drawing card for the fans and Owens recognized this. As a result, more appearance money was being required from the promoters or the team wouldn't race at their speedways.

The tour moved back to Daytona for the July 4 Firecracker 400. To Bobby's dislike, Owens' car was the only one in the field shod with Firestone tires. Realizing the tires' lack of dependability, Bobby voiced his opinion.

"I really think we should be on Goodyear tires instead of Firestones," Bobby said. "They seem to perform better on the track and can stay together better at high speeds."

"We've got a deal with Firestone," Owens responded. "We've got to use them."

"But the Firestones are slower and fly apart," Bobby said. "We shouldn't have to run a tire that renders us non-competitive.

"Look at Petty. He switches back and forth every week. Why can't we? I don't think this is the way to race."

"We're on Firestones and that's the way it is," Owens said as he walked away.

Once the green flag fell, Bobby started the event in 11th position and steadily moved into the lead by lap 23 for only five laps. Suddenly, his right front tire exploded, as he had expected. Bobby coasted into the pits for fresh tires and found himself a lap down to the leaders. But timely caution periods kept him from falling many laps down.

Throughout the afternoon, he fought with exploding tires but managed to stay just in contention against four factory Fords driven by Cale Yarborough, Dick Hutcherson, Darel Dieringer and David Pearson as well as the Dodge of Bobby Isaac and the Mercury of Lee Roy Yarbrough. Lap after lap, his arms would turn the wheel in an attempt to keep the car out of the wall.

To further complicate matters, there were two delays for rain — one of which lasted for four and one-half hours.

During the first lengthy delay, Bobby lined up his Dodge in its current running order, along with the other cars brought to a halt by NASCAR officials.

After a quick exit, Bobby found a seat on the pit road wall, where Sam McQuagg, driver of the Nord Kraskopf Dodge, approached Bobby and stood beside him. McQuagg had already fallen out of the race with engine problems.

"How are you feeling?" McQuagg asked.

"Fine," Bobby said.

"Cotton walked over to me a few minutes ago and said you were sick," McQuagg said. "He asked if I could get in your car at the restart."

But McQuagg realized immediately Bobby was in good health and some sort of mixup had taken place.

"Hey, I'm fine, really," Bobby said with arms raised as if presenting himself for inspection.

"Well, I told Cotton that I wouldn't run a single lap until he put Goodyears on that car," McQuagg said. "I told him to forget it otherwise. So he said he would get me some Goodyears."

"Thanks anyway, Sam," Bobby said. "I'm gettin' back in, probably on those old Firestones."

"Well, OK then," McQuagg said. "I'm here if you need me."

When the checkered flag waved some eight and one-half hours after the race began, Bobby was seventh, two laps down to eventual winner Cale Yarborough. Two more tires exploded before race's end.

Disgusted and tired from a long day's work, Bobby changed his clothes and flew home to Alabama.

Early the next morning, Owens called Bobby with an idea.

"Have you still got that old Chevelle you used to run?" Owens asked.

"No, I sold it to some friends but I'm sure they'd let me drive it if I wanted," Bobby said. "But I don't see where I have a reason to want to."

"Well, here's the deal," Owens said. "You take the Chevelle on the Northern tour so we can really get ready for the race at Bristol (Tenn.)."

"But Cotton, everything is ready, cars and equipment," Bobby responded. "All three cars are set to race right now. We changed all the Coronets over to Chargers with a lot of manual labor from me and Eddie and some of your people. We did everything we could think of to those cars."

"Now, Bobby, I'm sure there's work to be done," Owens said. "Believe me, they just aren't finished. Look, if you'll take the Chevelle up north, we'll have a car for you at Bristol that can win the race."

Bobby paused for a few seconds, took a deep breath and finally said, "OK, I'll do it."

To take the Chevelle north meant loading his own truck and trailer with equipment, as well as hiring people to transport it. But there seemed to be no other choice. Owens insisted his cars required more work.

On July 10, Bobby Walker, public relations director for Oxford Plains Speedway, invited Bobby and Judy to stay at his parent's house while in town for the race. The Allisons had just come from Trenton, N.J., for the race there — Bobby finished ninth — and were tired from the trip.

At two a.m., Walker knocked on the guest room door to summon Bobby to the telephone. Immediately, there was concern a loved one was sick or an emergency of some sort had transpired at home.

"Hello, Bobby," came the caller's voice. "This is sports writer Frank Vehorn. Why did you quit Cotton?"

Vehorn's question hit Bobby like a ton of bricks and brought him wide awake.

"I haven't quit Cotton," Bobby responded.

"You must have because you're up north with your Chevrolet," Vehorn said.

"I haven't quit Cotton," Bobby re-emphasized. "I made a deal with Cotton to come up here while they get the car ready for Bristol."

"That's not the case, Bobby," Vehorn said. "I've got a press release here that says you're unhappy with Dodge automobiles and that you've decided to return to Chevrolets.

"It also says that Sam McQuagg is now Cotton's full-time driver."

At that point, Bobby realized he had been set up.

Walking back into the bedroom, Judy knew the look on Bobby's face well, for she had seen discomfort many times.

"What is it, Bobby?" Judy asked.

"That call was from Frank Vehorn, a sportswriter back in Virginia," Bobby said dejectedly. "He told me that Cotton is going to put Sam McQuagg in the car at Bristol."

"Oh, no," Judy said. "Why do things like this have to happen? We've done a nice job for Cotton and Dot and were just starting to become good friends with them."

"I just don't know," Bobby said. "I should have seen what Cotton was doing by sending me up here with this Chevelle. But I trusted him. I had no idea this was what he had in mind. I guess I was just blind to it. I didn't even see it coming, even while I was talking to him."

Even though disillusioned, Bobby left Maine with a bit of pride in himself, as he emerged victorious at Oxford, winning the 300-lap event by a full lap over Petty.

Two days later, the Northern Tour provided Bobby with a second-place finish at Fonda, N.Y., and a sixth at Islip, N.Y., by week's end.

A few months passed and Bobby experienced a series of near

wins, disappointing finishes and crashes. Soon, he found himself welding and patching the old Chevelle in hopes of completing the season.

After a fourth-place finish at North Wilkesboro, N.C., Bobby accepted an invitation to drive a Nord Kraskopf-owned Dodge and finished 13th in the Oct. 15 National 500 at Charlotte, N.C.

On Saturday afternoon, Oct. 21, 1967, Bobby had secluded himself behind a welding mask in his shop in Hueytown when the phone rang. Continuing his work, he simply flipped the welding visor up and reached for it.

"Yeah, hello?" Bobby answered.

"You're going to get a phone call in a few minutes," said the unidentified voice. "Say, 'Yes.' Bye."

But Bobby knew the voice well. It was Ralph Moody, someone he had respected since his days as a teenager. He was also part-owner of the famed Holman-Moody race car factory operation in Charlotte.

At first, Bobby wasn't sure if he was being gouged, for Moody was bad to play tricks to get a laugh.

But the phone did ring again and this time, the caller was Fred Lorenzen, a former superstar driver who had retired from active competition in April.

"I've talked Ford Motor Co. into giving me a car for the race at Rockingham (N.C.)," Lorenzen explained. "I'd like to know if you'll drive the car there."

"Yes," came Bobby's quick answer. Moody had already told him what to say.

"Great. When can you get together with me?" Lorenzen asked.

"How about tonight around eight?" returned Bobby.

"Ah, super!" Lorenzen said. "Then meet me at the Holman-Moody shop in Charlotte. We'll talk there."

Bobby removed the welding shield from his head and flipped the switch on the welder. Directing his comment to no one in general, Bobby yelled through the shop area to those working on several unfinished tasks, "Hold up on what you're doing 'cause there's been a change in plans. Everybody take some time off. I've got to go to Charlotte."

Normally, the crew would have worked through the upcoming Tuesday in order to leave on Wednesday for second-round qualifying for the American 500 on Oct. 29 at North Carolina Motor Speedway in Rockingham.

The word having been passed, Bobby began to ready his single-engine plane for the trip.

Later that evening, Bobby arrived and was greeted by Lorenzen. Each took a chair in one of the vacant offices, as no one was around on a weekend.

"As you well know, Petty's beating the socks off of everybody and Ford wants to put a stop to it," Lorenzen said. "We feel you're the only driver that's beat him outright this year."

"Yeah, the others who have won against him did it after he fell out of the race," Bobby added.

"Well, here's my offer," Lorenzen said. "There's no salary, just race winnings. This is a new venture and Ford just wants to see what happens. We'll take it race by race."

"OK by me," Bobby said.

Other points, such as car chassis setups and race strategies, were discussed in the two-hour meeting. Once the meeting broke up, Bobby had a new liking for Lorenzen because of his honesty and his "no excuses" dedication to race-car preparation. Prior to their conversation, Bobby respected Lorenzen but did not particularly like him, as the two had battled one another on the race track before Lorenzen's retirement. Bobby's opinion, however, changed quickly about the Elmhurst, Ill., resident once he got to know him.

At Lorenzen's suggestion, Bobby flew to Charlotte, met Freddie, and went to the Holman-Moody shops where four Grand National cars were lined up to choose one from. There was one blue and gold Ford Fairlane with No. 11s, two Fairlanes numbered with 17s, and a metallic light brown Fairlane number 66.

"Take your pick, " Lorenzen said, casting a hand toward the cars in front of them.

"You pick for me," Bobby said with a smile, "cause I can win in any of them."

"Let's take the No. 11 because it has the 396 (cubic inch) engine," Lorenzen said. "Under the NASCAR rules, it gets to run with less weight."

From the minute Bobby strapped himself inside the team's Ford Fairlane, he knew immediately the car was going to be good.

Many times during his career, he had driven cars that were fast but lacked the ability to handle in the corners — so much so that when the wall would approach him lap after lap, the hair would stand up on the back of his neck. Other times, the car would handle beautifully but would not be fast. Lorenzen had the knowledge to get both speed and handling to come together in the same package.

David Pearson was in the other Holman-Moody car and one of the first to qualify. Pearson had been employed there since leaving Cotton Owens' team earlier in the year and Holman hired him to help stop the Petty dominance.

Bobby and his car were in top form during qualifying and he was sure he would get the pole position until Pearson's team reported Lorenzen to a NASCAR official. The safety inner liners from the tires on all the Fords had been removed for qualifying. This gave the Fords a slightly quicker qualifying lap. Even though he and Pearson were teammates, the finger was still pointed out of competitiveness. All of the other Ford teams had their qualifying tires put away when the NASCAR inspectors wanted a look at them.

Once the race began, Bobby's premonitions of having a strong car proved true, as he gained the lead for the first time on the 1.017-mile track on lap 13. Ultimately, he led a total of six times for 164 laps and was victorious over Pearson by one lap.

The marriage set up by Lorenzen made the Ford executives smile even more the next week at Asheville-Weaverville Speedway near Asheville, N.C., as Bobby won the pole position and led the first 121 laps before going head to head in a fender banging bout with Petty in the exciting season climax.

With six laps to go, Bobby managed to slip under Petty to take his second straight victory.

Crew chief Lorenzen was overjoyed at the team's second success and stated, "As far as I'm concerned, Allison has a lifetime job."

As the late afternoon sun sat just above the tree tops around Asheville-Weaverville, Bobby returned to the cockpit of his airplane sure his dreams were finally coming true.

But little did he suspect there were dark clouds on the horizon. Corporate politics would soon engulf his career.

CHAPTER EIGHT
A First Class Factory Effort

With the success realized at the end of the 1967 season in the Holman-Moody Ford effort managed by former driver Fred Lorenzen, Bobby was shifted over to the Bondy Long operation based in Camden, S.C., one of several teams maintained with H-M support.

Long, considered a playboy of sorts with the DuPont family fortune behind him, dabbled in various interests.

In years past, Ned Jarrett was able to capture the 1961 and '65 Grand National championships while driving Long's cars.

Dick Hutcherson, Long's driver in 1967, retired from driving at the end of the year, thus clearing the way for Bobby to join the team.

The initial deal handed down from Ford Motor Co. called for Bobby to run the first seven races and an evaluation would be made after those races had been completed.

If the team found its ranking in the point standings high, there would be a strong chance of campaigning the full schedule — something Bobby had always wanted to do.

In an interview just after the Allison-Long announcement was made, Bobby said, "I just hope to be able to run all the races. I want to go after the Grand National championship. Maybe we can do well enough so Ford will send us to every race. I don't want to run just some of the races."

Allison started off the season with a victory at Macon, Ga., on November 12, 1967, and set the stage for what everyone billed as the

"Superteam" of 1968.

In that season opener, Allison took the lead from David Pearson on lap 452 of the 500-mile event at the .534-mile facility and went on to take an early lead in the point standings.

But if that was exciting for Bobby, this tickled everyone's fancy: Federal and state agents seized a lucrative moonshine operation built in a tunnel underneath the race track. Entrance to the illegal still could be obtained through a ticket booth positioned in the north end of the track.

Agents climbed down a 35-foot ladder leading from a trap door. Once at the next level, they found the 125-foot tunnel where the still was located.

"This is one of the most cleverly run moonshine operations I have ever seen," said a Federal agent.

Following the investigation, it was discovered the still was capable of producing 200 gallons of whiskey every five days. At one end of the tunnel was a 2,000 gallon cooker, a 1,200 gallon box fermenter and a 750 gallon fuel tank for cooking. The operators had installed yellow lights to keep bugs from getting into the mash.

Track president H. Lamar Brown Jr. was charged with possession of apparatus for the distilling of illegal liquor.

The case went to trial on Dec. 12, 1968, with Brown being found not guilty after a two-hour deliberation by the jury.

After receiving a sizable amount of "show money," Richard Petty entered the 100-lap race at Montgomery, Ala., on November 26, 1967 and won the event, but only after Bobby's engine began to sputter on lap 143 of 200 laps. Bobby nursed his ill-sounding Ford and managed to hold onto second place in the final rundown.

Next came the event at Riverside International Raceway and in only three years after Bobby saw the track for the first time, he managed to score a solid fourth-place finish behind Dan Gurney, Pearson and Parnelli Jones. It was the fifth time Gurney wheeled his car into victory lane at the California road course.

The traditional qualifying races, usually run before the Daytona 500, were rained out on Friday, Feb. 23 and had to be run under a hurried agenda the day before stock car racing's most prestigious race.

More talk of the Bondy Long team being of championship caliber was fueled by a third-place finish in the 500. When the race concluded, Allison was in the same lap with race winner Cale Yarborough and second-place Lee Roy Yarbrough. With just a bit more horsepower at the end, Bobby could have possibly won the race. He led laps 77-78 as well as 167-171. Even though only briefly, he was able to show the team's strength.

Bobby only ran 41 of 500 scheduled laps at Bristol, Tenn., on March 17 due to a blown engine in his Ford Torino. The result was a last-place finish in the 36-car field.

On March 31, Bobby was running third at Atlanta International Raceway when he blew a right front tire and crashed hard into the frontstretch wall on lap 291. Repairs were made in the garage area leading to a 19th-place finish.

The team sat out races at Hickory, N.C., on April 7, Greenville, S.C., on April 13 and Columbia, S.C., on April 18 due to the limited funding agreed upon with Ford.

But at North Wilkesboro, N.C., on April 21, Bobby returned to action. There, another blown engine sent him to 29th place in the 35-car field.

At Martinsville, Va., Allison suffered yet another blown engine for a 26th-place finish and continued the string of bad luck at Darlington, S.C., with a faulty clutch for a 26th-place finish there.

At Charlotte Motor Speedway on May 26, another engine was lost for a 28th-place finish.

For Bobby, the situation was becoming intolerable.

As he walked to the showers located just past the sheltered garage area, he considered quitting the team. He reasoned he had worked hard to obtain a factory ride in Grand National racing, but having to constantly park the car due to faulty parts was doing him no good.

Bobby was beginning to feel resentment about the performances he had suffered over the first few weeks of the season. More so, he was feeling bitter at not being able to race until the word came down from Ford Motor Co. executives. There were many short-track events he had not entered which could have helped to put food on his table.

At Birmingham, Ala., Bobby rolled through the gate with his trusty J.D. Bracken Chevrolet in tow and a wide smile on his face.

He slipped out from behind the wheel of the transporter into a barrage of questions about where he stood with the Bondy Long operation.

"I've left that factory effort," Bobby said. "When I took the ride, I had a deal for 32 races. Then it went down to 22. Next thing I knew it was reduced to 15 races. I want to race. Just sitting around has driven me nuts. I want to drive in front of my hometown fans, so I quit

Ford and I brought my Chevrolet out of the closet."

Petty won the Birmingham race by leading all but one of the 160 laps at the 0.625-mile race track. Bobby was the only other leader.

Suddenly, it felt good to him to be back on his own once again.

"I was in a situation with the Bondy Long team where I had to stand at attention in the corner someplace and had to salute when some wheel walked in the room. And I had to keep my mouth shut and wasn't able to offer any thoughts about how to set up the car or what might make it run faster.

"At first, it was positioned as a sweet sort of deal because Ned Jarrett had been there and so had Dick Hutcherson. But I was shifted to the team at the start of the '68 season without a salary and had to live off of a cut of the purse. That wasn't very lucrative with engines popping all over the place. And too, we had restricted factory backing.

"I wasn't able to run any extra races like sportsman or modified racing. I had to run just the races they (Ford) want me to run. I tried to negotiate at times for another race or two along the way with little success.

"Because the Fords were running so strong in 1968, I tried to hang in there and work it out. But after a while, I could see the situation wasn't going to get much better. I wasn't going to stay home and not get paid. So I threw up my hands and said, 'See you all later. I'm gone.' That's when I dragged that old Chevelle out of moth balls again."

Swede Savage, a 21-year old rookie from San Bernadino, Calif., took over the Bondy Long ride.

On June 16, it was an Allison show with both Bobby and Donnie dicing for the lead throughout the 500-lap event at Rockingham, N.C.

In the end, Donnie bested Bobby, who finished second by two laps.

On July 4, Bobby suffered through a week of bad luck during the return trip to Daytona Beach, Fla., and broke an axle in the 160-lap event. In the final rundown, he was listed as 31st.

But his luck changed dramatically at Islip, N.Y., on July 7 with a victory in the 300-lap race on the 0.2-mile speedway.

Allison took the lead from David Pearson, in a factory-backed Holman-Moody Ford, with 28 laps to go.

But it was also the site of another confrontation with the Pettys. A genuine feud was brewing even after many felt all hostilities had ended with the dramatic '67 battle at Asheville-Weaverville.

"Richard was coming up on me to put me a lap down, but I was

still running in second. I found myself in some pretty tight traffic so I put up a finger to tell him to give me a minute, then I would get out of his way.

"Well, they tell me you didn't do that to Richard Petty. He hit me in the rear. But when he did, his fender cut right into his front tire and was rubbing badly. He had to go to the pits and I went on and won the race.

"I guess Petty didn't like the fact that the new guy was telling him to wait a minute. But as it worked out, he ended up losing the race because of it."

Bobby left the makeshift victory lane ceremonies and walked between the team trucks. Suddenly, he was struck by both Maurice Petty, Richard Petty's older brother, and another crew member.

A scuffle ensued and soon Bobby was on the ground.

He winced when he felt a hard kick to the center of his back.

Then came his rescue in the combination of Bobby's father's aunt and her twenty-pound pocketbook. Approximately 90 years old at the time, Bobby's great aunt closed her eyes and began to swing at anything in her path.

The fight ended, but the hot tempers remained.

"I guess it was a blowoff or one of those things that build up over a period of time," Maurice Petty said. "It started last year at Asheville-Weaverville when Bobby roughed up Richard real bad and got away with it. You might say we settled an old score."

Bobby considered calling the police and having both Petty crew members arrested for assault, but was persuaded by a high ranking NASCAR official not to do so.

"I don't hold grudges," Bobby said. "I think Maurice was led into the deal by Dale Inman, who is a great crewman and loyal to the Pettys. But he's an agitator. They both got me."

The month of July was one of feast and famine. Bobby scored a third-place finish at Fonda, N.Y., and repeated that effort at Trenton, N.J., three days later. But a faulty battery and electrical system caused a 25th-place finish at Bristol, Tenn., on July 21 and lack of oil pressure relegated Bobby to 17th at Maryville, Tenn., on July 25. But at Nashville on July 27, there was a third-place finish.

Bad luck didn't go away with the start of August. Bobby's Chevelle suffered a burned rear end and fell off the pace after 167 of 334 laps.

It continued. Bobby suffered a faulty distributor at Columbia. S.C., on Aug. 8, lost an engine at Winston-Salem, N.C., on Aug. 10

and eight days later, a transmission failed at Asheville-Weaverville Speedway.

On August 23, there was another 16th-place run at South Boston, Va., after rearend failure. But Bobby was able to close out the month with a fourth-place finish at Atlanta International Raceway in Hampton, Va.

On Sept. 2, Bobby logged his best finish at Darlington, S.C., with a seventh after qualifying a dismal 18th. He struggled throughout the 364-lap event and found himself 12 laps down to eventual winner Cale Yarborough.

The short-track events continued to produce a mixture of finishes, as a sway bar broke at Hickory, N.C., on Sept. 6. But there was a fourth-place finish at Richmond, Va., two days later.

Bobby managed to log a second-place finish at Beltsville, Md., after the Roy Trantham Ford driven by David Pearson was discovered to be too light. NASCAR officials checked Pearson's Ford after the race, found the error and changed the order of finish.

There was a sixth-place finish at Hillsborough, N.C., on Sept. 15, but once again, another blown engine sent Bobby packing early at Martinsville, Va., on Sept. 22. He had led 12 laps before falling to 14th place in the final rundown.

Once at North Wilkesboro, N.C., Bobby was given the opportunity to drive the Friedken Enterprises Plymouth engineered by longtime friend Bill Ellis, a local resident of Wilkes County. As part of the arrangement, Bobby brought brother Eddie along as one of the team's mechanics.

After winning the pole position at 104.525 mph, he finished a strong fourth behind Petty, Pearson and Lee Roy Yarbrough.

Bobby continued the streak in the Friedken Plymouth with a second-place finish at Augusta, Ga., on Oct. 5, where he earned the pole position and led the first 108 laps until he lost the lead to Pearson during a caution flag. The lead was lost when the Friedken crew had difficulty with a two-tire pit stop.

His efforts for the weekend caught the eye of Mario Rossi, who was searching for a driver for 1969.

"Did you know Ellis and Friedken are planning to fold their operation at the end of the season?" Rossi asked Bobby.

"I have to say I haven't heard that," Bobby replied, a bit confused by Rossi's statement.

"Well, it's true," Rossi said. "But if you'll come with me, Chrysler is willing to give us some support. But only if you'll come. They want you and so do I."

Bobby agreed to join Rossi after Ellis confirmed his plans to close. But the agreement had a stipulation — one which delighted Bobby. There had to be a concentrated effort to succeed. There could be no other way. Rossi agreed and the deal was set.

Bobby scored another top-five on Oct. 13 at Charlotte Motor Speedway after a rain delay due to the effects of Hurricane Gladys.

Charlie Glotzbach drove a Cotton Owens Dodge to victory after an eight-year drought. Also, country music star Marty Robbins drove his first superspeedway event and finish an impressive 12th in a car fielded out of Bobby's Hueytown shop. Robbins had campaigned on short tracks around his home when his hectic schedule would permit.

The arrangement for Robbins to enter the race was considered one of the most unique trades in NASCAR history.

Bobby traded a Grand National Dodge Charger, a trailer for the car, and a truck in exchange for Robbins' Late Model Sportsman race car and trailer, a pickup truck, a Lincoln Continental with a "lizard skin" roof and one Black Angus bull.

A fifth-place finish at Rockingham, N.C., on Oct. 27 put Bobby in a contender's role for the fourth time in four races and established him as a threat to win among his peers.

Petty scored his only superspeedway win of the year in that race at North Carolina Motor Speedway, ending a 13-month slump. Pearson captured the 1968 Grand National championship.

In the final race of the year, Bobby settled for a 27th-place finish at Jefferson, Ga., due to a blown engine, as his Plymouth lasted only 64 of 200 laps.

Even though he had occupied cars with three different teams throughout the turbulent season, Bobby found himself 11th in the Grand National point standings.

It was accepted that Rossi had the equipment to find victory lane more than once in the coming 1969 season. Even so, Bobby felt something he could not explain; something ominous. As it evolved, he had good reason.

CHAPTER NINE
The First Chance At Stardom

By joining Mario Rossi's operation, Bobby gained a degree of stability to which he had been unaccustomed. Chrysler needed a team to support after its star, Richard Petty, jumped ship to Ford Motor Co. Petty could not deal with what he felt were insurmountable obstacles inherent in the contract offered him by Chrysler. Needless to say, he was welcomed by the rival automaker.

Even so, Chrysler had ammunition. In fact, it had a secret weapon.

This, the company felt, was sure to have great influence on the history of stock car racing. Chrysler engineer Bob Rodger played a significant role in the design of a new Dodge; a design many felt was too radical. It was the first time an automaker had designed a car specifically for the race track, then later made the street version available to the public. Many months would pass before it would be available for retail sale.

Fighting a bad case of the flu, Petty captured the first victory of the season at Macon, Ga., on Nov. 17, 1968.

Bobby entered the event after striking a deal with Bill Ellis to drive the first few races of the season. Ellis still had enough money in the budget to at least start the season. Bobby continued to work with the Friedkin team since Rossi did not plan to enter the opening short-track events.

But at Macon's Middle Georgia Raceway, Bobby suffered another rear end malfunction and fell to 19th in the 30-car field.

A victory came the next week at Montgomery, Ala., in a Friedkin-owned Plymouth.

Once on the superspeedways, Petty was victorious at Riverside International Raceway in the Petty Enterprises Ford Torino.

Bobby's employment with Rossi began at Riverside and produced a 15th-place finish after the car sustained a broken rear end with 27 laps remaining.

Bobby entered the second of the two 125-mile qualifying events at Daytona International Speedway on Feb. 20 and led many of the early laps until his engine expired 19 laps from the finish, sending him to 22nd in the 24-car field.

A close duel developed between Lee Roy Yarbrough and Charlie Glotzbach in the closing laps of the Daytona 500 on Feb. 23. Bobby was not in position to challenge.

After only 45 of the scheduled 200 laps, another engine was lost, sending Bobby back to 43rd in the 50-car field.

Bobby found himself embroiled in a bit of controversy at North Carolina Motor Speedway in Rockingham, N.C., on March 9.

David Pearson led the final 130 laps of the 500-lap event at the one-mile paved speedway.

Pearson finished almost a full lap ahead of Bobby. But Rossi cornered a NASCAR official on pit road after the race and requested a check of the score cards. He was convinced Bobby had passed Pearson and not been given credit for it by NASCAR scoring.

"I honestly felt like we won the race," Rossi said. "When Pearson hit the wall, Bobby passed him. About four laps later, the caution flag came out and Bobby made up a lap. When Bobby passed David at the end of the race, I believe it was for the lead."

NASCAR's Joe Epton, the chief scorer, sat quietly in the scoring stand, studying each of the two drivers' score cards. After only a few moments, he placed the cards on top of one another and announced his findings:

"After carefully going over the score cards before me, it is my belief that the No. 17 car (Pearson) is our winner."

Perhaps the situation was created during an early caution period, when NASCAR officials in the tower attempted to determine which driver was leading. The process consumed 22 laps.

Each crew chief from the cars in the lead lap bent the ear of chief steward Johnny Bruner. This created more confusion and the sanctioning body opted to keep the yellow flag displayed until it was satisfied with the findings.

Finally, Cale Yarborough, driving the Wood Brothers-owned Ford, was declared the leader at the time. But many of the journalists in the press box were outraged. Said veteran sports writer Benny Phillips of High Point, N.C., "Even a computer couldn't have proven Cale was in the lead."

From there, the race was run amid a rash of ill will toward NASCAR from team owners and crew chiefs — Rossi among them. But as the race resumed, Pearson had no trouble disposing of the field with the horsepower under the hood of his Holman-Moody Ford.

Still, Rossi remained unsatisfied.

Bobby finally scored his first victory of the year for Rossi's team at Bristol, Tenn., on March 23, only after drivers Bobby Isaac and Pearson suffered problems late in the race.

A full capacity crowd of 28,000 witnessed Bobby win by four laps over second-place finisher Lee Roy Yarbrough.

A radiator hose popped off Isaac's Dodge and resulted in a blown engine. Pearson followed suit with smoke trailing from his Ford.

"It happens all the time," Allison said. He spoke from experience. "I figure I've lost more than I've won this way."

The strength of Rossi's Dodges was beginning to surface. There was a fourth-place finish at Atlanta on March 30. But the team sat out races at Columbia, S.C., Hickory, N.C., Greenville, S.C., and Richmond, Va., before returning to victory lane at North Wilkesboro, N.C., on April 20.

In that 400-lap event at the .625-mile Wilkes County track, Bobby first struggled during qualifying and finally found the chassis setup he was looking for.

He found it by gambling on an untested idea.

"We went to several setups," Bobby said during the winner's interview. "Toward the end of the last day of practice, we went to one we had discussed but never tried. We didn't have time to try it out. It was strictly a shot in the dark."

Allison took the lead from Buddy Baker on the 299th lap and held the lead for the remaining distance. He finished eight seconds ahead of Lee Roy Yarbrough.

Even with the successful gamble on setup, the real key to victory was excellent pit stops which kept Bobby in contention throughout the day.

"They put me in the lead twice," Bobby said. "It was a close race all the way and the pit stops made the difference. We had a long day of pit stop practice last week and it really paid off."

There was a third-place finish at Martinsville, Va., on April 27 and a fourth at Darlington, S.C., on May 10, even though an accident very late in the race wiped out the team's superspeedway car.

It was another Allison-Lee Roy Yarbrough duel for the lead with four laps left which resulted in a three-car spin across the race track. Bobby hit hard against a concrete structure, while Yarbrough spun but touched nothing.

"I saw Bobby up against the rail and he was coming down," Yarbrough said. "I tried to get by him, but he hung me in the door. Then we both spun off.

"I was lucky, real lucky to continue on. Bobby wasn't that lucky."

Bobby exited his battered machine and stood at the bottom of the race track. He was not happy. As the man whom he felt instigated the wreck circled by, Bobby gave him a message by simply pointing his finger.

It was not cast in the direction of Lee Roy Yarbrough, but rather, Cale Yarborough, who supposedly made contact with Bobby seconds before the crash occurred.

By all accounts, Bobby had the race won after leading laps 104 through 279 of the 291-lap event. He was holding a one-lap lead when he made his final green flag pit stop. Donnie Allison, driving in relief for Richard Petty after Petty had sustained injuries in a crash at Weaverville, N.C., the week before, blew his engine as he came down pit road. With that, Yarborough made up a lost lap.

Bobby led the restart on lap 286 while Yarborough found himself two car lengths behind and trapped in heavy traffic. As the pack of cars sped into the first turn, Yarborough dove under Bobby's Dodge. Bobby tagged the wall and then bumped Lee Roy Yarbrough. Cale was able to continue and made up a lap which allowed him to finish second. Lee Roy Yarbrough got tagged by Allison but had some quick pit work done by Junior Johnson's crew to take the win under caution.

There was more bad luck at Charlotte, N.C., in the World 600 on May 25. There, a faulty radiator sent Bobby to the garage area after only 15 of 400 laps.

Still feeling the desire to campaign in all the races, Bobby entered his trusty Chevrolet at Macon, Ga., on June 1 and again four days later at Maryville, Tenn. In those races, there were finishes of sixth and 16th, respectively.

Bobby returned in Rossi's Dodge at Michigan International Speedway in Brooklyn, Mich., on June 15, but once again lost an engine for a 30th-place finish in the 38-car field.

Obviously, that day at Michigan was insignificant to Bobby's career. However, another trip to Michigan would not be, nor would it be for Grand National competition.

On Thursday, Aug. 14, three days before the inaugural Yankee 600 at MIS, 11 drivers met in Ann Arbor, Mich., to form the Professional Drivers Association. It was an organization created strictly for the protection and benefit of the sport's drivers in such areas as retirement and insurance plans — the former nonexistent and the latter considered insufficient.

As a result of that meeting, Richard Petty was elected president of the organization with Cale Yarborough and Elmo Langley as vice presidents.

Bobby, along with brother Donnie, Buddy Baker, Lee Roy Yarbrough, David Pearson, Pete Hamilton, Charlie Glotzbach and James Hylton were elected as the board of directors. Strangely, Bobby Isaac, known as a prominent driver on the circuit, was not told of the meeting. Some of the drivers felt Isaac could not be trusted because he was considered a loner. When approached about forming the organization, he initially showed little interest.

Also, Lawrence Fleisher, a New York attorney, was retained as general counsel. He was chosen for his work with other professional athletes as well as his interest in the Restaurant Associates in New York City.

Unknown to the participants at the time, the strength of the organization would be heavily tested in the coming months.

On the return trip to Daytona on July 4, Bobby did not fare well in his Dodge.

Bobby was involved in a crash with Buddy Arrington and Hoss Ellington on lap 127. Arrington was hospitalized after the crash with a ruptured spleen and several cracked ribs. Ellington cut his forehead and Bobby bruised his left knee.

In the final rundown, Bobby finished 22nd, Arrington 23rd and Ellington 24th. Lee Roy Yarbrough was victorious, due in part to his exhaust pipes being positioned out the rear of his race car as opposed to being funneled underneath the passenger door. With this arrangement, it was difficult for rival drivers to draft due to the heat from his exhaust pipes blown into their radiators.

Immediately after the race, NASCAR instituted a rule banning rear exhaust pipes.

A couple of months had passed since ground was first broken on the proposed Alabama International Motor Speedway, located in Talladega, Ala., about 60 miles form Bobby's home in Hueytown.

On several occasions, Bobby dropped by to check the progress on the 2.66-mile, high-banked structure. He felt great concern each time he looked over the mammoth facility. To date, no tire had been developed to handle the speeds it would undoubtedly produce.

On July 13, the tour moved to the 1.5-mile speedway in Trenton, N.J., and even though a lap down to Pearson, Bobby wheeled Rossi's Dodge to a second-place finish.

A multicar crash stopped Bobby's efforts at Bristol, Tenn., after only 32 laps, forcing a 26th-place finish.

Cale Yarborough started the event from the pole position and led the first 32 laps. On the next circuit, the Timmonsville, S.C., driver hooked the bumper of Jabe Thomas' Ford and blocked the high-banked short track. The majority of the field was involved in the crash, and only 10 cars were able to finish.

On July 24, Bobby became the first driver to actually drive a vehicle around Alabama International Motor Speedway. While in a passenger car, he noted immediately how bumpy the track's surface was. It seemed very unsafe at a mere 80 miles per hour.

From there, the tour moved to superspeedways in Atlanta and Brooklyn, Mich., where Bobby posted a sixth and fifth, respectively, behind race winners Lee Roy Yarbrough and Pearson.

The Alabama International Motor Speedway officially opened for practice on Aug. 4 and the Ford and Mercury teams began rolling in. Lee Roy Yarbrough and Donnie were shaking down Fords at Bill France's new facility.

"This place is rough as a cob," Donnie said after he climbed from his Banjo Matthews-prepared machine. "It would be a beautiful speedway if it was smooth. The roughness bounced the car around so much it feels like it's tearing the wheels off in the corners. Going into both corners and where the gate is on the backstretch is where it's so rough. And the only way they're going to fix it is to repave it."

As tests continued, Bobby wheeled a Dodge Daytona to a scary 197.5 mph on the new track on Aug. 21.

The Sept. 1 Southern 500 at Darlington, S.C., was shortened to 316 miles due to rain and impending darkness and won by Lee Roy Yarbrough with a last-lap pass on Pearson.

Bobby finished fourth after an early spin coming off turn one.

Also involved in the crash was brother Donnie and sophomore driver Richard Brickhouse.

While at Darlington, a Professional Drivers Association press release was issued, targeted toward those drivers who would likely join.

But France, founder and chief executive officer of NASCAR, expressed surprise when he saw a copy of the release.

Petty made sure France knew no demands had been made and no strike threats had been communicated. According to Petty, the PDA was not to be looked upon as a bully organization, but rather, one that would help to solidify the sport.

But France was sure the organization was planning something.

Between practice sessions, Bobby was questioned by a group of reporters who had just gotten wind of the new organization.

"We formed the organization because we felt we were foolish in not forming one," Bobby told them. "Every other major sport has its players organizations. There are definitely things that we have grievances about. I don't feel the purses match the gate receipts on any of the big tracks and some little ones.

"And we have no pension plan. Insurance is inadequate. A guy devotes his life to racing, and he gets only $7,500 if he gets an arm torn off. If he gets killed, his wife gets $15,000. We've never had a voice in planning or scheduling. They might have a 500-mile race and two days later, a 100-miler a thousand miles away."

The sign-up process continued and involved many Grand Touring competitors as well as those from the Grand National ranks. Each member was required to pay the $200 initiation fee.

Rossi had no plans to enter his car in the Richmond 400 at Richmond Fairgrounds Raceway on Sept. 7. But with careful persuasion, Bobby finally talked him into taking a car there. After all, he still felt frustrated. He was not able to run all the races as he had hoped when he took the job.

The result was his fifth victory of the year in the race the team very nearly missed due to mechanical problems.

Bobby blew an engine in a late practice session, requiring another motor to be brought to the track from the team's shop in Spartanburg, S.C. But it did not arrive until 10 a.m. race morning.

A police escort was used to get the engine to the garage area and once there, the crew worked feverishly to get it installed. Meanwhile, Bobby handled such "details" as signing autographs and later getting dressed into his driver's uniform. There was little else he could do.

Finally, the red and gold Dodge was rolled into the 25th starting spot just as pole position winner Petty put his Ford into first gear and began to move off pit road to begin the event.

Bobby came from last to first by taking the lead from Petty on the 171st of 462 laps. He miraculously led the rest of the way, even though he was involved in two pit-road accidents.

At the checkered flag, Bobby held a four-lap lead over Sonny Hutchins and had won with an average speed of 76.328 mph.

"If hard work had anything to do with it," said Rossi, "then we deserve this one. Some of the crew and myself haven't had three hours sleep in the last three days."

Two days before Bobby won at Richmond, France filed an entry as a driver for the Sept. 18 Talladega 500. His ride came in the form of a Ford Torino purchased from the Holman-Moody operation that was driven earlier in the year by Bobby Unser and Mario Andretti in USAC competition.

France had his reasons. He had heard the grumblings over the unsafe conditions of his new speedway. And, too, there was the matter of the PDA.

In Richmond, France struck up a conversation with Bobby.

"He asked me if he drove in the race, could he join the PDA," Bobby recalled. "I think he's serious about it. He told me he had a car and he had filed an entry."

On Sept. 9, teams began checking into Alabama International Motor Speedway and were given garage assignments.

Early tests sessions showed an alarming number of tire problems which obviously made the cars unsafe at the speeds they were generating.

The next day, time trials began. Only nine cars were uncovered in the garage area, ready to make an attempt. That group did not include Bobby or his brother Donnie.

Executives from both Goodyear Tire and Rubber Co. as well as those from Firestone Tire were quickly on phone lines to discuss the situation with their respective headquarters, as the situation was grave. Soon chartered flights were in the air, equipped with tires carrying a different tread compound.

On Friday, Sept. 11, 14 more cars attempted time trials with the new tire. But there was no decided difference. To the competitors, the danger hadn't gone away.

As the evening sun was making its way downward, Donnie and Charlie Glotzbach agreed to conduct tests; one car equipped with

Goodyears, the other with Firestones. Every four laps, the two drivers would change to a different compound in search of one that would be suitable for the 500-mile race.

"My heart was in my mouth the whole time," Donnie said. "That was the most scared I've been in all my life."

Firestone finally made the decision to pack its gear and withdraw from the event. It felt it could not provide safe tire compounds.

Goodyear elected to try one last compound. It had tires flown in and made the stipulation they would not be raced at speeds over 190 mph. Any car which exceeded that speed would not be allowed to have tires mounted.

On Saturday, Sept. 12, Petty and France twice met in the garage area and engaged in very heated arguments. According to France, there would be a race the next day, even if he had to use the Grand American drivers who were there for the Saturday event.

Petty made it clear he would not have any part of it. France told him to leave if that were the case.

Eight hours later, a deep baritone voice echoed through the garage area. It belonged to France.

"All those who are not going to race, leave the garage area so those who are going to race can work on their cars."

Within a few moments, the engine of Petty's transporter could be heard. Soon, a sea of headlights flooded the area. Thirty-two haulers were headed out the garage gate.

Rossi tightened the straps on the rear of his transporter and bid farewell to Bobby, who proceeded to his passenger car for the hour-long drive home.

Some NASCAR Grand National drivers remained and joined the Grand American drivers for the race.

The winner was Richard Brickhouse, an independent driver who joined the PDA but remained behind. His dream had been to someday drive a factory-backed race car. It was his only Grand National victory in 26 starts. It cost him dearly. He was no longer accepted by his fellow drivers.

"The PDA really had nothing to do with tire problems at Talladega. We just happened to be organized to address other issues we felt we weren't being considered. We were all very concerned about what would happen to our families if we were hurt or killed in a race-related accident. The PDA allowed a voice for such issues.

"But keeping the drivers safe was the key to us even forming the PDA. The tires we were provided with simply wouldn't hold up to the

speeds we were turning. Something had to be done and walking out seemed to be the only answer. Bill France simply wouldn't listen to anyone. He wanted to have a race there that weekend."

On Sept. 28, Bobby lost yet another engine at Martinsville, Va., in a rare short-track appearance by Rossi's team.

But once at Charlotte Motor Speedway on Oct. 12 for the National 500, Bobby and Donnie staged an incredible race until Bobby was forced to pit late in the race due to a blistered right front tire. Donnie's margin of victory was 16 seconds at the conclusion of the duel between members of "The Alabama Gang."

Twenty laps into the Oct. 26 American 500 at Rockingham, N.C., Bobby found himself spinning the wrong direction in turn two after being collected by the Chevrolet of John Kennedy. At the time of the accident, Bobby was running second in one of only four winged Dodge Daytonas.

On Nov. 9, Bobby was able to score a short-track victory at Macon, Ga., after both Pearson and Petty collided with only 12 laps remaining.

The season concluded at College Station, Texas on Dec. 7. It marked the first superspeedway victory for Bobby Isaac, who had collected several short-track victories.

Allison's Dodge Daytona lasted for 163 of the 250 laps at the two-mile speedway, as the engine erupted in smoke.

With the season finally concluded, Bobby had logged some respectable finishes. But would he be able to progress further in 1970?

Only time would provide an answer.

CHAPTER TEN
A Shot At The Title

The arrangement between Bobby and Mario Rossi seemed to be working. Even though the team walked away with a 20th-place finish in the 1969 Grand National point standings, there were five victories and $69,483 in winnings.

Bobby looked back on the past nine months with a degree of satisfaction. But still, his nemesis once again had been a lack of strength in the engine department. The problem desperately needed to be addressed.

The winged Dodge Daytona was back in the fold for the Allison/Rossi effort, but Richard Petty had left Ford and was again in the Chrysler camp with a Plymouth Superbird.

The season opened at Riverside International Raceway on Jan. 18 where Parnelli Jones captured the pole position with a record speed of 113.310 mph in the Wood Brothers Mercury.

A bit of controversy surfaced after his run. Being a Firestone dealer, Jones qualified with "limited edition" tires, ones not readily available to the public or other competitors — if they were available at all. NASCAR had decreed them ineligible for competition. The sanctioning body did not approve of their insufficient quantity.

As punishment, Jones was forced to begin the 193-lap event from the 35th starting spot, giving the pole position to Dan Gurney, five-time winner of the event.

Jones, however, gained the lead by the 43rd circuit, but fell out when clutch failure sidelined him on lap 168.

Bobby had gotten behind the wheel of his Dodge certain he would have a good run. The tests on the engine dynomometer during the winter produced a feeling that the team would be stronger on the superspeedways. For the second straight year, Rossi had elected to bypass the short tracks.

Despite his optimism, Bobby's hopes were dashed when, on lap 165, he suffered a cracked bell housing.

The Rossi crew was deeply dejected over the engine loss and thus the season started off poorly. That was, and is . . . nothing new in racing; often results fall short of expectations.

In the case of the Rossi team no fingers were pointed and no harsh words were spoken. But there was something . . . something just not right.

Five hours, 11 minutes and 19 seconds passed before A.J. Foyt parked his Ford in Riverside's victory lane.

Two accidents marred the event, both of them serious.

Buddy Young, a talented driver from Fairfax, Va., tumbled the L.G. DeWitt Ford end over end just past the start-finish line after the Plymouth driven by Dick Brooks blew its engine and laid a sheet of oil over the track. Once Young crossed the line on lap 37, he could not avoid the spill and suffered internal injuries and a concussion as a result of the crash. The severity of the accident ended his career.

Jim Cook, of Norwalk, Calif., was critically injured when his Ford hit a concrete wall on lap 94. His injuries included fractures of both arms and legs.

On Feb. 19, Bobby found himself involved in the second qualifying race for the Daytona 500 and led one lap of the 50-lap event before falling to third behind race winner Charlie Glotzbach and Buddy Baker.

That race was blackened by the death of Talmage Prince, a rookie driver from Dublin, Ga.

Prince had purchased his Dodge Daytona from James Hylton two weeks before Speed Weeks and had limited track time on the high banks of Daytona International Speedway. On lap 18, the car slid sideways into the high groove and was collected by a Ford driven by Bill Siefert.

According to track physician A.A. Monoco, Prince died instantly of a broken neck. Siefert suffered cardiac contusions and a concussion.

Unknown to anyone at the time, there would be a surprise winner when the Daytona 500 received the green flag on Feb. 22.

Pete Hamilton, of Dedham, Mass., a newcomer to the sport who had been given a shot in a Petty Enterprises Plymouth Superbird, captured the prestigious event after a late-race caution set up by Dick Brooks. Once the green was displayed, the Ford of veteran David Pearson slipped in the fourth turn with two laps remaining, giving Hamilton, the 1968 "Rookie of the Year," the lead.

Bobby placed his Dodge within striking distance throughout the race and showed his strength by leading twice for four laps.

Consistency seemed to be falling into place by March 8 when the tour moved to the North Carolina Motor Speedway at Rockingham.

On March 6, Bobby captured the pole position with a record speed of 139.048 mph and led five times for 162 laps.

But as the 492-lap event progressed, Bobby found himself having to adjust to a variety of problems. Two flat tires, ignition failure and finally, a broken wheel, took him from contention.

Still, he was able to score a third-place finish behind Richard Petty and Cale Yarborough.

At Savannah, Ga., on March 15, Bobby worked a deal with car owner Jabe Thomas to enter the race since Rossi had no plans to campaign the short tracks.

Bobby qualified Thomas' Plymouth fourth, but fell out due to a loss of brakes and ultimately finished 19th in the 21-car field.

Once at Atlanta International Speedway for the next event, Bobby was able to log his 17th career Grand National victory after being a full lap behind with 10 laps remaining.

Cale Yarborough, in the dominant car of the day, entered the pits on lap 318 of the 328 lap event. Simultaneously, Donnie suffered engine failure in the Banjo Matthews Ford, trapping Yarborough in the pits for a splash of gas.

Once the yellow flagged was displayed for Donnie's smoking Ford, Rossi, by pit board, directed Bobby into the pits for tires and fuel.

Suddenly, Bobby was on the lead lap with Yarborough and when the green flag was displayed on lap 323, Bobby was able to make the pass for the win. Once Johnny Bruner waved the checkered flag, Bobby led by a mere 50 feet.

"That was really a break," Bobby said. "Cale pitted just as the yellow came out. That allowed me to make up the lap I was behind. I was scheduled for a regular stop four laps later."

It was Easter Sunday, and only 22,000 people were in the stands to watch the race.

Bobby once again rented a Plymouth owned by Thomas and finished second to Donnie at Bristol, Tenn., on April 5.

The stands were filled to a capacity of 32,000 when Donnie won the event with an average speed of 87.543 mph.

Thomas, teammate to Bobby who was in another one of his Plymouths, drove down pit road and stopped in Donnie's pit during the closing laps.

Seeing car owner Banjo Matthews standing quietly, watching the race, Thomas motioned Matthews over to the driver's side window and yelled, "How much will you pay me not to spin Donnie out?" Thomas, one of the great jokesters in racing, wasn't serious.

Matthews waved Thomas back to the track with a backward flip of the wrist.

As Thomas entered the first turn, Matthews grabbed some chalk from the tool box, marked "50 cents" on the pit board and flashed it to Thomas with a wide smile. Matthews, too, had a sense of humor.

The next lap by, Thomas returned to Donnie's pit and extended his hand.

Matthews handed Thomas two quarters. A wealthier Thomas continued and finished 12th.

On the return trip to Alabama International Motor Speedway on April 12, tire problems similar to those in September of 1969 were expected. But since the track had undergone a repaving job tires held together. France had apparently gotten the message.

Allison's Dodge challenged eventual winner Hamilton, again in the Petty Enterprises Plymouth, throughout the event. But engine problems sidelined him after 126 of 188 laps.

Bobby wheeled the Robertson Plymouth to a sixth-place finish at North Wilkesboro, N.C., on April 18. There had been little hope of catching Petty, who led from lap 52 through lap 400 in front of a live national television audience.

The frustration of having to negotiate a ride on the short tracks was mounting and prompted Bobby to build his own Dodge for the short-track events.

His Dodge made its debut at Columbia, S.C., on April 30 and finished second to Petty, who once again dominated by gaining the lead on lap 97 and holding it for the duration of the 200-lap event.

In the early going of the Rebel 400 at Darlington, S.C., on May 9, Bobby set the pace and appeared to be the driver to beat.

But the needles on the gauges began to rise suddenly and soon Bobby found himself amid smoke and fumes as another engine let go after 146 of 291 laps and caused a 20th-place finish.

The race was marred by a horrifying crash involving Petty, who flipped several times down the frontstretch on lap 176. The Level Cross, N.C., driver suffered a broken shoulder after being knocked unconscious in the accident.

For Bobby, a pattern was becoming clear with a third-place finish at Beltsville, Md., on May 15 behind Bobby Isaac and Hylton. In his own equipment and with engines he had built himself out of his Hueytown shop, the consistent top-five finishes seemed to be coming more often.

More evidence came at Hampton, Va., on May 18 with a second-place finish to Isaac in a 300-lap event on the 0.4-mile speedway.

There was a scary moment at Charlotte, N.C., during the World 600 on May 24.

After posting a qualifying speed good enough for the outside front row, Bobby's engine expired in the Rossi Dodge on lap 17.

While at full speed, the engine compartment exploded in flames, causing Bobby to spin the car in the second turn, which put the flame out. But before coming to a stop, Bobby crashed into a concrete retaining wall.

"I was becoming quite agitated with the fact that our engines were simply not holding together in Rossi's Dodges. They would run strong in the opening laps of a race but always seemed to blow within the first 100 laps or so. It seems Mario tried everything to keep them strong, but nothing seemed to work.

"After I started running my own Dodge on the short tracks, engines were never a problem. I tried to apply some of what I had learned in my own engine department but being the driver, Rossi never was crazy about me adding input as to how his engines should be built."

Bobby's former team manager from the 1967 and '68 Grand National seasons came out of retirement to compete in the World 600.

Fred Lorenzen, a superstar in his own right, qualified a Dodge Daytona owned by track promoter Richard Howard. The Elmhurst, Ind., native finished 24th in the 40-car field after his engine expired on lap 252 of 400 laps.

At Maryville, Tenn., Bobby qualified in the pole position with a speed of 82.558 mph, but was passed by Isaac before the field reach the third turn on the first lap. Eventually, Bobby had a tire to go flat and caused him to hit the fourth-turn guardrail.

Isaac led all 200 laps. Bobby, however, found himself struggling back from his meeting with the guardrail on lap 75 after a tire blew. The crash caused extensive damage but not enough to stop him from posting a 12th-place finish.

Isaac continued his streak at Martinsville, Va., on May 31 and was almost a full lap ahead of Bobby's Dodge at the finish. The race was hit hard by heavy rains and stopped twice. Finally, a third delay came on lap 337 of the scheduled 500 laps. But darkness had begun to settle over the 0.526-mile speedway and NASCAR officials declared the event complete.

A scoring snafu plagued the running of the Motor State 400 at Michigan International Speedway.

But for Bobby, that scoring problem proved academic, as his Rossi-owned Dodge never performed as a contender and finally finished 17th, 21 laps behind race winner Yarborough.

Bobby scored another pole position on the return trip to Riverside, Calif., on June 14. But on the first lap, Bobby lost control of his car and spun off-course, losing valuable time.

Petty clearly had everyone outmatched in speed and went on to record the win while Bobby finished a distant second.

Back in the driver's seat of his own Dodge at Hickory, N.C., on June 20, an oil leak caused a 15th-place finish among the 22 cars which entered the 276-lap event.

That was followed by a fourth-place finish at Kingsport, Tenn., on June 26, a second at Greenville, S.C., on June 27 and a third-place finish at Daytona Beach, Fla., on July 4, which marked the return to the Rossi Dodge.

At Albany-Saratoga Speedway in Malta, N.Y., on July 7, Bobby found himself in the lead with five laps remaining, but was forced to pit for fuel, giving Petty his seventh victory of the season.

Bobby came out of the pits a lap behind, but was able to secure the second position at the finish.

From there, Bobby logged a seventh-place finish at Thompson Speedway in Thompson, Conn., and returned to Trenton, N.J., on July 12 for a second place finish.

At Bristol, Tenn., on July 19, Bobby returned to victory lane while once again driving his own Dodge.

The summer heat had taken its toll on several drivers and with that in mind, Bobby pitted on lap 370 of the 500-lap event and turned the car over to Dave Marcis, who had lost the engine in his Dodge on lap 83.

"I saw what Lee Roy Yarbrough and Petty were doing (calling for relief)," said Allison after joining Marcis in victory lane. "I decided I was foolish to try it by myself. It was hot and I was getting tired. I saw Marcis in my pit and I couldn't think of anyone I'd rather have in my car."

Marcis gained some exposure for himself, even though the victory officially belonged to Allison.

"I was familiar with the car," said Marcis. "Bobby let me drive this car last week at Trenton. All I had to do here was keep it in front. Bobby put it in the lead."

A faulty fuel pump took Bobby out of the 200-lap event at Maryville, Tenn., on July 24 and dictated a 17th-place finish.

But there was a bit more luck for him at Nashville, Tenn., on July 25.

Isaac stayed out of trouble and easily won the event after several drivers, including Bobby, suffered blown tires. Despite the difficulty, he managed to finish second, two laps off the pace.

The race at Atlanta International Raceway on Aug. 2 was in danger of being canceled due to the financial problems experienced by the speedway.

Under the direction of Larry LoPatin and American Raceways, the track's principal owners, AIR's purse was short by many thousands of dollars. Action was taken by NASCAR officials.

The speedway was plagued by several unpaid bills. Before the race, Federal agents were in place to padlock the facility once the race came to a conclusion.

Richard Howard, general manager for Charlotte Motor Speedway who had become wealthy through private business interests, came to AIR's rescue. He paid the outstanding debts as well as the needed funds to start the race.

Even though he was five laps down to race winner Petty, Bobby was able to finish in the seventh position.

Two short-track races put Allison back in his own Dodge.

In those events, there was a third-place finish at Columbia, S.C., on Aug. 6, followed by an 11th at Ona, W.Va., where Bobby led the first 26 laps after starting from the pole position.

On Aug. 16, Bobby wheeled Rossi's Dodge to a second-place finish at Brooklyn, Mich., which was followed by a 13th-place finish at Talladega, Ala.

Allison drove his Dodge to a second place at Bowman Gray Stadium in Winston Salem, N.C., and followed that with a third-place finish at South Boston, Va.

At the 367-lap event at Darlington, S.C., on Sept. 7 — the venerable Southern 500 — Bobby could only muster a 10th-place finish after falling 19 laps down to eventual winner Buddy Baker.

There was a third at Hickory, N.C., on Sept. 11, a second at Richmond, Va., on Sept. 13 and a second at Dover, Del., on Sept. 20.

Bobby took a 1970 Dodge to Raleigh, N.C., for the final NASCAR event staged on a dirt track. In that race, he finished sixth.

Rossi elected to take his Dodge to North Wilkesboro, N.C., where Bobby finished fourth, five laps off the pace set by Isaac, who was well on his way to capturing the championship.

But Isaac's victory was marred by the death of Curtis Turner, 45, whose private airplane crashed in the Pennsylvania mountains near the small township of Punxsutawney. Clarance King, 51, a professional golfer, was also on board.

According to the Clearfield County deputy coroner Robert Young, both Roanoke, Va., residents were pronounced dead at the scene.

Bobby felt a great hurt upon learning of Turner's death. Even though the two had engaged in some fierce racing in the past, Bobby felt a immense respect for the elder motorsports veteran-both because he was a fellow racer and fellow aviator.

Of the five NASCAR Grand National races remaining on the schedule, Bobby logged a victory at Atlanta International Raceway as well as two seconds, a third and a fourth.

Even though success was apparent, Bobby once again felt the urge to race his own equipment.

The relationship between Bobby and Rossi wasn't strained at the end of the season, but it certainly was not the best it could be.

Bobby would have a new car owner in 1971 — himself.

CHAPTER ELEVEN
On His Own Again

Dressed in jeans, plaid shirt, loafers and white socks, Bobby exited his house through the basement door and walked just down the hill to the entrance of his shop. Once inside the doorway, he reached for the metal light box on the wall and flipped the switch. A double row of fluorescent bulbs flickered briefly, then came to life overhead.

The smell of fresh acrylic enamel automotive paint filled the air, for located in the center of the room sat two Dodge Chargers, each glistening with bright red sides accented by gold tops, hoods and trunk lids.

Only minor adjustments were required to finish one of the cars in time for the road course race at Riverside, Calif., just one week away.

Before removing his jacket, Bobby stood with his hands in his pockets and stared at the cars before him. The thought of being his own boss once again caused a slight twinge of nervousness in his stomach. There were obvious advantages and disadvantages to being a car owner/driver in NASCAR Grand National racing. Even though there were complications from time to time, at least there was control. There wouldn't be a pink slip from a disgruntled car owner.

Mario Rossi, Bobby's car owner from the season just completed, was now out of the picture. Their "mutual agreement" to part ways at the end of the '70 campaign was one of the few points upon which the two men ever agreed. They had experienced some success together, but there was a bit of relief as the new season dawned, for the discord between Allison and Rossi was finally history.

A burden remained, however: The thought of facing the unknown as a car owner — again. After all, great turmoil was beginning to surface between the automotive giants of Detroit and NASCAR. There had been many obstacles for NASCAR to overcome since its birth on December 14, 1947. But the present situation seemed to bear little hope of a decisive answer.

On Nov. 19, 1970, Ford Motor Co. announced its intention to withdraw from stock car racing entirely for the 1971 season, while Chrysler would reduce its support dramatically.

The only Grand National equipment Bobby owned sat right before him. But whether a Dodge, Ford, or any make of car, factory support was seemingly a luxury of the past. Now, it couldn't be found in the budgets of any of the big three automobile manufacturers. Even though light, Bobby had financial support from Coca-Cola. The sponsorship was carried to the team from Rossi's operation after the Atlanta-based soft drink company test-marketed its product in four races during the '70 season with favorable results.

Ironically, Bobby finished second to Bobby Isaac for the 1970 Grand National championship, but neither the runnerup nor the champion would have factory support for '71. The entire picture looked mighty bleak. Many of the veterans of the sport predicted they would be forced to return to the local short tracks if they wanted to race anything at all. And some speculated NASCAR racing wouldn't exist by the start of the '73 season unless financial support could be drummed up from a major corporation.

Then, like a bright star on the horizon, R.J. Reynolds Tobacco Co. promised support in the way of sponsorship of NASCAR's Grand National division. Junior Johnson contacted the Winston-Salem, N.C., based firm for sponsorship of his own team, but marketing executives realized stock car racing as a whole offered them a much broader arena in which to sell their products. One of their first executive orders was a drastic reduction from 52 to 29 events on the Grand National schedule.

Part time racer and full-time farmer Ray Elder scored a major upset by winning the first race under the new Winston Cup Grand National banner. At the race's finish, Bobby felt optimism over his team's strength, as he led 39 of the 191 laps and lost the lead with only 12 laps to go. He finished second.

Once at Daytona for the 125-mile qualifying race on Feb. 11,

Bobby's Dodge didn't fare well. At the end of the 50-lap event, his Hueytown-based team found itself four laps down in 24th place, behind race winner David Pearson. The finishing position translated into a 31st-place starting spot for the Daytona 500 three days later. In the race, a sour engine relegated Bobby to an 18th-place finish, 13 laps off the pace behind Richard Petty, who scored his second Daytona 500 victory.

Eighteen days later, the refurbished tour moved back to California for the Miller High Life 500 at Ontario Motor Speedway. But there, a faulty ignition sent Bobby back to 39th place after he completed only 78 of 200 laps. His payday for the costly trip to the west coast was $1,400.

There was a fourth-place finish at Richmond, Va., on March 7, but another engine problem sidelined the Dodge. Then came a 30th-place finish at Rockingham, N.C., a week later.

At Bristol, Tenn., Bobby finished fourth to start a string of top-10 finishes during the month of April. But he was used to winning, not falling 15 or more laps down at the finish. That seemed to happen with distressing regularity.

Bedecked with Confederate flags, the 1.366-mile Darlington (S.C.) Raceway had come to life in preparation for the May 2 Rebel 400. From the minute Bobby pulled his car transporter through the entrance, however, problems surfaced. It should not have been a real surprise. The seeds for such difficulties had been planted months before.

Throughout the 1970 season, Bobby's engine parts had been ordered from the Chrysler's parts distributor Ray Nichels, owner of the Plymouths campaigned by Paul Goldsmith. Usually, if a part was needed, it would be delivered promptly, without red tape or excuses.

But in 1971, Petty Enterprises, Bobby's direct rival, took over the distribution duties and service immediately went downhill. On more than one occasion, a key piece necessary to the construction of an engine, such as a piston, would mysteriously disappear from the box while en route from Level Cross, N.C., to Alabama.

The remedy called for a mixture of used parts to "get by," but just getting by went totally against Bobby's nature.

Predictably, the engine in his Dodge ran poorly and finally erupted on the 177th of 293 laps.

Bobby coasted silently to a halt in the garage area. On the way, he loosened the seat belts and removed his helmet.

Crew members raised the hood for a quick glance only to see

smoke, oil and water covering the engine compartment with liquids draining from underneath. Without reaction, those gathered around the front of the car returned the hood to a horizontal position by holding onto the pin cables.

Bobby emerged from the racer disgusted and walked away with one thought in mind. He decided then and there to quit NASCAR Grand National racing and return to the Alabama short tracks where he was winning races in routine fashion every week when the Grand National schedule allowed him to be home. At that very moment, he had had enough of the frustrations, the disappointments and the heartaches that came with campaigning a race car in the big leagues. He reasoned he could put money in his bank account and would be within a hundred miles from home and shop. And best of all, his feet always seemed a bit warmer in his own bed in Hueytown.

A camera crew from a local television station suddenly appeared and interviewed Bobby as he wiped his face with a faded red shop rag. As the interview concluded and he began to turn away from the camera, there was only one thing left for him to say: "That's it. I'm broke."

But as he was walking through the infield to leave the speedway, Ralph Moody spotted him from the doorway of his motorhome. Moody was part of the famed Holman-Moody operation, a large factory based in Charlotte, N.C., that built stock cars in assembly-line fashion for other competitors who raced on the circuit.

"Why don't you park that pile of shit and drive a real race car?" Moody shouted.

Bobby broke his gaze at the pavement in front of him. He looked at Moody. He tried desperately not to show the disappointment he was feeling.

"All you've got to do is give me one," Bobby replied.

With a wave of his hand, Moody motioned for Bobby to come in and as the two long-time friends talked, Bobby spoke of all the problems he had experienced and his desire to return to the Alabama short tracks.

Later that day, Bobby took brother Donnie to Indianapolis where Donnie had a ride with A.J. Foyt for the 1971 Indy 500. While Donnie's racing career looked to be flourishing, Bobby's spirits were so low he became physically ill.

When Donnie set the private plane down on the runway at Bristol, Tenn., for refueling, Bobby excused himself and found a nearby restroom where he vomited for what seemed like hours.

Upon their arrival in Indianapolis, the Allisons met with Foyt and Elmer George at the airport. Both were there to give them a ride to the motel. But Foyt and George had an ulterior motive in mind.

"What do ya' say we all go out and get some dinner?" George asked. "I know a great place just down the road apiece."

"Sounds good to me," Donnie said.

"I don't know, guys, I'm feeling kind of puny," Bobby said.

"Come on, we won't be gone long," Foyt said.

George drove the four men to a Lion's Club meeting some 75 miles away where the three race drivers signed autographs and spoke. The evening meeting did not conclude until past midnight.

Once Bobby came dragging into the motel in the early morning hours, the message light glowed brightly on the telephone.

"Yes, this is Bobby Allison in room 16. You got a message for me?" he asked the clerk at the front desk.

"Yes, Mr. Allison," the clerk said. "You need to call your wife immediately. She said the minute you came in. She sounded urgent."

"OK, thank you," Bobby said.

He pushed down the button on the cradle of the phone and soon placed the call to Hueytown.

"Hey, what's upside down now?" Bobby asked Judy.

"Nothing," Judy said. "Ralph Moody has been looking for you all day. You need to call him right away."

Once again, he hung up and quickly placed a call to Moody. After several rings, a disgruntled voice answered.

"Yeah, who the hell is this?" Moody asked.

"This is Bobby. Judy said you were looking for me."

"Who?," Moody asked again.

"Bobby. Bobby Allison."

"Oh, Bobby. What time is it?" Moody asked.

"One fifteen in the morning," Allison responded.

"Can you come back down to Charlotte tomorrow?" Moody inquired.

"Yeah," Bobby said.

"What's your deal with Coke?" Moody asked.

"I'm not sure," Bobby said. "I told them I was out of business. I'll call them tomorrow and ask. But I thought David Pearson was your driver.

"Pearson quit at Darlington while you were talking to me in my motorhome. Well, how do you feel about driving for me?"

"Yes, yes, yes," Bobby said with great enthusiasm. "That would be great. See ya' tomorrow."

The next afternoon, Bobby met with Moody and agreed to a deal to drive for him in the remainder of the superspeedway races in 1971. Pearson departed because he felt the H-M Fords were non-competitive. But if anyone could figure out a problem with a race car chassis, Bobby Allison could and Ralph Moody knew it.

Bobby had driven for Holman-Moody in 1967 under the direction of Fred Lorenzen and then moved over to the Bondy Long operation based in Camden, S.C., which was an extension of H-M, in 1968. But by May of that year, they were only running a few races a year and Bobby departed to campaign his own Chevelle. Now, he was being offered another chance with a more powerful race car under him and a better financial deal as well.

With his own cars parked race-ready in his shop in Hueytown, Bobby brought his sponsorship package from Coca-Cola to the Holman-Moody operation for a schedule of selected events. Amazingly, he didn't begin his employment with H-M until May 16, 1971, but he still managed to give the team eight wins in 22 starts, all but one on superspeedways. And that didn't count the two victories he'd earned in his own equipment coming at Riverside, Calif., and Houston, Texas.

For Holman-Moody, there were wins at Dover, Del., Talladega, Ala., Darlington, Macon, Ga., two at Charlotte and two at Michigan.

One victory did not count in the official NASCAR Winston Cup Grand National records, however. Bobby won a race at Bowman-Gray Stadium in Winston-Salem, N.C., but NASCAR had not counted the win since he was driving a Grand American car owned by Melvin Joseph, declared legal before the race as to assure a complete field. A post-race protest on Bobby's part to have his Ford Mustang declared the winner came to no avail.

Ironically, Tiny Lund was victorious during the season while driving a Grand American car—and the win was counted by NASCAR. On Aug. 28, 1971, Lund drove a 276-lap event at Hickory, N.C. in a 1969 Camaro owned by Ronnie Hopkins. Elmo Langley, driving a Grand National Ford, finished in the lead lap but was officially recorded as finishing second.

For Bobby, however, he earned a personal career high in number of victories for one season.

During the season, one light-hearted evening stood out as a very pleasurable experience for Bobby. Even today, it always brings a smile.

The Friday before Bobby's Winston Cup Grand National win at Talladega, Ala. on Aug.22, Bobby found himself hanging around with country music singer Marty Robbins. After the races had concluded at Birmingham International Raceway on Friday, Aug. 20, the two men stopped at a local pizza parlor in Midfield, Ala. for a late dinner.

As they entered the room, Robbins spotted a piano in the far corner and asked the owner of the establishment if he could play it.

Robbins gave the restaurant's patrons a free unexpected concert as they enjoyed their meals. Before very long, the place was rocking.

But the hour was getting late and the owner had had a long day.

"Mr. Robbins," the proprietor said, "it's close to midnight and I've got to be up early tomorrow. Can we call it a night?"

"Hey, my man, we're having all kinds of fun," Robbins said. "Can't we keep going for a while?"

"Well, I don't know. . . I. . ."

"Hey, just tell us where you want us to leave the key," Robbins said. "We'll lock up. Go on home."

"I can't do that," the restaurant owner said. "C'mon, we need to call it a night."

"Why don't you sell me this piano and I'll play it in the parking lot," Robbins said.

"I can't do that," the owner said. "I'm sorry, you'll have to leave."

"OK, sell me the restaurant?" Robbins asked.

"C'mon, let's go," the owner said. "Out! I've got to close."

The packed house protested wildly as Robbins stood, bowed and walked away after making every effort to continue.

A few days after his return from Texas World Speedway for the year's final race on Dec. 12 — where he finished third —Bobby returned to Charlotte. While in town, Bobby stopped by the race shop. John Holman, the other half of Holman-Moody, waved him into his office.

Once in the room, Bobby stood for a moment until being directed to a chair by a point of a finger.

Holman remained silent for a moment, then spoke with a look of stone.

"So how do you feel you've done this year?" Holman asked.

"I'm pretty pleased," Bobby responded with a smile.

"You and your buddy (Moody) have had a silver spoon up your ass, that's why," Holman said.

Bobby sat motionless and said nothing. But he was very uneasy.

"Do you have Coca-Cola for next year?" Holman asked.

Bobby simply said, "Yes.".

"Well, you can take your sponsorship and your buddy and go up the road someplace and get something to drive because you're not driving for me anymore," Holman said with a wave of his hand. "Now, get the hell out of here!"

Even though he had experienced the most lucrative season of his career with 11 victories, Bobby found himself out on the street looking for employment. In Holman's eyes, Bobby's success in no way guaranteed job security, especially if you were a friend of Ralph Moody's. Had there not been a deep running feud between Holman and Moody through the past 15 years, things might well have been different.

But they weren't. And since Holman held the upper hand at Holman-Moody, his decision was final.

During hours of shooting pool and relaxing at Moody's home in Charlotte, Bobby pondered the direction of his career. One minute he was on top of the world and the next at its lowest depths.

The next day, Moody's telephone rang just after breakfast. The phone was given to Bobby and the voice of the caller came as a complete surprise.

"Hello, Bobby? This is Junior Johnson. Can we meet before you go back to Alabama?"

"Yes, we sure can," responded Bobby with a smile.

"Good," Johnson said. "Do you know where Richard Howard's furniture store is in Denver, (N.C.)?"

"Yes," Bobby said.

"Can we meet there today around two o'clock?" Johnson asked.

"Sure. I'll be there," Bobby said.

He returned the receiver to its cradle and looked up at Moody.

"What do ya' think he wants?" Bobby asked. "Charlie (Glotzbach) is his driver. Why's he calling me?"

"Looks like you'll be racing a Chevrolet next year," Moody said.

CHAPTER TWELVE
Recognized As A Winner

In December of '71, Bobby drove from Moody's home in Charlotte to the home of Richard Howard, located in the small community of Denver, N.C. Howard was the promoter at Charlotte Motor Speedway and a business entrepreneur as well as a NASCAR Winston Cup Grand National team owner.

Bobby knocked on the front door and soon, Howard greeted him and invited him into his living room. Junior Johnson was seated on the sofa when Bobby arrived. Each man greeted the other and proceeded with business.

"So, the reason we're all here is this," Howard said. "As Junior may have told you, we'd like for you to drive for us next year."

Bobby looked at Johnson inquisitively and said, "No, he didn't mention it, but that sounds great to me. A couple of years ago, I begged you for a ride. Why are you giving me one now?"

"Because you proved you could win on the superspeedways," Johnson said. "Before, I didn't think you could."

Bobby studied Johnson's reply and accepted it as an open and honest answer to his question.

Immediately, however, there was a problem; one that threatened to end the deal almost as quickly as it was mentioned.

"How much money does Coca-Cola want to put into the deal?" Howard asked.

"Their top dollar is $75,000 for the entire season," Bobby explained.

"That's not going to be enough," Johnson added quickly. "We need $100,000."

"I'll talk to them and see what I can do," Bobby replied.

By the first of the next week, Bobby phoned his connection at Coca-Cola corporate headquarters in Atlanta and the pitch for a higher sponsorship package was made. The soft drink corporation upped the ante to $85,000, but no more. So Bobby removed the additional $15,000 from his personal bank account to cover the needed funds. With that, the three men signed a deal for the 1972 NASCAR Winston Cup Grand National season.

During the 1971 season, Johnson had campaigned what was first considered a prehistoric dinosaur with Chevrolet as it re-emerged on the Winston Cup Grand National circuit after a three-year absence.

Johnson encountered various problems while attempting to make the car competitive, including the loss of his engine builder Bob Allman, who took one look at the engines and refused to waste his time with them. With that, Robert Yates, an employee of the nearly-defunct Holman-Moody operation, was hired to fill the void.

Johnson called upon the driving services of Charlie Glotzbach for a schedule of 19 events that year. On July 11, Glotzbach scored the team's only victory at Bristol, Tenn., in the newly acquired Chevrolet Monte Carlo (with the help of relief driver Friday Hassler) and went on to capture seven top-five finishes and 10 top-10s as well as two pole positions.

As the 1972 season dawned, Bobby had the knowledge of such mechanics as Herb Nab, Yates, and "Turkey" Minton at his disposal, all highly respected for their chassis and engine expertise. Coupled with Bobby's own stellar abilities behind the wheel along with his keen knowledge of chassis setups, many considered the team a powerhouse from the onset.

At Riverside, Calif., to begin the season, the premonitions of the fans and media alike held true as Bobby finished a strong second behind Richard Petty in the Winston Western 500 on Jan. 23. Unknown at the time, the finishing order of Petty and Allison would be repeated many times and would transform into a bitter rivalry before season's end.

On Feb. 17, Bobby claimed victory in the first of two 125-mile qualifying races held at Daytona International Speedway, sharing the double bill with Bobby Isaac. In that 50-lap event, Bobby held the lead for all but the first lap which was taken by pole winner A.J. Foyt in the Wood Brothers Mercury.

Next on the schedule was Atlanta International Raceway where the Atlanta 500 was held March 26. There, Allison drove the No. 12 Chevrolet Monte Carlo to its first superspeedway victory. While he smiled and waved to the crowd en route to victory lane, female fans seated in the hospitality suites high atop the race track wrote "Chevy Is Back" with various colors of lipstick on the large plate glass windows.

On April 9, winning looked easy as Bobby took the lead for the final time on lap 187 of the 500-lap event at Bristol, Tenn., and took his second victory of the season.

Bobby's red and gold Chevrolet was listed among the top-five positions on the leader board for 445 of 500 laps on the .533-mile oval. A backlash of complaints from Bobby's rivals was expected before the start of the season, as the Chevrolet was new to the tracks and hadn't been raced since 1968. At issue were the wedge-type engine and larger carburetor opening.

Isaac drove the Nord Kraskopf-owned Dodge to a stop on pit road after posting a second-place finish. As he removed his helmet and goggles and emerged from the car, he said, "It was the best we could do. That Chevy is supposed to win. That's the way the rules are written."

Richard Petty also lodged a complaint, saying, "NASCAR has jacked the rules around so much to help that Chevy. Just once I'd like to be even with them."

But while seated in the press box fielding questions from the media, Bobby, who had expected the comments, countered by saying, "We win two races and everybody's saying we have an advantage. I guess that's to be expected."

The winning continued, as Bobby returned to victory lane on June 4 in the Mason-Dixon 500 at Dover, Del. The win came after a classic Allison-Petty duel was staged. But Bobby gained the upper hand on lap 416 of the 500-lap event and held the lead for the remainder of the race while Petty suffered problems with a faulty transmission.

Instead of just showing up on the leader board during the return trip to Bristol on June 11, Allison led 445 of 500 laps and dominated the Volunteer 500 in another easy victory. That feat moved him into second place in the Winston Cup Grand National point standings, just 71.05 points behind Petty. The championship that year was partly determined through points given for laps completed.

For the race at Trenton, N.J., on July 16, Bobby had convinced Johnson to use one of the Monte Carlos that had been built in Bobby's shop in Hueytown and later sold to Howard for Jim Paschal's use in the World 600 at Charlotte Motor Speedway. He then held off a late-race challenge by Isaac to win his fifth race of that season by a 1.4-second margin. He led 50 of 200 laps.

Allison earned a sweep of both Atlanta races with his return trip there on July 23, where he was again victorious over Petty. Pole winner Pearson experienced engine problems in the final 100 miles and finished third but had proven to be Bobby's toughest competition. The victory was Bobby's sixth of the season.

At Nashville, Tenn., on Aug. 27, yet another Allison-Petty duel ensued. But in the end, Bobby held on to win, despite having to negotiate a gaping hole in the track surface. Petty's demise came when a heavy group of cars exiting pit road blocked his path and caused him to be ultimately held up by a NASCAR official as the field rolled by. The incident cost him one lap. Petty passed Bobby to move back into the same lap, but trailed by 10 car lengths at the end.

During the post race interview, Bobby admitted, "I wasn't sure I was going to win this race until I was 103 feet from the finish line."

Of all the wins that year, the brightest moment came at Darlington, S.C., on Sept. 4 in the Southern 500. Throughout the 367-lap event, Bobby dueled Pearson, who had joined the Wood Brothers in April, for the win and emerged victorious after taking the lead with six laps remaining. The two veteran drivers swapped the lead 13 times in the final 300 miles and separated themselves by seven laps over the remaining cars in the field.

During the final laps of the race, Bobby trailed Pearson by 3.8 seconds following his final pit stop. But steadily, he ran the Spartanburg, S.C., driver down and retook the lead.

After the race, Allison said, "I was concentrating on not making any mistakes. All I could think about was getting the most out of my car. I knew I was closing in and I knew that I could win if I didn't make any mistakes."

The pressure felt between Bobby and Petty came to a boil at North Wilkesboro, N.C., on Oct. 1 and even though Bobby finished second, the race was noteworthy.

The final five laps saw Bobby's Chevrolet and Petty's Plymouth bash heavily into each other more than once. With three laps remaining, Bobby ducked under Petty in the hope of making the pass, but Petty shut him off, using the Ford driven by Vic Parsons as a blocker.

As Petty did so, he and Bobby fused together and crashed into the wall.

They quickly recovered and Bobby emerged with the lead. But Petty was in close pursuit. The two cars went into the first turn and crashed again. Once more they recovered and Petty went on to cross the start-finish line just two car lengths ahead.

After the race, Petty said, "He could have put me in the boondocks. There's not going to be any more trouble until he hurts someone. If he does that, there's going to be real trouble. He's playing with my life out there. That I don't like."

Bobby, on the other hand, saw the incident in a different light.

"The other competitor had to wreck me in order to win, and that's what he did," he said. "I had so much smoke in my car I could hardly see."

As Petty prepared to take part in the victory lane ceremonies, an intoxicated spectator attacked him and was warded off by a swing of Petty's helmet.

Bobby sat quietly on the back of a flat bed truck in the infield with a white towel draped around his neck. A large group of his fans surrounded him and one suggested to the others they find Petty and settle the score. Allison quickly halted the fans from any violence, saying, "No, no. We're not going to have anything like that."

His final two wins of the year came at Charlotte, N.C., in the National 500 and at Rockingham, N.C., in the American 500. At Charlotte, he was victorious over Buddy Baker, while staging yet another victory over Petty at the North Carolina Motor Speedway.

Even though success was obvious for the Johnson/Howard team with Bobby behind the wheel, there had been tense undercurrents, which pulled hard throughout most of the season.

From the moment the car was rolled off the transporter for the first test sessions at Riverside in January, communication between Bobby and Johnson was always strained.

Bobby would stand alongside crew chief Nab and Johnson for consultation sessions before races. But direct comments from Johnson were rarely heard.

"Herb, tell Bobby that we need to put a different set of springs in the car before we test again," Johnson might say with Bobby standing alongside.

"Herb, tell Bobby to meet me at Richmond to test next week," Johnson would say, again with Bobby standing close by.

Bobby made repeated attempts to make Johnson aware of the

fact that he could talk with him directly, but Johnson would just walk away.

Halfway through the season, Johnson made yet another comment directing Nab to talk with Bobby, who stood in Johnson's presence. But Bobby was exasperated with the treatment and when the three met to talk again, he countered by saying, "Herb, tell Junior to kiss my ass." The treatment stopped, but communication never improved.

The final straw came while Bobby was in Riverside for a Trans Am race. It was five o'clock in the morning California time, eight o'clock in North Carolina.

Bobby, asleep in his motel room, was awakened by a phone call.

"Yeah, hello?" Bobby said.

"Me and Junior are talking," Howard said. "We want to know yes or no. Are you going to drive for us next year? If you're not, we have a chance to get the best driver in NASCAR right now."

Bobby, not fully awake at that moment, replied, "Get him," and hung up.

Bobby played the phone call from Howard in his mind countless times during the return trip to Alabama. He thought to himself, "Had I been awake, I would have addressed the question a million different ways. They already had the best driver in NASCAR today."

Then he felt himself grow a bit angry when he realized the time the phone call was placed was more than coincidence.

Johnson had never expressed a desire to have Bobby return for the 1973 season, and Bobby had never expressed a desire to do so. But Johnson did know that Bobby was looking to form a Chevrolet team with Moody for '73.

Perhaps the two could have talked and resolved their differences. Perhaps they could have come to some sort of agreement for 1973. But lack of communication was nothing new, for it had shadowed everyone's efforts all season.

It hardly mattered, though.

While Bobby enjoyed his breakfast in California, Johnson and Howard were introducing their new driver to the media back in North Carolina at a prearranged news conference.

Once again, it seemed Bobby Allison had been set up.

CHAPTER THIRTEEN
A Change In Plans

Bobby's eyes studied the gauges on the instrument panel of the Aerostar and then his attention drifted to the soft white clouds around him. They seemed peaceful during the lengthy flight back from the West Coast.

There was something else — a name — that kept surfacing in his mind as well. It was his longtime friend, former race driver Roger Penske. He had known Penske from racing circles long before leaving Riverside International Raceway. After being introduced to the prominent Indy Car owner in the mid-sixties, he felt great respect for him. Ironically, as a result, that chance meeting left Bobby with a lucrative offer for the future in a form of racing totally foreign to him. No doubt, it would be an exciting challenge.

But Bobby's thoughts quickly refocused on stock cars. He felt anxious to call Ralph Moody upon returning from California — the very minute he touched down in Hueytown, in fact.

Because he was, technically, a race driver without a team.

During the latter part of the 1972 NASCAR Winston Cup Grand National season, Bobby seriously talked with Moody concerning their possible reunion in '73. It would be another driver-car owner arrangement as it was in 1967 and again in 1971.

During those years, there were 19 victories. The thought of repeated success was appealing.

But had he been too hasty with his answer to Richard Howard about 1973? Should he land his plane and place a call to explain the time zone difference and that he simply wasn't awake when Howard called? He quickly dismissed the thought. What was done was done, and nothing else said could change the situation.

Unknown to Bobby at the time, Cale Yarborough was shaking hands and granting interviews about his new job — as Bobby's replacement in the Howard-Johnson Chevrolet.

Today, Bobby still ponders what could have come to pass with a reconciliation:

"Looking back, I would have probably answered that (Howard's) question a million different ways had I been awake. But it was pretty early in California; 8 o'clock or so on the East Coast. I've always thought there was a little more than coincidence surrounding that whole deal. With me in California, I was basically out of the way."

Upon arrival at the Hueytown airport, Bobby secured his aircraft and walked over to a nearby phone booth. There were two rings before a gruff voice answered.

"I guess you've heard about me and Junior," Bobby said.

"Yeah, I heard some guy named Yarborough got the ride," said Moody, knowingly. "It's been all over the news."

"So what's our deal now?" Bobby asked. "Can we start getting things in order to run the whole season?"

"Well, Bobby there's a little bit of a problem," Moody said dejectedly. "The deal isn't coming together like I'd hoped. We're doing all we can, but . . ."

Bobby felt disappointment as Moody told him of his abbreviated plans.

"What do you mean, Ralph?" Bobby asked. "I thought things were looking good."

"We just simply can't run the whole deal," Moody said. "A lot of that hinged on John Holman and he seems to be singing a different tune now. But if you can get your own equipment going, I can provide you with engines. Me and Waddell Wilson have teamed up to build a few this year."

"OK, Ralph," Bobby said. "We'll play it by ear and see how it goes. I'd like to think we can still give 'em a run for it."

"With my engines and your equipment, we can," Moody said. "That seems like the best way to play it right now."

Bobby placed the receiver back in its cradle. He stared out onto the short runway for a few moments and pondered Moody's words. Since meeting many years before, Bobby always respected the elder car owner for his fairness as well as his stellar talents with a race car.

In other words, Ralph Moody "hung the moon" as far as Bobby was concerned. Not only was he a business associate but a genuine friend he could trust.

The thought of operating his own team again meant hiring people, building cars and buying a truck to transport the car over the road. Bobby could not help but feel an uneasiness about the situation. He had basically given up the ride with Johnson and Howard to team with Moody. Earlier talks between them indicated it would be a powerhouse organization, possibly better than what he had during his previous stints at Holman-Moody. Bobby was to provide the sponsorship while Moody provided a complete team at his disposal. But now, there was a difference in Moody's voice, as parts of the plan simply did not materialize due to lack of financing, mostly held by Holman. A chance to re-create the magic of the past seemed to be out of the question.

Like so many times in the past, the wheels were put into motion for Bobby to resurrect his own team.

The first order of business was to decide which car would be best to campaign for the '73 season. There was the newly-created Chevrolet Laguna, but the sleeker Malibu was more appealing to many of the teams. With no factory support to speak of, Bobby did not have loyalties to Chevrolet but felt the car was supported well in the NASCAR rule book.

Exhaustive work took place until two cars were complete; one for the ovals and one for the road courses. There was little time between seasons and some teams were already doing winter testing at Daytona.

The season began Jan. 21 at Riverside International Raceway and while there, Bobby and Penske crossed paths again — indirectly. It was Penske's car that had bested him on the California road course.

In only his fifth start in NASCAR competition, road racing specialist Mark Donohue won the Winston Western 500 in Penske's lightly regarded American Motors Matador.

In his first outing with his new team, Bobby turned some heads with a second-place finish, one lap down to Donohue at the end. As it was in years past when Bobby fielded his own cars, strength surfaced immediately.

But the difference was the brake system on Donohue's car, as each wheel carried a disc brake.

"It made all the difference," Donohue said. "I could carry the car deeper in the corners and that's what it takes on a road course."

Penske conveyed his thoughts by saying, "One of the reasons Mark is so good is because he can evaluate what you're doing on the drawing board," Penske said. "You might call him a built-in reliability factor. He's the most consistent driver in the business. He's not driving 102 percent — over his head — it's more like 98 percent. There is always something in reserve."

Two months prior to the NASCAR Winston Cup Grand National race at Riverside, Penske had expressed his appreciation of Bobby's talent behind the wheel of a race car, especially those automobiles he drove for the first time. So it was the Riverside outing that set the groundwork for Penske's offer.

Bobby had been invited to drive one of the Peter Brock-owned Datsuns in a special SCCA (Sports Car Club of America) event. Also on the schedule was a Can-Am race, a division with which Bobby was quite unfamiliar.

Don Nichols entered his driver, Jackie Oliver, and had three spare cars for the race. Nichols quickly became friends with Bobby and offered him a chance to test one of his machines.

Bobby strapped himself into the Can-Am car, a delicate machine much different and more expensive than the stock cars to which Bobby was accustomed. Immediately, he felt comfortable and his times were very fast. His speed caught the eye of Penske, who had entered a Porsche for Donohue.

Ironically, Bobby's time was the day's third fastest. Since he was inexperienced in such a high-tech division of racing, his performance caused Oliver to become a bit uneasy, if not embarrassed that a rookie had bested him.

"You must think you're really good coming in here showing everyone what a hot shot driver you are," Oliver said.

"Look, I'm just here having some fun," Bobby said. "Look, you drive it. I didn't intend to upset anyone."

Oliver walked away without saying another word.

Bobby then struck up a conversation with Nichols. He turned around and saw Penske standing close by. He joined the discussion.

"Boy, you really went fast in that thing," Penske said.

"The car really felt good to me," Bobby responded. "I didn't realize I was turning laps so fast until I came back into the pits."

"What would you say if I told you I thought you should get in an Indy Car?" Penske asked.

"Well, I don't know," Bobby said. "I've never driven one before."

"Well, if you can run that fast in one of these, you could do well in an Indy Car," Penske said. "From what I see, I think you've got the talent for it."

Bobby smiled at Penske's flattering words.

"We're going to be testing at Ontario Motor Speedway in a couple of weeks," Penske said. "Why don't you come on out and give it a try?"

"We'll talk soon," Bobby said. "Let me check my schedule."

But the offer intrigued him and Bobby soon found himself landing his plane at the airport in Ontario. With him was Tom Gloor, his long-time friend who first helped Bobby many years earlier by allowing him to work on his race car at his dealership in Bessemer, Ala., as well as one of Bobby's former car owners in the early days of his career.

Upon arriving, Bobby and Gloor exited the plane and found the crew which was preparing the car for warmup laps. Bobby was finally allowed to slip into the tight cockpit and checked the steering and the positioning of the gauges. He became familiar with his surroundings and eased the car around the race track to get the feel of the machine. But he was instructed not to drive the car too fast. According to the fifteen-minute lecture from the crew chief in attendance that day, Bobby was a stock car driver with no experience and he would probably kill himself if he did so. But he could go ahead and take it out anyway — slowly.

The next practice session was scheduled for a few hours away. During the break, Bobby invited Gloor to go with him to nearby Big Bear Mountain, located near the speedway, for some sightseeing.

When he returned to the track, the car was ready for some harder laps. Bobby immediately became comfortable with the car and turned in some impressive times.

He slowed coming down pit road and came to a stop in the selected pit stall. He was not prepared for the words expressed by his crew chief.

"You lied to me," he said.

"No, I didn't lie to you," Bobby responded.

"Nobody has ever been in one of these cars for the first time and turned laps nearly as fast as the veterans are turning," the crew chief said. "Peter Revson and Mark Donohue are turning 192 mph and you are already at 191 mph. You lied to me."

"No, I didn't lie to you," Bobby said. "The car just felt really good and I just drove it."

"You lied to me," the crew chief insisted one final time and walked away, getting in the last word.

Penske was not in attendance for the test session but heard of Bobby's remarkable times. But the veteran Indy Car owner was not at all surprised. He already had seen him in action.

Preparation for the Daytona 500 began. Bobby consistently turned fast laps and was looked upon as an early favorite. Closer inspection of the engine scheduled for use in the race proved the manifold was not correct. Another was removed from the engine used in the previous Thursday's Twin 125-mile qualifying race and placed on the race engine.

During the process of changing the manifold, the standard practice was to place shop rags over the tappets and push rods to guard against trash falling or blowing into the motor.

The change was soon completed but almost immediately, Bobby detected something was amiss. He continued to allow the engine to idle in the garage area in hopes of detecting the problem.

"Something is wrong with it, Ralph," he said dejectedly. "I'm not exactly sure what it is, but the engine is really pulling and sounding sour."

"OK, let's tear into it," Moody said to no one in particular. A half hour passed before Moody discovered the problem.

"We think we've found small pieces of shop rags in the oil system," Moody said. "From the looks of it, they were left in the engine when the manifold was put back on."

Bobby was greatly disturbed over such a careless oversight. Operating funds were already tight and there was never any margin for such an error. The shop rags were simply left inside an engine and never caught before the process of reassembling was complete. Someone's carelessness cost him many thousands of dollars for repairs as well as one less engine for use at Daytona. That fact alone created the need for Bobby to race a bit conservatively in the 500. After all, the race at Richmond Fairgrounds Raceway was a week away. There was no time to completely disassemble the engine, so the crew elected to resort to a backup.

The two who accidentally left the rags in the engine were Bobby's employees at the Hueytown shop and not the engine specialists out of Moody's shop in Charlotte. One of them left the team as a result, while the other received heavy criticism from the other crew members.

Bobby's approach was not to point fingers, but rather, to keep the team in harmony. Too much was at stake for ill feelings to surface and possibly create war among the crew.

The team did not fair well in the 500. A second engine change was made but the fresh race engine erupted after 141 of the 200 laps. Bobby started the race in 29th place and gained only four spots before falling by the wayside. While coasting back to the garage area, Bobby's mind was already on the race at Richmond, scheduled for the next week.

Once there on Feb. 25, Bobby seemed to have his engine problems solved and placed his Coca-Cola Chevrolet in the pole position at 90.952 mph. He led the 66 laps of the race, but was caught in a tight traffic situation. The bumping caused extensive damage to the right-front fender and front end. He eventually finished 15th behind race winner Richard Petty, 49 laps off the pace.

Back a second time from California, Bobby entered the Carolina 500 event at Rockingham, N.C., on March 1. But it was David Pearson who dominated the event by leading 499 of the 500 miles. Bobby led the one mile Pearson didn't and eventually finished fourth, two laps in arrears.

After only 52 laps on the 0.533-mile Bristol (Tenn.) International Raceway for the next race, heavy rain brought the race to a halt with Cale Yarborough in the lead.

On the return trip on March 25, Yarborough, in the Junior Johnson-Richard Howard Chevrolet, led all 500 laps for the win. It was the first time a driver had led a NASCAR event from start to finish since Darel Dieringer accomplished the feat at North Wilkesboro, N.C., on April 16, 1967.

Bobby brought his Chevrolet home third, five laps off the pace. Even though down laps at the end, Bobby's new team was improving.

After only 103 laps at Atlanta on April 1, Bobby pulled behind the wall with a blown engine. It was the first lost engine of the year, other than the one accidentally infested with shop rags at Daytona.

From there, a couple of top-five finishes developed. There was a fourth at North Wilkesboro on April 8 and a third at Darlington, S.C., on April 15. But an oil leak sidelined Bobby at Martinsville, Va., after only 30 laps.

Then came the most frightening race in NASCAR history, the '73 Winston 500 at Alabama International Motor Speedway on May 6.

On the eighth lap of the 188-lap event, 21 cars were involved in a crash that left several drivers injured, the worst of whom was Wendell Scott, who suffered broken ribs, a lacerated arm and a cracked pelvis.

Bobby started the event from the fifth position and was quickly swept into the crash when race leader Buddy Baker and second-place Yarborough slid through oil on the backstretch from a blown engine in Ramo Stott's Mercury.

From there, a chain reaction ensued.

Bobby regained his composure and met with reporters in the garage area amid a sea of badly damaged vehicles. He blamed the 60-car starting field as the culprit.

"The extra 10 or 20 cars were needed to fill up the track," Bobby said. "Well, they did — all over the backstretch.

"The whole system is wrong. The yellow flag should be official. When you see it, you should start putting on the brakes. But the way the rule is, you're forced to keep racing to the start-finish line."

Bobby was given credit for finishing 42nd with a paycheck of $3,055. But the total loss of his race car made the trip to Talladega a costly one.

At Nashville, Tenn., on May 12, Yarborough claimed yet another short-track victory in dominant fashion. It was the first race on the newly redesigned 0.596-mile paved speedway. At the request of many drivers, the 35-degree banks were lowered to 18 and made for safer and more competitive racing. Bobby brought the Chevrolet home fifth, nine laps off Yarborough's pace.

Local star Darrell Waltrip started 10th in the field for his first-ever Winston Cup Grand National race, but went out early with handling problems. He finished 24th in the 28-car field.

Bobby received a lucrative monetary offer — he was going to miss the World 600 at Charlotte Motor Speedway on May 27 — and signed a two-race contract with Penske to drive the 1973 and 1974 Indianapolis 500s.

The team entered Indy's gates with an Offenhausen I-4 powered McLaren. But nothing seemed to go right for any of the competitors. It was a month of disappointment and destruction.

The horror began during the first day of qualifying. Art Pollard, a close friend of Bobby's, entered turn one and crashed into the retaining wall. His machine flipped violently. Pollard sustained head and chest injuries and died en route to the infield medical center. The loss was extremely hard for Bobby and placed a cloud over his first trip to Indy.

To no one's surprise, Bobby was the fastest rookie, qualifying 12th with a speed of 192.308 mph. But the weather was miserable most of the month and created several false starts in practice and in the race itself, which was postponed and completed on Monday, May

28.

Coming out of the second turn on the first lap, Bobby's engine blew and crudely ended the team's hopes of a solid finish. At that point, all preparation had been for nothing.

To further add to his disillusionment, Bobby lost another close friend before race's end. Swede Savage was killed after being involved in a multicar crash. The two had first met when they both drove stock cars as teammates for Holman-Moody six years earlier.

A final heavy rainstorm halted the event on lap 133 and Gordon Johncock was declared the winner.

Once in the garage area, Penske found Bobby and Judy, preparing to return to Hueytown.

"Well, we didn't fare so well today but we'll get 'em next year," Penske said.

"Roger, I don't want to ever come back here — ever," Judy said, clearly upset over the deaths of Pollard, Savage and a crew member of another team during the race. "This is just not where we want to be. This type of racing is just not for us."

Penske could see how disturbed Judy had become and retrieved Bobby's contract from his leather briefcase. Placing his hands at the top of the contract, he ripped the document into two pieces down the center.

"Judy, Bobby will never have to come back here if you don't want him to. I consider Bobby's obligation to me fulfilled," he said.

Still feeling great disappointment at Indy, Bobby prepared his Chevelle and returned to NASCAR action at Dover, Del., on June 3. He led 50 laps but was three laps down at the finish due to a slight chassis problem. He ultimately finished third.

Another engine erupted on June 10 at College Station, Texas, in the Alamo 500 at Texas World Speedway. It was a frustrating weekend to say the least. Bobby led only one of 250 laps at the two-mile facility.

On June 17, Bobby experienced his best race of the year with a victory at Riverside International Raceway.

Richard Petty held a commanding lead in his Dodge for much of the 153-lap race, until the Level Cross, N.C., resident smacked the ninth-turn retaining wall.

The lead was then given to Yarborough, but a blown engine sidelined his Chevrolet on lap 113, thus giving the lead to Bobby.

Petty mounted a valiant charge to regain the lead lap, but still found himself one minute, 13 seconds behind Allison at the finish.

Once he rolled to a stop in victory lane, Bobby exited his car to the cheers of the crew around him as well as those of the 43,700 fans in attendance.

"I knew all the other guys were having trouble," Bobby said over the booming public address system. "We were running well all the way. So near the end, I decided to save the car as much as possible. I didn't think anyone could catch me."

Bobby collected $12,750 for the victory.

He scored yet another top-five finish at Michigan International Speedway on June 24, but fell out of the Firecracker 400 at Daytona on July 4 after placing his Chevrolet on the pole. Once again, engine problems plagued his efforts.

During the return trip to Bristol on July 8, Bobby hit the second turn wall hard on lap 343 of the 500-lap event. As he dropped low down the backstretch and drove into turn three, he lost control and was hit by Yarborough's Chevrolet. The two drivers finished 19th and 20th, respectively. Only five drivers in the 30-car field did not require a relief driver.

At Atlanta on July 22, Donnie Allison wheeled the Chevrolet of the newly formed DiGard Racing, Co., to a third-place finish. But once again, Bobby was sidelined by a faulty engine after starting second alongside pole winner Petty. He completed 205 of 328 laps but finished 27th in the 40-car field.

The second event at Talladega on Aug. 12 proved to be almost as exciting as the first, but was marred by the death of rookie sensation Larry Smith.

As Smith entered the first turn of the 2.66-mile speedway on lap 14, his Mercury hit the wall in a single-car accident. The 1972 Rookie of the Year was killed upon impact.

Observers were shocked to hear of Smith's death. The right side sheet metal was flattened but all roll cage parts were solidly intact. His crew chief, John Green, was working to get the car back in the race when he was informed of Smith's death. The Lenoir, N.C., native died of massive head injuries and a basal skull fracture.

On lap 90, Bobby Isaac radioed his car owner, Bud Moore, and told him to find a relief driver for his Ford. The Matthews, N.C., driver complained of hearing voices telling him to get out of the race car.

"Something told me to quit," Isaac said. "I don't know anything else to do but abide by it."

On lap 159, both Allison brothers were eliminated when their Chevrolets crashed into one another. Both were considered serious contenders for the win. Donnie hit the wall with both the front and rear of the DiGard entry while Bobby escaped with less damage — but too much to continue.

Three days before the race, car owner Jimmy Crawford hired California native Dick Brooks to wheel his black No. 22 Plymouth. Crawford did not have the experience to race Talladega, according to NASCAR officials.

Remarkably, at the end, Brooks was the winner over Baker and Pearson. That surprised the entire motorsports community. It was Brooks' first-ever Winston Cup Grand National victory.

For the second time during the season, Bobby returned to near-by Hueytown with a great deal of disappointment and a badly damaged race car.

On Aug. 25, the fourth engine failure of the year sent Bobby's Chevelle behind the wall at Nashville, Tenn., and to a 22nd-place finish.

But then there were three top-10 finishes in as many weeks; a sixth in the Southern 500 at Darlington on Sept. 3, a third at Richmond on Sept. 9 and a second at Dover on Sept. 16.

Bobby's fortunes rose higher at North Wilkesboro, N.C., on Sept. 23. There, he made up a lap with 47 circuits remaining and went on to capture his second victory of the season over Petty.

He relinquished the lead on lap 352 for a four-tire pit stop, caused by an increasingly slick track surface. The fresh tires proved to be the winning factor, as Bobby chased down Petty after the pit stop and found himself on his rear bumper as the two cars crossed under the white flag. By the time they entered turn one, Bobby had retaken the lead and held it for the win.

"We decided to change all four tires," Bobby said in the post-race interview. "We knew we would lose some time to Petty, but we figured we'd be able to make it up by having better traction. It was getting real oily out there."

By this time, some things began to come to a head — at least for Bobby.

Throughout the season, he had been feeling he was losing races because other teams were blatantly twisting the rules in their favor and getting away with it. Other times, the rules weren't considered at all, and the 400-mile event at Charlotte Motor Speedway on Oct. 7 confirmed Bobby's feelings.

The day before the race, Bobby sought out Bill Gazaway, technical director for NASCAR, for a consultation.

"Bill, I feel there are some funny things going on," Bobby said. "I can tell you now I'm legal as the day is long, but I know some of these other guys aren't. I'd like the top cars torn down for inspection after the race tomorrow and here's the $100 protest fee in advance."

"No need for that, Bobby," Gazaway said. "Put your money in your pocket. We're going to tear down the first three anyway and maybe a few more."

Bobby returned the five $20 bills back in his wallet and for the moment, felt satisfied restitution was forthcoming.

After talking with Gazaway, Allison spoke to reporters.

"I'm running faster than I've ever run here and if I finish the race with no problems, I want to look at any car that finishes ahead of me. I'm curious as to how I get blown off the track as much as I am this year. It just gets you to wondering," he said.

The next day, Bobby found himself three laps down in the final stages of the race to the front two cars — Yarborough and Petty, who led 310 of the 334 scheduled laps.

But there were questions to be answered.

Bobby stopped his car in the garage area and pulled the seat belt pin. He exited still wearing his helmet and chased down Gazaway with $200 in his hand.

Once he found Gazaway, Bobby said, "Here's a hundred to look at the No. 11 (Yarborough) and a hundred to look at the No. 43 (Petty)." But Gazaway returned the $200 to Allison. The inspection was now an order of NASCAR.

Bobby's Chevrolet, which finished third, was also to be inspected and moments later, his car was joined by Petty's Dodge and Yarborough's Chevy after victory lane ceremonies had concluded.

Twenty minutes passed and Bobby's Chevrolet was released as perfectly legal. Petty's and Yarborough's cars, however, were kept in the closed and guarded garage for several hours.

After loading his own car for the return trip to Alabama, Bobby stayed close by in hopes of getting the results of the inspection before he departed.

Bobby stood outside the inspection station with a group of newspaper reporters, all waiting for the results from NASCAR.

"I guess now's as good a time to tell you guys this as any," Bobby said to no one in particular. "I followed Petty into the pits after the race and was going to park in the garage right beside of him. But some of his crew ran out in front of me before I got stopped. Anyway, I saw members of Petty's crew raise the hood and jerk the air breather of and run away with it. I saw a NASCAR official with his knees against Petty's car watching it all. Now he says he didn't see anything.

"I'm satisfied I know how Petty was beating the game. Now I want to know about that No. 11."

While most of the reporters ran back to their typewriters to record Bobby's comments, a NASCAR official exited the building. Bobby grabbed his right elbow and pulled him closer.

"What's the verdict?" Bobby asked.

"I'm not supposed to tell you this," the official said in a low voice, "but Petty's engine is a whopper and Yarborough's is bigger than that."

At 10:15 p.m., Gazaway emerged to greet the haggard reporters who remained, along with various crew members and onlookers. He unfolded a small white piece of paper and began reading a prepared statement.

"The official measurements of the engine size of the No. 11 has been sent to Daytona Beach," Gazaway said. "A final decision will be made tomorrow. I have no further comment."

"What about the other two cars?" asked one of the reporters.

"Excuse me gentlemen," Gazaway said. "I meant to say that the measurements on cars Nos. 11, 12 and 43 have been sent to Daytona Beach and a final decision will be reached on Monday. Now I have no further comment."

All parties had no choice but to return to their respective homes. No further news would come until morning.

But everyone was left waiting until 5 p.m. the next day, just in time for NASCAR's ruling to be reported on the evening newscasts.

A written communication from NASCAR said: "The decision to let the results stand was made following a meeting of NASCAR officials after reviewing information that showed in a post-race inspection the procedure used to check all of the engine sizes in the pre-race inspections proved inadequate.

"Since the purpose of the pre-race inspection is to determine that the cars in competition conform to the rules prior to the actual running of the race and that this procedure was in effect for the Charlotte race, the results are official."

Upon learning of NASCAR's position, Bobby exploded — and rightly so, according to many observers. Of the top-three finishers, Bobby's Chevrolet was the only one perfectly legal. But he was beaten by two cars which, apparently, were not. It appeared the cards had been stacked.

When contacted by phone at his home in Hueytown, Bobby said, "I figured they would lie out of it. It stands to reason that those cars did not conform to the rules. Otherwise, it wouldn't take six hours to inspect them if they were legal. The time spent on their cars wasn't whether they were legal or not, but how to worm their way out of it. We were lied to and cheated out of the money. The first two cars were cheating and that's a fact."

By 11 p.m., Bobby had answered many phone calls from reporters across the country and expressed one thought; his desire to quit NASCAR racing.

The following day, he withdrew his entry from North Carolina Motor Speedway in Rockingham, N.C., for the American 500 scheduled for Oct. 21.

"On account of NASCAR's arbitrary and capricious conduct, I find it necessary to withdraw from the remaining races this season," Bobby said. "They need to satisfactorily resolve the matter of rewarding people for running illegal engines and penalizing others for staying within the rules."

On Oct. 11, Bobby made the statement that opened everyone's eyes. He announced his intent to file a lawsuit against the sanctioning body.

"NASCAR has stolen money from me and permanently damaged my career," Bobby said. "NASCAR has stolen a minimum of $39,000 and maybe as much as $65,000 from me considering point bonuses by covering up for the two other cars involved. I am quite sure I have a good case. I have arranged legal counsel on the assumption of filing a suit.

"If you use the standards utilized by NASCAR, we ought to give Spiro Agnew (former Vice President of the United States) his job back. If you get caught cheating, it doesn't seem to matter in NASCAR's eyes. I'm just one of 38 who got cheated. I feel sorry for the other 37, but I can't speak for them."

But in the meantime, Bill France Jr., President of NASCAR, made himself available after taking the position of "unavailable for comment" throughout the episode.

France agreed to meet with Allison in Atlanta, Ga., on Monday, Oct. 15 in hopes of resolving the situation before court proceedings began.

The meeting lasted several hours. Late in the night, France and Allison emerged from the room and issued a formal statement.

"Grand National stock car driver Bobby Allison, who had previously withdrawn his entry to compete in the Winston Cup Grand National stock car race to take place at Rockingham, N.C., North Carolina Motor Speedway, Sunday, Oct. 21, 1973, has announced his intentions to compete.

"This change came as a result of a meeting Allison had with Bill France Jr., president of NASCAR, Monday night.

"The purpose of the meeting held in Atlanta was to discuss the official outcome of the National 500 stock car race at Charlotte Motor Speedway, Oct. 7, 1973.

"As a result of the meeting," Allison said, "I am confident that NASCAR will take positive steps in the future to avoid any misunderstandings about the rules and penalties and that the meeting was most constructive for the good of stock car racing.

"Furthermore, France reaffirmed his previously stated position released last week 'that a study into all inspection procedures is being conducted at this time.'

"In addition to the procedure, France said that at the Rockingham event 'there will be a post race inspection on the carburetor plates, air cleaners and engine size.'"

The statement came jointly from Allison's office in Hueytown and NASCAR's headquarters in Daytona Beach.

All Bobby could do was hope the situation wouldn't repeat itself at Rockingham and trust France to fulfill his end of the agreement.

"A lot of people thought I walked away from that meeting with some sort of financial settlement from NASCAR. But for the first time, I'll talk about it here.

"The fact of the matter is I didn't receive one dime from NASCAR. Instead, I got a solemn promise from Bill France Jr. that there would never again be a race winner with an illegal engine or illegal gas tank.

I had to accept that because there wasn't anywhere else (another sanctioning body of the magnitude of NASCAR) that I could go to.

"To me, it was so important to establish some sort of degree of fairness. I couldn't just walk away and say nothing after the two cars in front of me were clearly illegal. I felt like walking away and doing nothing could create more damage later on. The situation had to be addressed right then."

In the final race of the season at Rockingham, Bobby finished fourth, four laps behind eventual winner David Pearson.

Benny Parsons was awarded the Winston Cup Grand National championship, even though he was involved in a violent crash that threatened to sideline him for the day. His crew, along with members from several crews, repaired the car and returned him to the race, where he logged the necessary completed laps to win the title.

It had been a tough year for Bobby. More equipment had been destroyed than any other year in his career. But if NASCAR went through with the plans that had been circulating in the garage area, everything he had worked for in the past wouldn't matter anyway. Bobby would be out of business.

CHAPTER FOURTEEN
A Different
Breed Of
Race Car

All the NASCAR Winston Cup Grand National team owners and drivers began the 1974 season with a shallow rule book and a complicated point system.

Although there was a need for change, the same rules were in place that had existed throughout 1973. NASCAR's Executive Vice President, Lin Kuchler, said the sanctioning body was prepared to make changes in the rules but the fuel shortage created by the oil embargo had reached international proportions. It gained virtually all of NASCAR's attention.

With auto racing considered by some a waste of precious fuel on the race track, NASCAR was faced with a dilemma; one which threatened to halt stock car racing across the country, at all levels of competition.

Bill France Sr. delivered some surprising figures in a study conducted at the United States Government's request. Auto racing consumed 93,639,696 gallons of fuel annually. But other professional sports, such as horse racing, basketball and football, consumed far more. Those figures included spectator travel and chartered flights to get teams to their respective contests.

Well-trained in the arena of politics, France represented the entire auto racing fraternity when he negotiated with officials of the

Federal Energy Office.

In a prepared statement, France said, "While auto racing used only a minimal amount of fuel in contrast to other leisure time activities, we are anxious to cooperate in the overall curtailment of fuel consumption.

"Auto racing is a highly visible sport and has a public relations problem inasmuch as we are very vulnerable. We feel it is important to cooperate with the government's request to exceed the 25 percent overall cut if possible. I am sure the quality of NASCAR racing for our fans and our competitors will be unaffected."

France immediately canceled the 24 Hours of Daytona and cut the distances of NASCAR Winston Cup Grand National events by 10 percent — or 50 miles in most cases. Further, he established a 30-gallon limit of fuel for practice. Starting fields also were reduced.

The energy crisis aside, NASCAR teams had serious concerns to address in the form of carburetor plates and a point system overhaul which proved complicated to follow.

The carburetor plates would be removed from all cars and replaced with special carburetors built especially for Winston Cup Grand National racing. It would be placed on engines larger than 366 cubic inches in displacement — which meant most of the engines used in competition. It was billed by NASCAR officials as the only rule change of the year, but that was not to be.

Bobby found the Chevrolet Malibu to be more competitive and made the body switches on his equipment during the winter months. There were no sponsorship changes, as Coca-Cola elected to remain with his Hueytown-based team.

The Winston Western 500 opened the season at Riverside International Raceway, but the 50-mile reduction in length did not go into force until the second race of the year — the Daytona 500.

The 191-lap event was staged in two parts; 63 laps being run on Jan. 20 and the remainder completed on Jan. 26. When the cars rolled to a halt in heavy rain showers during the scheduled race date, Bobby found his Chevrolet out front. But since the race had not reached its halfway point, it was not declared official.

Cale Yarborough drove an unsponsored Chevrolet to victory over Richard Petty on the 2.62-mile road course. David Pearson was third in the Wood Brothers Mercury, Benny Parsons was fourth for car owner L.G. DeWitt, while Bobby salvaged a fifth-place finish after encountering transmission problems. He only had high gear in his red and gold Chevrolet and lost three laps to Yarborough at the end.

A blown engine after 97 laps of the 200-lap Daytona 500 on Feb. 17 sent Bobby home with a disappointing 30th-place finish. Donnie looked to be on his way to victory until he encountered problems in the form of Bob Burcham's Chevrolet. That car suffered a blown engine and spread parts over the racing surface. The debris cut down both Donnie's front tires with only 11 laps remaining. He ultimately finished sixth behind eventual winner Petty, who captured his fifth Daytona 500.

But it was Bobby who won at Richmond, Va., in the next race and stopped Petty's win streak at seven. He drove his Chevrolet into the lead on lap 409 and held it for the remaining 91 laps. It was Bobby's first win of the year.

For the race, Bobby had hired a new crew chief. Bill Hamner took control of the team and used a strategy quite different from what Bobby had utilized throughout his career.

"He told me to take it easy and save the car for the finish," Bobby said as he sipped a Coke during post-race interviews. "I don't like to race that way. I'd rather go racing from the start. Petty has won a lot of races that way, so we tried it. It worked."

Bobby logged a third at Rockingham, N.C., on March 3 and a fourth at Bristol, Tenn., on March 17. But the next day, Monday, March 18, the new engine rules became effective. They had been created to eliminate the big powerplants and that's when trouble began for everyone.

Once the teams arrived at Atlanta International Raceway for the Atlanta 500, Pearson wheeled the Wood Brothers Ford to a speed of 159.242 mph to take the pole position over Gary Bettenhausen in a newly-prepared American Motors Matador. The odd-shaped machine was built for car owner Roger Penske by the Hutcherson-Pagan race car fabrication operation based in Charlotte, N.C.

Bettenhausen's speed was 156.160 mph, more than three miles per hour slower. That alone dictated a possible runaway by Pearson in the 328-lap event.

As expected, Pearson led most of the scheduled laps. But an extra pit stop cost him certain victory as Yarborough scored his second win of the year.

Bobby, however, did not fare well with the large-block engine. It erupted on lap 147 and relegated him to 26th in the final order.

Bobby had the April 7 Rebel 500 at Darlington, S.C., in his back pocket until his Chevrolet began to sputter out of fuel on the backstretch with only 11 laps remaining. Pearson took the lead and went on to victory. Bobby's engine fell silent during the final lap but he managed a second-place finish.

Bobby did well on the short tracks — at North Wilkesboro, N.C., on April 21 and at Martinsville, Va., on April 28. For both races, he logged third-place finishes behind race winners Petty and Yarborough, respectively.

The day after Martinsville's Virginia 500, another rule change was handed down from NASCAR. Virtually all the front runners had spent thousands of dollars to switch to the smaller motors, but NASCAR's new rule fell in favor of the large engines.

"We feel the larger engine could use more help, so we've given it a little more carburetor to intensify competition," were the words from NASCAR.

Many of the top teams felt they had been ambushed by NASCAR and more than one voiced its displeasure over the unstable rules.

When the tour moved to Alabama International Motor Speedway for the Winston 500 on May 5, Bobby once again found himself watching the race from the garage area. Another blown engine sent him home to nearby Hueytown in 31st place.

Pearson and Benny Parsons had finished one-two with small-block engines.

Soon after, Pearson drove both the Richard Howard-Junior Johnson Chevrolet and the Nord Kraskopf Dodge in private tests requested by NASCAR in hopes of making the small and large block engines equitable.

As a result, more rule changes were forthcoming. But all the while, those changes had cost Bobby many thousands of dollars. Being a car owner and driver, he was feeling the pressures of fielding a competitive race team and the constant rule changes were pulling his team down. His new equipment was becoming more obsolete by the minute.

Effective May 20, two different size carburetors would be implemented for the large engines, depending upon the size of the track on which they competed. NASCAR made a second announcement and said this would be in effect on June 24. By then, the maximum size of the small-block engine would be reduced from 366 cubic inches to 358 cubic inches.

The outcries of anger rang out from virtually every driver and car owner.

At Nashville, Tenn., on May 11, rain stopped the event after only 127 laps. Bobby had dueled closely with Yarborough before the red flag was displayed.

But when the race resumed the next day, a Sunday, Bobby found himself in the second-turn wall, his car too damaged to repair. Before he parked his battered Chevrolet for good and unstrapped himself from the driver's seat, he had completed 217 laps.

Petty increased his lopsided point lead over Bobby, who was ranked fourth in the standings and had gained only a third of Petty's point total. It was a two-man battle for the championship, if that. Petty had a stranglehold on the lead.

After only 90 laps at Dover, Del., on May 19, Bobby's engine began to overheat and just 10 laps later, he once again found himself behind the wall.

The performances were becoming a bit frustrating. To win the Winston Cup Grand National championship would be virtually impossible under the best conditions. Bobby had no chance with continued mechanical failures.

The situation seemed to get better at Charlotte for the 600-mile event on May 26. Surprisingly, Bobby's engine held up for the longest race of the year. He still found himself five laps off the pace to leaders Pearson and Petty.

At Riverside, Calif., on June 9, Bobby found an unexpected wind in his sails and had one of his better performances of the season. Had he not been forced to pit with seven laps remaining, the victory would have been his. But low fuel dictated the move and put him nine seconds behind Yarborough near the end. Before the checkered flag fell, however, Bobby had muscled his way through several packs of cars and closed the gap to a mere 2.7 seconds.

At Michigan International Speedway on June 16, the engine rule had taken its toll on many of the teams, especially the independents, those without significant sponsorship. Bobby settled for a 23rd-place finish after losing yet another engine. The rules had rendered him helpless. The future looked bleak and with low operating finances, a curtailment of the schedule seemed imminent. There was no choice but to fill in the missed Winston Cup Grand National races with short-track events whenever possible.

But while at MIS, Bobby's luck changed dramatically.

Bettenhausen had another motorsports commitment to fulfill and would not be available for the July 4 race at Daytona Beach, Fla. Roger Penske, owner of Bettenhausen's American Motors Matador, needed a driver and asked Bobby to do the job. Bobby gladly accepted and after some consultations with Coca-Cola, he carried his sponsor over to the Matador's rear flanks. It was some relief from the bad luck he had experienced with his own Chevrolet.

Days before the race, Bobby studied the Matador closely at Penske's Reading, Pa. stock car facility. It was a foreign looking object compared to the customary Chevrolet and Fords. The odd looking machine sported large round headlight openings with a sloped rear end and a small rear opera window. Many had their doubts the car could be competitive, but Bobby felt good about the red, white and blue machine.

"I didn't particularly think the Matador was ugly and didn't downgrade it because it came from a relatively small company and our racing effort was a particularly small company in Alabama. It was completely different from the Fords and Chevys and I thought that was pretty neat. It had a lot more potential than it showed but a few minor things happened later on that really hurt the car's effort.

"It was an underdog but I think we won some races with it and showed some things during those years. "

The results were immediately favorable. Bobby wheeled the Matador to a fifth-place finish, one lap behind the close duel between Pearson and Petty for the win. Another duel ensued for third place between Buddy Baker and Yarborough. As they hit the start-finish stripe, they were dead even. They were officially scored as tied for third.

Bobby returned to the Chevrolet at Bristol on July 14 and posted a fifth-place finish, six laps off the pace. His engines simply were not competitive. He was not accustomed to watching his rivals run away virtually every week.

At Nashville Fairgrounds Raceway on July 20, controversy surfaced and robbed Bobby of a victory that was rightfully his.

Yarborough drove to victory lane only to find Bobby's Chevrolet sitting there. Bobby still had a leg inside his car when officials began trying to turn him away. Bobby wasn't about to concede, especially when there was proof of victory in his hand.

Yarborough claimed he won the race by leading the final 31 of the 420 laps. But earlier in the race, Yarborough had cut down a tire and after he returned to the track, a caution was displayed for the spinning cars of J.D. McDuffie, Buddy Baker, Walter Ballard and Roy Mayne.

The pace car picked up the wrong leader and did not notice Charlie Glotzbach, driver of the Junie Donlavey Ford, as well as Yarborough.

Noticing the infraction, Bobby brought his car to a halt on the frontstretch in hopes of rectifying the problem with NASCAR officials.

"Hey, you know he's (Yarborough) a lap down?" Bobby asked.

"OK, Bobby," said Chief Steward Johnny Bruner. "We'll fix it. Don't worry. We've got everything under control."

But the pace car picked up only Glotzbach — again bypassing Yarborough.

Bobby stopped his car once again.

"We still don't have it fixed," Bobby yelled out the window opening at the screen net. "You got the No. 90 car but what about the No. 11? He's a lap down, too."

"Look, if an error has been made, we'll correct it after the race," Bruner said.

"After the race means the race will be over," Bobby shot back. "When the checkered flag waves, it's over."

Bruner cut a glance and walked away. His decision would stand.

Yarborough was given the checkered flag with Bobby trailing in second, less than a lap behind.

Later, with Bobby's car occupying victory lane, Yarborough became angry.

"I've always been raised to believe that the guy who wins the race should go to victory lane," Yarborough said, now close in Bobby's face.

"The car that won IS in victory lane," Bobby replied.

"They gave me the checkered flag," Yarborough retorted.

"It's simple," Bobby said. "They gave the race to the wrong man."

At that point, the track announcer gave the microphone to each man to let him explain his side of the story. When Bobby concluded his statement, the crowd 18,000 cheered strongly, while Yarborough received only boos.

"It's obvious that I'm in Allison country," Yarborough muttered.

Bobby's Chevrolet was removed from victory lane and replaced with Yarborough's. Bobby walked away in search of another official to argue his point.

Four days later, NASCAR issued a statement. The sanctioning body agreed with Bobby that Yarborough had regained his lap illegally, but the win would stand.

Bobby voiced his displeasure over NASCAR's ruling.

"They said it would be rectified afterwards. But it was never done. It doesn't make any sense, but why should it? It's what you expect from NASCAR", he said.

"I feel like that situation at Nashville could have been handled much differently. If Johnny Bruner had listened to what I was telling him about Cale, it would have never come to that. I knew Cale was a lap down because I passed him at least once and maybe even twice. There was no way he should have been in victory lane that night. I knew I was right and I showed it to NASCAR on the score cards and showed them exactly where the error was made. But at the time, it really didn't do any good."

On Aug. 4, Bobby erupted another engine at Pocono, Pa., but managed a third-place finish at Talladega, Ala., on Aug. 11.

At Michigan on Aug. 25, Bobby returned to Penske's AMC Matador and finished fifth. Bobby always recognized Michigan as a good place to post a strong finish since most of Detroit's automotive brass attended races there on a regular basis.

Pearson went to victory lane over Petty, Yarborough and Baker.

The Matador fell silent after completing 80 of the scheduled 367 laps in the Southern 500 at Darlington on Sept. 2. Bobby made contact with Yarborough, the eventual winner of the race, which caused great damage to the front of Bobby's car. It was a long day for everyone, as only 12 cars finished the grueling race. A total of 101 laps was run under caution.

It was Yarborough's third career Southern 500 victory.

The point system which decides the Winston Cup champion came under more fire. Petty received more points for finishing 30th than Darrell Waltrip for finishing second, due the fact emphasis was placed on the number of starts multiplied by basic prize winnings. Bobby had long since dropped out as a contender for the title as a result of his string of blown engines and misfortunes.

Bobby had no choice but to keep his team home from Richmond, Va., on Sept. 8. The purse simply didn't warrant the long trip from Hueytown. Secondly, the rules pertaining to the engines had contributed heavily to his decision to park his own equipment until something could be settled in a fair and uniform manner. Bobby continued to pay the price, for rules had rendered many Winston Cup Grand National powerplants useless.

He made the decision to only run the races Penske wanted him to run, which consisted of the superspeedways. The remaining would come in the Sportsman ranks. But Penske was not in favor of Allison campaigning cars in any other division. It was a standard rule for all of Penske's drivers in various forms of motorsport.

Penske called on Bobby once again for Dover, Del., on Sept. 15.

Bobby worked hard throughout the 500-lap race and found himself in second with only 23 laps remaining. Then, without warning, his oil pump locked up and sent him behind the pit road wall.

Penske had great hope for a win at Charlotte Motor Speedway on Oct. 6. It proved to be a wild melee for most of the drivers when Baker crashed on the second lap. Many cars suffered extensive damage and were eliminated from the race.

But Bobby started eighth and missed the wreck behind him.

Baker had spun the Bud Moore-owned Ford on his second qualifying lap earlier in the week. According to NASCAR rules, he was required to start the race on his qualifying tires. But since they were flat-spotted, Moore asked for permission to change them. Permission was denied. At that point, Moore pulled out a knife and cut his own tires. Baker was then moved to 41st position by NASCAR officials.

In an effort to return to the front, Baker collected Dick Brooks and started the wild spin.

Bobby's hope of winning fell short with a fifth-place finish, one lap down to Pearson, the race winner. Petty was second, followed by Waltrip and Donnie.

A fourth-place finish at Rockingham, N.C., on Oct. 20 continued the mediocre streak Bobby had been suffering. Five laps down to Pearson at the finish was discouraging.

Just over a month passed before the teams fired their engines for the final race of the year at Ontario, Calif., on Nov. 24. During that time, a lot of preparation had been done by all Winston Cup Grand National teams. The time span allowed every nut and bolt to be checked, especially by those running for the championship.

Bobby qualified on the flat 2.5-mile Ontario Motor Speedway in the fourth starting position. He ran a steady race, but did not grab the lead until lap 169 and held it for his second victory of the season.

The usual victory lane celebrations took place, both for the winner of the race and the winner of the Winston Cup Grand National championship. Richard Petty was crowned champion under the confusing system by 567.45 points over Yarborough.

After granting the final interview and giving an autograph to a nearby fan, Bobby left for the Los Angeles airport, where he boarded a commercial flight to the East Coast. A wide smile crossed his face as he thought there was hope for the Matador. He had always had faith in the equipment of the small American Motors car and it looked like it had a great future in Winston Cup Grand National racing.

In routine fashion, Bobby buckled the seat belts and waited for the aircraft to taxi to the runway. In a brief moment of meditation, with head bowed and eyes closed, Bobby made a Sign of The Cross with his right hand, an act to summon divine guidance during the pending journey.

But unknown to him at the time, the situation at OMS was becoming tense.

When Bill Gazaway, NASCAR's Technical Director, asked to see and inspect one of the Matador's valve lifters, a crew member handed him a cold one from out of the tool box. Being cold, there was no doubt that it did not come from an engine that had been raced for nearly four hours.

"This one is cold," Gazaway said. "It could not have possibly come from that engine. I want to see what's in that engine."

A crew member then removed a valve lifter from the engine and handed it to him. At that point, no words were necessary from either party. Both new the part was an illegal roller tappet.

Bobby landed at 6 a.m. in Atlanta. After locating his luggage in the baggage claim area, he passed by a nearby newspaper box and stopped dead in his tracks at the sight of the headline over the Los Angeles Times newspaper: "ALLISON'S MATADOR ILLEGAL AT ONTARIO." The subhead read: "Penske Fined $9,100 by NASCAR."

At that moment, Bobby dropped the hang-up bag that was steadied over his shoulder, fished some coins from his pocket and retrieved a paper.

After reading the article carefully, Bobby found a nearby pay phone and placed a call to Penske in Reading, Pa.

"Roger, where did the roller tappets come from?" Bobby asked.

"They (the engine building firm based in Los Angeles called Traco Engines, Inc.) put them in there," replied Penske. "We've seen them on some of the other cars in the garage area and no one has said a word about not using them."

"Not until we win with them," Bobby replied.

"Well, we'll just pay the fine and not make any excuses. Just don't say anything until I talk to NASCAR," Penske said.

"OK, Captain," Bobby said sternly. "I won't say a word until you tell me to."

Later in the day, Penske placed a call to Bobby to state he had talked with NASCAR. The fine would stand and he had accepted its ruling.

When contacted by reporters, Penske said simply, "We had a modification to our lifter which did not meet NASCAR specs. They found it and they fined us."

Bobby was contacted late in the afternoon, Alabama time. His words echoed much of what Penske had said. But there was clearly no intention to cheat.

"Roger shows up with the car and I show up with a helmet," Bobby said. "I can't tell you anything about it because I was on my way home when it was inspected. It appears we were guilty and we got caught. We have to suffer the consequences."

Some of racing's insiders speculated the only way to make the Matador competitive was to bend the rule book. Penske would park the modern-day Hudson Hornet and not return to action in 1975 if that were the case.

But Bobby had a feeling he would be back with Penske in AMC equipment. The next time, it would be stronger and more competitive than before — in its own right, without illegal engine parts.

It was time he knew what went into his race engines before he raced them. He did not like having his name associated with so-called "cheating" of any kind. He would know from then on.

CHAPTER FIFTEEN
Success With The Matador

T he growing costs of auto racing seemed to have ill effects on every level of stock car competition. Within a time span of six seasons, NASCAR had lost such prominent car owners as Holman-Moody, Ray Nichels, Cotton Owens, Mario Rossi, Ray Fox and Banjo Matthews.

Junior Johnson also had officially called it quits. But thanks to the funding from businessman Richard Howard, his doors remained open.

Another team was considered prominent. It fell under Rossi's direction. It was called DiGard Racing Co., and was owned by Bill Gardner and Mike DiProspero with Bobby's brother Donnie hired as the team's driver. The fledgling operation was based in Daytona Beach, Fla.

Some of the top independent drivers, those without factory backing who ran on a shoestring budget, were forced to pull out of racing as well.

Some of them were Neil "Soapy" Castles, John Sears, Ben Arnold, Earl Brooks, Wendell Scott and Roy Tyner.

Bobby once again was teamed with Roger Penske with American Motors Corporation the selected automaker.

Some questioned Bobby and Penske's use of the Matador, as it clearly had been an underdog — especially during the very tough times for owners whose cars had been tested over many years of use.

Being the eternal optimist, Bobby looked at the Matador as an automobile with undiscovered advantages.

Those thoughts were confirmed at Riverside International Raceway on Jan. 19. Bobby virtually dominated the 191-lap event and led all but 18 laps after starting on the pole position with a speed of 110.382 mph.

It was Bobby's 45th career NASCAR Winston Cup Grand National victory.

Richard Petty had applied most of the pressure early on but fell from contention on lap 33 when he backed into the turn-nine wall while chasing Bobby.

The victory gave Bobby the lead in the national point standings going into the Daytona 500 on Feb. 16. But only 12 NASCAR Winston Cup Grand National drivers had made the trip out west due to the lack of finances. The remainder of the field was filled by NASCAR Grand National West entries.

Once back in Daytona Beach, an upset victory ensued when David Pearson made contact with Cale Yarborough with less than three laps remaining, causing Pearson to spin.

That left the victory for Benny Parsons, who had been running strong in the top-five throughout the 200-lap event.

Bobby never led any of the 500 but was able to take a distant second-place finish once the checkered flag waved.

Even though Bobby's points lead had been enhanced by the stellar performance at Daytona, Penske elected to sit out the Richmond 400 on Feb. 23 due to the low purse.

When asked to comment, Bobby said by phone from Alabama, "I was hoping to get the chance to run all the races. I guess I'll keep busy in Sportsman racing. But at this stage of my career, I'm not doing it for the money. Grand National racing is a disease and I guess I've got it."

Bobby was forced to sit out races at Rockingham, N.C., and Bristol, Tenn., but returned on March 23 at Atlanta International Raceway.

Bobby was able to lead the first two laps after starting on the outside front row, but the Matador went behind the wall with engine problems by lap 73.

At Darlington, S.C., on April 13, Bobby found himself two laps behind in seventh with 40 laps to go when his fortunes changed dramatically.

Parsons and Pearson made contact as the two drivers battled hard for the lead going into turn two. Both cars slid and came to a halt at the top of the turn, with Pearson's Wood Brothers Mercury pinning Parson's L.G. DeWitt Chevrolet up against the retaining wall.

With the leaders having crashed in the second turn, the remainder of the field returned to the lead lap and Bobby was at the head of the pack when he crossed under the caution flag at the start-finish line.

Once the race was restarted with six laps remaining, Bobby held off challengers Darrell Waltrip and Donnie by a mere 10 feet.

"Looking back on that particular race, we were struggling. I had been in a distant top-10 car all day and just couldn't seem to get the handling in the chassis down exactly right.

"I have to say I was a bit surprised to see them crash out of the race like they did. When I saw them going into the turn, I was probably just getting ready to come off the front straightaway.

"When I saw them crashed and smoke coming from both cars the next lap around, I just threw up my right hand and said, 'Thanks, guys. Thanks a bunch. I do appreciate the win very much.'"

Penske decided to enter the Matador at Martinsville (Va.) Speedway on April 27, even though it was a short track, only 0.525-miles in length.

To everyone's surprise, the Matador finished behind Petty, Waltrip and Yarborough, respectively.

At Talladega, Ala., on May 4, tragedy struck the Petty family.

On lap 140 of the 188-lap event at the 2.66-mile facility, Petty's Dodge had burned a right-front wheel bearing and was forced to make an unscheduled pit stop to extinguish the fire.

Knowing the part was critical and would need extensive repair, Petty exited the car and was headed over the pit-road wall to take a seat on a nearby tire.

But just as his right leg crossed over the wall, he looked up and saw an explosion; one very near him.

In an attempt to douse the fire, Randy Owens, Petty's wife's brother, turned a valve on a pressurized water tank and it exploded, sending chunks of metal through the air. Owens was struck immediately by shrapnel, which also caused head lacerations for Gary Rodgers, a crew member for Parsons who was standing close by.

Medical teams administered treatment but the 20-year-old Owens died en route to the infield medical center.

"I had just gotten out of the car and stepped across the pit wall," said Petty, fighting to restrain his tears. "Randy reached over to turn the pressure on and the thing blew up. That's close to home. He was just a kid and had those two, little-bitty boys. The bad part about it is somewhere along the line it could have been prevented."

Bobby had already left the race track when the accident in Petty's pit occurred. The Matador only lasted 47 laps before the engine expired.

The next day, Bobby contacted the Petty family by phone and extended his condolences.

Throughout the month of May, Penske had other plans for Bobby, and they didn't involve racing stock cars. There was an Indy Car with Bobby's name on it at Indianapolis Motor Speedway.

In order to fill that obligation in his contract, Bobby missed Winston Cup Grand National races at Nashville, Tenn., Dover, Del., and the World 600 at Charlotte, N.C.

After many months of negotiating, Penske had been successful and got Bobby to commit to Indy Car competition for 1975. Bobby would run races at Ontario, Calif., Indianapolis, Pocono, Pa., Michigan and Ontario again at the end of the year.

Almost immediately, Bobby began to apply his knowledge of stock car chassis setup to the Indy Car and as a result, increased his speeds dramatically. But he had a new crew and crew chief for his 1975 venture and there was a great deal of resentment toward him. At Ontario in March of 1975, the car ran fast and after a qualifying race, Allison found himself starting sixth. But the car never made any lasting impression, as the engine expired after only 30 of the scheduled 200 laps.

Unlike NASCAR, green-flag conditions remained on the track unless there was an accident, which was extremely annoying to a stock car driver not used to such a procedure. Once his car rolled to a stop in the backstretch grass, Bobby got out. A young security guard quickly appeared on a motor scooter and reprimanded Bobby for leaving his car. But Bobby had quickly thought of a reason to exit and passed it on to the guard.

"I had my helmet off by this time," Bobby said. "I just leaned over to his ear and informed him there was a snake in my car and that I had to get out.

"With that, the security guard ran over to get a glimpse of the snake, and I jumped on the guy's motor scooter and returned to the garage area and left the speedway. I was flying over El Paso, Texas, in my Aerostar when the race was over. "

A couple of weeks later, Bobby went to Indy along with then-Penske driver Tom Sneva to test for the 500, which was two months away.

For the 1975 Indy 500, Bobby found himself in the 23th starting position, again in the Offy-powered McLaren. Communication was obviously strained but finally Penske allowed Bobby to get the chassis set-up adjusted to his preference

But after a couple of days off, Bobby returned to the track for scheduled carburetion tests only to find his car's chassis returned to the standard Indy setup. An argument ensued with the crew and the chassis was returned again to the way Bobby wanted it.

By lap 23, Allison found himself leading the Indy 500, as many of the frontrunners had pitted for tires and fuel. When he pitted just a few laps later, near tragedy struck. The fuel vent valve broke, sending methanol over his body when he left the pits.

"I said, 'Wow, what am I going to do? These things can often catch on fire when they stop and I'm bathing in this fuel.' It was so bad I could feel the fuel sloshing back and forth in the sleeves of my uniform," Bobby recalled. *"At that point, I began to search out every fire truck all the way around the track and determined the ones I thought would be the quickest to get to me if I did have a fire."*

On his next stop, the crew plugged the hole, but on his third stop, the plug handle broke and would not allow more fuel to be added to the car. The problems caused him to loose a lap. Upon re-entering the race, the car ran really well again. But just as he passed A.J. Foyt to return to the lead lap, Bobby's flywheel broke, which disengaged the transmission and ended his day.

Both Penske cars experienced problems. Sneva was involved in a frightening crash on lap 125 and the former high school principal was seriously injured. At that point, Bobby was not happy with his Indy Car arrangement but was committed to driving some more races.

At Pocono, Bobby blew another engine. But activities there convinced him never to return to Indy Car racing.

His car performed flawlessly in practice and lap times looked good enough for Bobby to seriously challenge for the pole position. But during his qualifying laps, the engine would not come up to full speed, thus causing a poorer qualifying effort than Bobby hoped for. He suspected his car had been tampered with. Statements made by someone not on the crew, but close to the situation, confirmed his fears.

Bobby quit the team but then was talked into staying by Penske, under the condition that Earl McMillian would immediately become his crew chief. Starting back in 12th for the 500 at Pocono, Bobby gradually moved toward the front. But another blown engine just as he got to the lead sent him to the sidelines.

The next Indy Car race was in August at Michigan International

Speedway. That day, they ran a 200 mile Indy Car race and a 200-mile USAC stock car race. Bobby would run both.

The Indy Car race was first and also the first time USAC would use the pace car during caution periods. Penske told Bobby that even though normally the stock car guys pitted under every caution that our Indy team would only pit when we had a scheduled stop. Bobby protested, but agreed to follow the team's plan.

According to the plan, Bobby would pit every 25 laps. The caution came out on lap 17. Bobby stayed on the track but teammate Tom Sneva pitted. On lap 25, Bobby pitted under the green. Sneva had taken the lead and as Bobby came out of the pits, Sneva lapped him. Bobby got right back around Sneva and as his car was really handling and running good fourteen laps later, he passed Sneva for the lead of the race. As he passed Sneva, the engine blew up. At that point, Bobby coasted to the pits.

"I coasted in and the crew wanted me to stop there on pit road," Bobby said. "But I just turned left and went straight into the garage area. I jumped out of the car and walked over to a nearby trash can. I took off my helmet and threw it in the trash. I took off my gloves and shoes and threw them in the trash can. I took off my fireproof uniform and fireproof underwear and threw them in the trash. I'm standing there in my boxer shorts when the crew got there.

"They asked, 'Why are you throwing that stuff in the trash?' I said, 'Because I will never, ever need them again. You can take that car and everything here in the trash and do anything you please with it. I'm through with Indy Cars.'"

Bobby went over to the stock car garage, strapped himself into his USAC Matador, and won the stock car half of the event.

Once he returned to the Grand National stock car trail on June 8 at Riverside, Calif., Bobby battled hard with Petty for the win during the second race of the year on the road course, but was forced to settle for second.

There were blown engines at Brooklyn, Mich., on June 15, Daytona Beach, Fla., on July 4, Pocono on Aug. 3 and Talladega, Ala., on Aug. 17, causing finishes of 22nd, 35th, 31st and 29th, respectively.

The return trip home from Alabama International Motor Speedway was one of great despair for Bobby. Just hours before, his friend and fishing companion Tiny Lund was killed on the sixth lap of the race after being struck in the driver's side door by the Chevrolet driven by Terry Link. Bobby and Lund had both run the sportsman event at Hickory Speedway the night before and the two had flown back to Birmingham together in Bobby's plane.

Bobby placed his Matador in fourth position at Brooklyn, Mich., on Aug. 24, again behind Petty, Pearson and Yarborough.

But the return trip to Darlington Raceway on Sept. 1 was as good as the first trip of the year in April. Bobby was able to master the Southern 500 to record his third victory of the season.

While others were suffering both physically and mentally during the long, hot, grueling race, Bobby came back from a two-lap deficit and found himself back in contention after attrition took several top competitors out of the race.

Bobby drove into the lead on lap 289 of 367 laps, led the final 78 laps and won by 48 seconds over Petty, who came into the race with the flu and had gotten some relief from Dave Marcis.

"We had the strongest car out there today," Petty said. "But they (Penske's Matador team) had the strongest driver. He was able to go all day. I couldn't."

Even so, with 50 laps remaining, Bobby's victory was in question.

"A part in the rear suspension broke," Bobby said after the race. "That made it kind of hectic, especially with a guy like Petty running behind you (actually, it was Marcis). We had to have luck to win today. Luck is always an important ingredient to winning."

Another engine expired at Dover, Del., on Sept. 14, causing a 28th-place finish in the 37-car field. But it was followed by a third-place finish at Martinsville, Va., on Sept. 28.

The feast-or-famine scenario continued at Charlotte, N.C., on Oct. 5. There, a 31st-place finish came after yet another blown engine on lap 123 of 334 laps at the 1.5-mile track.

There was a second-place finish at North Carolina Motor Speedway in Rockingham, N.C., on Oct. 19 after a hard fought battle with Yarborough in the Junior Johnson Chevrolet.

But at Atlanta on Nov. 9, another sour engine translated into a 26th-place finish.

With a fourth-place finish at Ontario Motor Speedway on Nov. 23 to end the season, Bobby met Penske for some closed tests at Michigan International Speedway, the track Penske owned.

Several changes were made to the car, all for experimental purposes. One key change came with the front grille of the Matador.

After a quick flip of the grille to place it inside-out on the front of the car, Bobby strapped himself back behind the wheel and took to the track.

That adjustment alone produced an increase in speed of 8/10ths of a second. To racers, that is a significant improvement.

Other tests were conducted, but the flip of the grille gave both Bobby and Penske great hope for 1976.

But in order to campaign the grille in such a way, it had to be installed as a standard part on the American Motors' passenger version of the Matador in order to be considered legal for NASCAR Winston Cup Grand National racing.

After the test, they went to Detroit where a meeting was scheduled among the president of AMC, the engineer in charge of the Matador's design, Bobby and Penske.

Once all were in the room, Penske presented his case.

"We've got some interesting news," Penske said. "After extensive tests at Ontario, we've happened upon a discovery that will really help our racing effort for next year and maybe give the Matador a great deal more exposure."

"What sort of discovery?" asked the engineer.

"By turning the front grille in the opposite direction, we were able to gain significantly in speed during our tests. The air flow seemed to enter the frontal area more smoothly, giving less aerodynamic drag which all race teams search for."

"Gentlemen, I'm the chief designer here and I quite honestly don't agree with your findings," he said as he stood. "Furthermore, I'll not have anyone tampering with my designs of the Matador. That car is my baby. I'll have no part of it."

"You're saying to me you'll not even consider making the change?" Penske asked.

"Well, yes. That's exactly what I'm saying," replied the engineer.

Penske looked over to the president of the company for some sort of support, but received none.

"Very well," Penske said. "C'mon, Bobby. We're going to find another car company."

Penske stood and was almost to the door when Bobby broke the silence.

"Wait a minute," Bobby asked. "Aren't we even going to discuss it with them, Roger? We've won with that car. It's got a lot of potential."

"We've discussed it and they said no," Penske said. "C'mon, Bobby. Let's go. We've got a lot of work to do. We've got to find someone who wants to race with us."

CHAPTER SIXTEEN
A Time
For Change

A pole position at Riverside, Calif., on Jan. 18 seemed to be an appropriate way to bid farewell to the American Motors Matador.

For years, it had been customary for many of the teams to enter equipment from the previous year, at least for the season opener. The final touches were being made to the upgraded race car sheet metal that would make its debut during Speed Weeks, scheduled for a month away.

Since the issue of the Matador's front grille had not been settled to Penske's satisfaction, Bobby was going to wheel a fleet of new Mercurys.

But the immediate goal was to win with the Matador one last time before it went into the USAC or ARCA ranks.

Many admired the team for its willingness to battle the competition with a car dubbed an underdog. But the Matador had proven to be competitive and, thus, there had been hope.

Bobby's qualifying speed on the 2.62-mile road course was 112.416 mph, good enough to take the pole position. His smile told the story back in the garage area.

Come race time, the Matador looked strong and remained in front for the first 18 laps. Initially, the 358-cubic-inch engine appeared to possess the power to leave the Winston Cup Grand National ranks a winner.

But as Bobby shifted down and entered turn five of the nine-turn course on lap 19, the oil pressure decreased sharply. Soon the inevitable occurred.

"Roger, it (the engine) just blew up," Bobby radioed to his pit. "I'm going to try to make it back, but it's a long way around."

"Once you get here Bobby, park it right behind the truck," Penske ordered. "We're going to drop another engine in. There's still some time left for a decent finish."

"OK, captain," Bobby said. "Whatever you say."

The red, white and blue machine crept to a halt, but before the wheels came to a complete stop, the crew converged upon the front end and quickly lifted the odd-shaped hood.

Bobby removed his goggles and hung them over the rearview mirror and put his solid-red helmet on the floorboard beside the fire extinguisher. He lowered the screen net and crawled out the driver's side.

"Any warning, Bobby?" asked a crew member.

"None," Bobby said. "Just a loud boom and a lot of smoke."

Sixty-three minutes had passed when Bobby crawled back into the Matador. Soon he was given the signal to fire the engine and all gauges looked strong.

He completed 149 of the 191 laps and finished 15th, but the second engine blew with only two laps remaining.

Independent driver Cecil Gordon placed his Chevrolet out front briefly, as did Chuck Wahl for a handful of laps. But the stronger factory supported cars of David Pearson, Cale Yarborough and Richard Petty returned to the point.

Pearson took the lead with 51 laps remaining and was never again challenged, holding off Yarborough for the win.

There was little fanfare when the Matador was returned to the hauler after the race, even though Bobby wanted to give the unique old racer a salute of some kind. It came to NASCAR Winston Cup Grand National racing amid the sound of laughter from those who competed against it. But it left the circuit a winner, on occasion besting everything the other Detroit automakers had to offer.

"The first Matador that Mark Donohue won with at Riverside was an AMC two-door sedan. It wasn't like the other Matador, but it was somewhat different from the standard taxi cab.

"When AMC and Penske designed the second Matador, I thought, 'Hey, this is kinda neat.' I had been a Studebaker fan from when I was a little kid. My Dad owned a Studebaker truck and his having it contributed heavily to me having one. The Matador wasn't a

Studebaker but they were a smaller company that had a pretty nice looking car. It had a fairly impressive V-8 engine and I had seen the thing go really fast on the straightaways.

"After that final race in Riverside, I walked away thinking I was going to miss being in it."

Two weeks later, Bobby arrived at Daytona International Speedway for Speed Weeks and found his name lettered on the roofline of a different brand of automobile. The Mercury nameplate had proven itself time after time out of the Stuart, Va., shops of the Wood Brothers, whose driver was David Pearson. Penske felt comfortable with the car as did the Mercury officials with him, and they welcomed him to their camp with open arms. With a talent like Bobby Allison at their disposal, Mercury executives bragged of a double chance of going to victory lane, having the second and fourth winningest drivers in NASCAR history in their equipment.

Penske's debut with the Mercury at Daytona proved disappointing. Bobby only completed 123 laps of 200 before the engine expired.

The race came down to a Pearson-Petty duel with the two crashing while racing for the lead just out of turn four.

Petty's Dodge stalled in the muddy area between the trioval and pit road, while Pearson, whose Mercury had come to a halt near the entrance to pit road, had the presence of mind to engage the clutch, thus keeping the engine alive. He passed Petty and took the checkered flag at just under 20 mph.

It was Petty in a runaway at North Carolina Motor Speedway in Rockingham, N.C., on Feb. 29. But before the 492-lap event was complete, the story of the day involved Bobby. Many members of the media, as well as those fans in attendance, were certain they had lost one of the sport's greatest ambassadors.

Immediately after a restart on lap 363, Bobby's Mercury was in the high groove next to the outside retaining wall. That would figure significantly in the moments ahead.

Bobby shifted into fourth as he entered turn two, building his speed for the long backstretch. But he didn't see Cale Yarborough's red and yellow Chevrolet to his right rear.

Suddenly, there was impact and Bobby found himself climbing the outside retaining wall.

Out of habit, Allison revved his engine, but the car had rolled upside down in the air and set the stage for a long and unpredictable trip.

Bobby tightened his grip on the steering wheel and tried to brace for the worst. The car hit the pavement hard with its roof and began a series of rolls and end-over-end turns, hitting many other cars in the process.

"I felt I had a very good shot at winning. I was really surprised when a car got into me and sent me into the wall and over and over and over. I remember how weird it looked through the windshield upside down and seeing people running in the grandstands."

Once the car came to rest just shy of turn three, Bobby was conscious but in severe pain, as he had suffered many deep bruises and some cuts, as well as a serious eye injury.

A cooler of Coca-Cola positioned behind the driver's seat sent the carbonated soft drink over most of Bobby's uniform through a clear plastic tube used for retrieving a drink during the race.

The liquid pouring over him worried Bobby. The pain caused him to go blind, and he immediately began to check for a gash as he thought the Coke was blood pouring from a wound. The soft drink was sticky and a bit warm to the touch.

A quick flip of the seat belt lever dropped Bobby to the roof which was quite hot from the friction it had encountered.

Bobby felt around and made his way out the driver's side opening. Upon reaching fresh air, Bobby announced to those he could not see, "I'm hurt and I'm blind. I need help."

Rescue workers were on the scene and quickly administered to Bobby's needs. He was soon driven to Moore Memorial Hospital in Pinehurst, N.C., 26 miles away, where the diagnosis was severe bruising of the chest from the seat belts and an eyeball badly cut.

By Thursday, March 3, Bobby was released from the hospital and sent back to Hueytown to begin his recovery. His eyesight returned after strong medication was administered.

Many felt he would miss the March 7 race at Richmond, Va. Surprisingly, however, Bobby showed his toughness and determination by attending the event.

Neil Bonnett, considered Bobby's protege, captured the pole position by wheeling Bobby's Mercury to a speed of 92.715 mph.

Once the race began, it proved to be a good day. Bobby got back into his Mercury and finished third, one lap down to race winner Dave Marcis and second-place Richard Petty. Many walked away calling his finish nothing short of a miracle.

Bobby finished fifth at Bristol, Tenn., on March 14, but except for leading the race from laps 38-42, he left little impression. At the end, Yarborough rolled into victory lane after dominating the 400-lap event. Bobby found himself struggling — he was five laps off the pace. The box-shaped Mercury simply didn't perform well on Bristol's .533-mile, high-banked surface. The crew needed more of an education on a car that was still new to it.

The problems continued in Atlanta on March 21. Another Penske engine expired after 188 of 328 laps. Bobby only led one lap — No. 23 — during the lackluster afternoon.

Pearson took the Wood Brothers Mercury to its third 500-mile victory in four starts.

Yarborough easily won at North Wilkesboro, N.C., on April 4. It was the usual domination of a Junior Johnson car at the Wilkes County short track. Bobby recorded a third-place finish, three laps off Yarborough's pace.

On April 11, the Rebel 500 at Darlington, S.C., was another Pearson benefit, the fifth win in as many superspeedway starts. But a series of wrecks eliminated several of the strongest cars — including Bobby.

On lap 80 of the scheduled 367 laps, Darrell Waltrip tagged the car driven by James Hylton in turn four. Bobby had elected to travel in the high groove the lap before and found himself pinned between the two spinning automobiles.

When he came to a stop on the apron of the race track, Bobby immediately noticed the heavy damage his car had suffered. The Penske crew already was headed for the garage area with tool boxes to rebuild as much of the wreckage as possible. All chances for winning the race were gone but a finish could help gain valuable Winston Cup Grand National points.

Bobby sat quietly on a nearby work bench in the garage area, fielding questions from reporters as they came by. Most of those questions consisted of his prediction as to when the Penske organization would produce a victory. The financial backing was there from Cam2 Motor Oil and any equipment from Penske, whether stock cars or Indy Cars, was obviously considered the best money could buy. There was no question Bobby knew how to win races. But something was missing, and all he could do was search for a diplomatic way to say he didn't know why the team wasn't winning.

Each crew member busied himself, either over or under the race car. Crew chief Travis Carter barked out an occasional direction while turning wrenches and ripping away sheet metal himself.

Many laps passed, but Bobby once again slid behind the wheel and completed a total of 328 laps. The crash shoved him to 18th position at the finish.

There was a sixth at Martinsville, Va., on April 25, a third at Talladega, Ala., on May 2 and a fifth at Nashville, Tenn., on May 8. They were respectable top-10 finishes, but they were not victories. Bobby saw the team struggling with the Mercury, which caused him great concern. The Matador had just begun to reach its highest plateau when Penske parked it because of something so minor as a disagreement over the configuration of the front grille.

Bobby found himself wishing the awkward-looking automobiles were still in Penske's shops. The team needed a win badly and at that point of the previous season, the Matador had been to victory lane. The Mercury, at least the one under Penske's roof, had not.

Waltrip played a wait-and-see game in the DiGard Chevrolet at Martinsville, Va., on April 25. He led the final 48 laps unchallenged to score the victory.

Bobby found himself 11 laps down to Waltrip in the end, but managed to score a sixth-place finish, nonetheless.

At Talladega, Ala., on May 2, there was little to smile about. Bobby managed to lead lap 53 and went on to score a third-place finish, one lap behind race winner Buddy Baker, who set a blistering average speed of 169.887 mph. The previous former record for a stock car race was held by A.J. Foyt for his 161.550 mph winning speed in the 1972 Daytona 500.

Yarborough continued his short track streak at Nashville on May 8, while Benny Parsons returned to victory lane at Dover, Del., on May 16.

On lap 252 at Dover, rookie Ricky Rudd lost control of his Chevrolet after he was hit from behind by Baker. Bobby jammed on the brakes to avoid Rudd but was hit hard by Parsons' Chevrolet in the rear, causing severe damage to both cars.

The impact caused extensive damage to the rear inner sheet metal which allowed exhaust fumes to fill the cockpit.

Donnie had retired the Hoss Ellington-prepared Chevrolet on lap 149 due to a faulty transmission. Seeing his brother was in need of relief, Donnie took over and wheeled the badly damaged Mercury to a third-place finish. Afterward, he required oxygen.

At Charlotte, N.C., on May 30, Pearson won his fifth race of the year and scored the victory by missing a three-car accident with only three laps remaining.

The top-five finishes continued for Bobby with a fourth place at Charlotte to his credit, but that didn't seem to matter. Fourth might as well be last, because a win had still not come. Penske's Mercurys were strong enough to contend but not strong enough for victory.

At Riverside, Calif., on June 13, that missing combination seemed to surface, even if just momentarily. At the road course, every competitor knew of Pearson's strength and quietly conceded the race to him.

Bobby was the only driver to come close to taking the victory away, especially when Pearson slowed to avoid the spinning Ford driven by Baker. Pearson knew Allison was closing fast and nearly lost the race when Cecil Gordon squeezed him momentarily. The lead dropped from six seconds to 1.6 in the closing lap.

After the race, Bobby said, "Pearson was just phenomenal. He could beat us all pretty bad. The only way anybody else could have won was if he fell out."

It was Bobby's closest shot at victory all year, which magnified the disappointment even more.

Bobby was third at Michigan, the Penske-owned race track, and logged a third-place finish at Daytona on July 4. Six days later, Bobby's racing strength was tested again.

While driving an American Motors Hornet in a Sportsman event at the third-mile speedway at Elko, Minn., in a "special appearance" race, Bobby struck a concrete abutment with great impact. He saw the car ahead of him blow its engine and as he attempted to avoid the other car, ran through a sheet of oil and found himself in trouble.

Bobby quickly approached the wall, which he then struck violently. He was knocked unconscious and severely injured.

Soon, rescue workers arrived on the scene and found Bobby unconscious and bleeding. Seeing the gravity of the situation, they worked feverishly to free him from the wreckage.

He regained consciousness en route to the hospital while in the ambulance, only to discover his uniform covered with blood. He also hurt badly all over, especially his feet.

He placed his hands on his face to discover a deep cut and at that point, he began to realize the severity of his injuries.

The extent of those injuries was three broken bones in his left foot, two broken bones in his right foot, three broken ribs, a broken nose, two facial fractures and a blow-out fracture to the right eye socket, causing double vision. Forty stitches were required to close the laceration in his face.

Bobby remained in the hospital for four days before making the painful trip home to Alabama. Two of Bobby's friends, Tom Gloor and

T.D. Howton, helped with transportation arrangements. They had flown to Minnesota on Howton's plane, allowing Gloor to fly Bobby's Aerostar back to Alabama with Bobby, Judy and the kids aboard. On Friday, they went to Nashville for the 420-lap Winston Cup Grand National race scheduled for July 17.

Neil Bonnett was tapped to drive in relief during the 420-lap race on the .596-mile short track in Nashville.

On Friday, July 15, Bonnett qualified Bobby's Mercury at 89.908 mph to capture the pole position.

In pain, Bobby was helped into the race car some 15 minutes before race time to ensure the utmost care would be taken with him. Of the injuries suffered, his ribs were the main concern, as a punctured lung could occur if not handled properly.

On the pace lap, Bobby held the point mid-way down the backstretch and dropped to the apron. Standing ready in his pit was Bonnett, who was poised to take the wheel once Bobby could be extracted from the car through the use of special cloth handles sewn to his uniform.

The exchange took less than one lap and Bonnett managed to bring the entry home seventh behind eventual winner Parsons.

Bobby entered the 500-mile event at Pocono, Pa., on Aug. 1, but had Bonnett in his pit in case there was a need for relief.

But the unexpected happened again — there was a botched pit stop.

Before the race, the crew chief said, "We'll only do two-tire pit stops. We'll not do any four-tire stops."

On lap 44, Bobby was notified by radio that his top on the next lap would consist of a four-tire change. But Bobby's radio was not working and he did not hear the transmission.

When Bobby rolled to a halt, he concentrated his eyes on the right front of the car where an adjustment was being made by a crew member. He did not notice the other crew members or what they were doing.

Unaware the left-side lug nuts had been removed, Bobby roared back onto the speedway when the jack dropped, as it was a customary signal for the driver to take off. He thought the stop to change two tires was all they were going to do on that stop. Several crew members waved their arms in an attempt to try to stop him, but he didn't see them. By the time he reached the tunnel turn, the wheels had flown off, dropping the left side of the car hard against the pavement.

Twenty-two laps passed before repairs on the exhaust pipes,

which were crushed when the car fell to the pavement, were completed. One hundred laps later, Bobby drove the car into the pits and once again was relieved by Bonnett, who finished the race 24th.

Petty staged a come-from-behind win when Pearson's Mercury bobbled due to a flat right-front tire in the tunnel turn with two laps remaining.

At Talladega, Ala., on Aug. 8, Bobby's engine expired on lap 152 and sent him to a 23rd-place finish. It was another dismal run after showing promise early, but the engines simply weren't holding up under the strain of the racing speeds.

Dave Marcis went on to win in the Nord Krauskopf Dodge.

The Wood Brothers had the only other prominent Mercury in the field. Having campaigned Fords and Mercurys since the team's formation, it was no surprise the cars were performing so much better than those from Penske's shops.

There was a fourth behind Pearson on the return trip to Michigan on Aug. 22, a sixth to Yarborough at Bristol, Tenn., on Aug. 29 and a ninth to Pearson at Darlington, S.C., in the prestigious Southern 500 on Sept. 6. All told, Pearson's Mercury had rolled into victory lane nine times with eight races remaining in the season.

Away from the NASCAR Winston Cup Grand National trail, Bobby continued to operate the Birmingham International Speedway, making him a driver and race promoter during the summer of 1976. He purchased a contract on the track and anticipated a successful financial venture.

But rainout after rainout posed great problems for the competitors who depended on the revenue generated by racing at Birmingham.

"I discovered promoting was as challenging as driving. It was a constant battle, as tough as trying to go out to get sponsors.

"In the two years we owned the track there, we had 44 race dates and 23 rainouts. And we probably had 10 more nights we should have called a ranout.

"On a bad night, a ranout or something, a competitor is out his expense money to get to the event. The promoter is out the initial expenses, often times needs to pay tow money to his competitors and has spent everything he would have spent if the event went off with a full house. The weather was a big factor. Things got very rough at times."

Many felt the reason for the bad luck came as a result of "Josie," a woman who thought she could practice voodoo against those who crossed her, or at least, those whom she thought crossed her.

"She came to the races all the time and she still goes to all the races there at Birmingham. Way back then, she was married to a tall, well built man and she pushed and pulled him around like a little puppy.

"But she was an incredible race fan. She knew what was going on and knew all the people. If she liked what was going on she would tell you and if she didn't like what was going on, she would tell you. In fact, if she really didn't like it, she might curse you out right in front of a bunch of people.

"As I remember, the deal she would do was what you would call voodoo, crossing her arms and hands over one another. I was a little unhappy about that even though I liked her and got such a kick out of her being such a race fan. I really did not like or appreciate the fact that she thought she could call down bad luck on you."

Understanding the racer's plight by being a racer himself, Bobby attempted to pay higher purses to the competitors and provide them with rules that would allow them to spend the minimum amount for race equipment.

Next to engines, tires were costly to the racers every week. Bobby worked to combat the problem and promote fairness.

"I met with Bob Newton at Hoosier Tire Co. and he said he would build me a track tire which he would put BIR in big letters and they would retail for about $60 a piece. So I went to Leo Mehl at Goodyear for the same deal and he said they couldn't help. I really understand that now, but back then I thought they ought to be able to do it. There was a key to that situation working. My brother Donnie won eight or nine feature races on a set of tires he used when he won his first feature race. That really impressed me.

"There was another rule that no one ever challenged me on. It was if a driver won a feature event, another driver could buy his tires simply by giving the winning driver a brand new set. If they thought all four tires were special, they could have all four. If they just wanted the right front or left rear, they could exchange tire for tire. I felt that was a very fair way to keep the competition even."

To Bobby's displeasure, there were some who felt the race promoter should not race against them, even though he won only one event.

"Donnie won those eight or nine races and I won the other one. It really wasn't good for the track owner to even be racing but that was my number one profession at the time — racing. I had resistance from *really good friends and a few of them boycotted the races. And that hurt me from the standpoint that these are my friends and now they are fighting me."*

In the end, the venture proved to be non-profitable, to say the least.

"I didn't make money and I didn't break even. I spent tons of money and recouped very little of it and sold the contract for less than I paid for it."

In his most aggressive charge of the season, Bobby posted a strong bid for the victory at Richmond on Sept. 12. Yarborough led the final 89 laps on the .542-mile oval, but Bobby remained right on his bumper and dogged him for the final portion of the race. There were several attempts made to get around Yarborough, but none were successful.

One of the race's highlights came from Richard Childress, a young upstart from Winston-Salem, N.C., who qualified his Chevrolet in fifth. He was forced out of the race on lap 271 with engine problems.

The hot and cold scenario continued up until the last race of the season at Ontario. In the final seven Winston Cup Grand National races of the year, there were three top-five finishes with three blown engines and a crash. Bobby's average finish was 18th.

Bobby's season record read 30 starts, 15 top-fives and 19 top-10s with total winnings of $230,169.72. Many teams would cherish such a record. But Bobby felt bittersweet about the season.

When time came to sign contracts for the 1977 season, Penske presented Bobby with a unique package. Under the guidelines of his new arrangement, he would drive 10 NASCAR Winston Cup Grand National races, 10 USAC events, gain a $125,000 salary and $25,000 more to start the Indianapolis 500 with 50 percent of the winnings incurred during the race.

It was a very lucrative offer for those times. But the contract would not allow Bobby to compete in any races other than specified in the contract. That would cut 70 short-track races from Bobby's annual schedule of events.

The accident at Elko National Speedway fueled Penske's argument that he did not want his drivers to compete in any other form of racing other than NASCAR Winston Cup Grand National or Indy Car competition. It was a hard and fast rule that Penske had somewhat waved as a stipulation for Bobby to join his organization. But for 1977, the rule would once again be enforced.

After a few days of serious consideration, Bobby met with Penske to discuss his decision.

"Roger, I'll not be back with you next season. As of right now, I'm officially resigning as your driver."

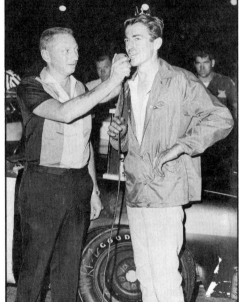

Bobby won many races in the Modified-specials before joining the NASCAR Grand National ranks fulltime. Those victories translated into four Modified championships.

BOBBY ALLISON collection

Bobby was victorious at Fonda, N.Y., on July 14, 1966, only two days after his Chevelle was badly damaged in a crash at Oxford, Maine. Note the primered front fenders and hood.

BOBBY ALLISON collection

Bobby takes a cup of water after finishing second in his first attempt behind the wheel of Cotton Owens' Dodge at Richmond (Va.) Fairgrounds Raceway on April 30, 1967.

BOBBY ALLISON collection

In the early stages of the 1968 NASCAR Grand National season, Bobby drove Fords for car owner Bondy Long of Camden, S.C. Here, he is shown making a pit stop at Riverside (Calif.) International Raceway. BOBBY ALLISON collection

During a black-tie function in the early 1970s, Bobby is shown with one of his closest friends, a country music singer, the late Marty Robbins.

BOBBY ALLISON collection

Bobby also wheeled the American Motors Matador for Roger Penske on the NASCAR Grand National circuit during the 1974 and '75 seasons.

As part of his arrangement with Roger Penske, Bobby wheeled Indy Cars in 1973 and '75, respectively. He is shown prior to the 1975 Indianapolis 500.

One of Bobby's worst racing accidents occurred on July 10, 1976, during a "special appearance" race in Elko, Minn. His AMC Hornet sustained heavy damage, while Bobby suffered severe injuries.

*Even though suffering from severe stomach problems, Bobby managed to log his
first of three Daytona 500 victories in 1978. To his left is his wife, Judy Allison.*

BOBBY ALLISON collection

*At the conclusion of the 1979 Daytona 500, Bobby (wearing white helmet) found
himself in close quarters with Cale Yarborough (right) and brother Donnie Allison (left).*

BOBBY ALLISON collection

In 1981, Bobby (No. 28) battled fiercely with Darrell Waltrip (No. 11) throughout the season for the coveted NASCAR Winston Cup championship. In the end, Waltrip took the title by only 53 points. GPC ARCHIVES Photo

The following year, Bobby's Buicks sported a new look. It was also the year he captured his second career Daytona 500 victory.

GPC ARCHIVES Photo

En route to the 1983 Winston Cup championship, Bobby mastered the turns at Riverside International Raceway and overcame a series of mechanical problems. GPC ARCHIVES Photo

After decades of Winston Cup competition, the championship was finally his. Here, he is shown with the champion's trophy of 1983. GPC ARCHIVES Photo

Bobby douses commentator Jack Arute in victory lane after his victory at Talladega, Ala., on May 4, 1986.

GPC ARCHIVES Photo

In one of the sport's most memorable finishes, Bobby (No. 12) bested his son Davey (No. 28) in the 1988 Daytona 500. It was Bobby's final victory.

GPC ARCHIVES Photo

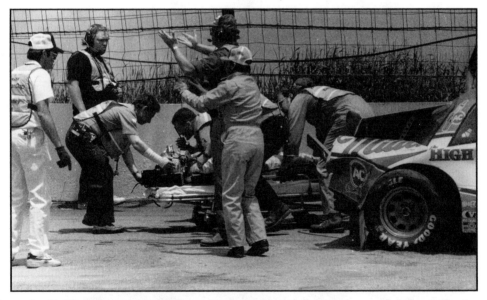

As Bobby was removed from the wreckage after the near-fatal crash at Pocono, every breath threatened to be his last. GPC ARCHIVES Photo

Today, Bobby enjoys his role as a NASCAR Winston Cup team owner.

CHAPTER SEVENTEEN
A Return To
The Underdog

With the turn of events transpiring, Bobby secluded himself in his office and made phone calls to a few of his closest advisors. Each heard news that a major change was in the works.

"I want you all to know something before the word gets out. I've officially quit Penske," Bobby told them in a solemn tone.

"As you know, we didn't win any races this past year and that really bothered me. I feel like I could do a better job in my own equipment and get back to doing what I enjoy most — winning races.

"I'm sticking my neck out again, but I think we can run the Grand National races as we see fit. I'm going to run some Sportsman races to supplement the program.

"Thirdly, I'm going to close the race-car building shop and concentrate on building my own cars. I've looked at the books from the past few months and the numbers don't look that impressive. I want to quit working on everyone else's cars and do what I like most — racing for myself."

"Finally, I'm going to let the fans decide what kind of car we run this next season."

Bobby was met with nothing but optimism at his suggestions. Everyone was willing to back his decision whole heartedly.

Just days after the completion of the last race of 1976 at Ontario Motor Speedway, sportscasters delivered the shocking news to stock car fans across the country.

Their reports topped the sports stories of the day with

announcements that Bobby had resigned from Penske's organization due to non-competitive race cars and also announced the plan to field his own cars once again from his shop in Hueytown. Many editorialized and questioned Bobby's judgment in leaving a prominent racing organization such as Penske's to race his own cars, which he did not presently have.

When questioned by the media about the sudden decision, Bobby said, "It's the first time in 10 or 11 years I haven't won a race. I've always had at least one win every year since 1965, but this year, that was not the case. I've made a lot of mistakes before, but I've always put competitiveness first.

"I'm going to let the fans decide the brand of car we run in 1977."

Penske, just days away from a scheduled test session when he learned of Bobby's decision to leave, voided his driver's existing contract.

"I don't want a driver racing for me who doesn't want to," Penske said. "So I let him go. Now we have to find another driver."

There was one lone, race-ready Chevrolet sitting in Bobby's shop. Neil Bonnett had driven the car in select superspeedway events during the '76 season with little success.

Before week's end, mail from across the country began to flood the post office in Hueytown. Each day, stacks would be read and sorted through, each categorized into car make. The results were a bit surprising.

Aggie, Bobby's sister and wife of Donnie Johnson, longtime business manager for Bobby Allison Racing, sat behind one of the large brown desks in his office at the shop. The business area was of humble surroundings, made up of one large room constructed of concrete blocks. The walls were painted white with a painted concrete floor. There were book shelves stacked with racing periodicals, model cars and planes, with a few photos gracing the walls.

Johnson had busied herself answering the phone, signing for parcel packages and checking over the results of the survey.

Bobby entered the office to make one of many phone calls but instead stopped long enough to be given the news.

"You may not believe it, but it looks like they want a return to the Matador by a pretty big margin," Aggie announced. "There's a few for Chevrolet, a few for Ford, but there's no doubt; the Matador is the winner."

"No kidding," Bobby responded.

"It's true. I'd say the entire 100 percent are glad you quit Penske and 80 percent want the Matador back."

Bobby found a nearby office chair and skimmed a few responses off the top of the stack. He reached in his shirt pocket for his silver-stemmed reading glasses.

He silently read each response in his hand, each of which proved to be a good representation of the pile in the center of the desk.

Bobby placed a call to the public relations department of American Motors Corporation.

"Hello. I've got a stack of mail here that says I should run the Matador again," Bobby said.

"Really?" came the answer.

"Yep. I've got the results of the survey involving the fans right here in a big pile on my desk. What do you think we might be able to work out?" Bobby asked.

"Bobby, let me call you back. I'll need to talk to a few people around here," was his answer.

"Super. I'll be around."

Several hours passed. Bobby finished the evening meal and stood up to put on his coat and return to the shop. But before he could get out the door, the phone rang.

"I've got somewhat of a green light from AMC," said the caller. "They said they'll work with you. What do you want to do?"

"Well to start off, I think it would be smart if we go to Riverside to start the year because we're always strong there," Bobby said. "Then I'd like to run the major races to see if we can do any good there."

"OK, here's what we'll do. We'll pay you to build the car for Riverside and we'll give you what you need to back you up for that. Then we'll take a look at the situation and see where we stand. That's the best I can do at this point."

"OK," Bobby said. "I'm willing to gamble on that."

The next day, the plan came together even more. An executive for First National City Travelers Checks called Bobby and asked if he had a ride for the 1977 season. Bobby informed him of his plans to once again campaign the Matador and that a deal was set to run selected events and they became the major sponsor of the team.

Within days, parts to construct the first Matador arrived from Detroit.

Bobby posted a decent qualifying effort on Jan. 14 at Riverside

International Raceway, but to his great disappointment, race day had an entirely different story line.

After only three laps in the Winston Western 500, Bobby's engine erupted, leaving him with a last-place finish in the field of 35 cars.

Bobby was already feeling uncomfortable about the chances of success for the season. There was something not right among those who turned wrenches on his engines. The enthusiasm seen in the past was not immediately evident and that type of attitude among any race team members usually proved detrimental.

Another engine expired during the Feb. 20 Daytona 500. Bobby completed only 167 laps of the 200-lap event and was credited with 15th in the finishing order.

There was a bit of optimism felt at Richmond, Va., on Feb. 27. Bobby put the Matador into the lead from laps 69-97 of the rain-shortened Richmond 400. He was running fifth when rain set in for the day.

Bobby had two more engines expire at Rockingham, N.C., on March 13 and Atlanta on March 20. Upon returning to the shop on March 21, a meeting took place between Bobby and his engine department. The job wasn't getting done and some adjustments had to be made.

The meeting was lengthy, but before everyone left the shop for the day, Bobby was made wiser of the team's true feelings about the Matador.

The majority of the crew had little faith in the independently manufactured machine from Detroit. They simply did not feel it was mechanically sound, especially in the engine department, to compete with the more established Fords and Chevrolets. The races at Riverside, Rockingham and Atlanta were evidence of what members of the crew secretly felt.

On March 27 at North Wilkesboro, N.C., Bobby posted a fifth-place finish, another typical short-track performance.

But with Darlington's Rebel 500 on April 3, a pattern was beginning to develop. Of seven NASCAR Winston Cup Grand National races completed to that time, Bobby failed to finish all four superspeedway events, those on tracks one mile and over in distance.

Due to a faulty battery, Bobby was forced to coast around the 1.366-mile Darlington facility at an unmercifully slow pace to get back to the garage area. Once there, the electrical system in the car had shorted and the day was finished — at least for Bobby's crew.

Bobby relieved Donnie in Hoss Ellington's Chevrolet Monte Carlo but found himself caught up in an accident with eight laps remaining.

Dick Brooks fought with the Junie Donlavey Ford in turn three and eventually pinched J.D. McDuffie into the wall, scattering debris behind both cars.

Bobby gained the lead with seven laps remaining but cut both right-side tires on Donnie's Chevrolet while passing by the crash site. Waltrip, riding in second, decided to go for broke and pushed the throttle, knowing the race could not be resumed and would finish under caution.

Bobby almost had the race won, but just before he crossed the line Waltrip slipped underneath.

"I thought I had it won when I passed Pearson," Bobby said once he vacated Donnie's car in the garage area. "But I should have known better. Anybody who has been in racing as long as I have knows that you never have a race won until you get that checkered flag."

With temperatures in the high 70s and cockpit temperatures reaching 140 degrees at Dover, Del., on April 17, Bobby called upon Ed Negre for relief driving services due to a stomach virus. Negre brought the Matador home sixth after the engine in his Dodge expired on lap 198 of the 500-lap race.

The Virginia 500 on April 24 at Martinsville, Va., saw Bobby struggle to a 19th-place finish, but the next big test came at Talladega, Ala., on May 1. Another dismal finish sent the crew home to Hueytown in 40th position out of 41 starters. Another engine had fallen by the wayside.

There was a seventh at Nashville on May 7 and an eighth at Dover, Del., on May 15. It marked the first superspeedway finish of the season.

On May 29, only 63 laps of 400 were completed at Charlotte, N.C., during the World 600. Once again, engine failure sidelined Allison for the day. With the Matador silent in the garage, Bobby did assist Benny Parsons in the L.G. DeWitt Chevrolet by driving in relief for the Ellerbe, N.C., resident.

The second road course race at Riverside International Raceway was an improvement over the season opener there, but not by very much. The best Allison could salvage was a 17th-place finish, seven laps down to race winner Petty.

Once at Michigan on June 19, there was reason to smile, at least slightly. Bobby finished 10th, four laps down to Cale Yarborough. To date, it was the best finish of the season on a superspeedway.

For the first time since 1949, three women entered NASCAR Winston Cup Grand National competition with the Firecracker 400 on July 4. None, however, finished the race.

Janet Guthrie was first out of the race on lap 11 with a blown engine in the Lynda Ferreri Chevrolet.

Belgian Christine Beckers lost the brakes on the Junie Donlavey Ford.

Italian Lella Lombardi parked the Charles Dean Chevrolet with gearing failure.

Bobby's Matador didn't perform much better than the machines driven by his female counterparts. As the checkered flag waved over Petty's Dodge, Bobby found himself eight laps down in 17th.

There were plenty of headaches where race scoring was concerned at Nashville on July 16. The confusion was due to a unique pit road arrangement. Cars would enter the pits close to the first turn and exit close to the fourth turn — just the opposite of the other pit road procedures in NASCAR.

Waltrip won the 420-lap event but many of the 17,500 spectators felt the Franklin, Tenn., driver was just a mere car length ahead. But instead, he was listed two laps ahead.

Initially, Bobby was credited with third place but a recheck of NASCAR's scoring cards proved a mistake had been made.

On Tuesday, July 19, Allison was elevated to second in the official rundown issued from NASCAR.

The brightest hope of the season came at Pocono International Raceway on July 31. For the first time, it looked as though the Matador could be made competitive.

After a hard fought battle, Bobby wheeled the Matador into fourth and finished in the same lap with race winner Parsons, second-place Petty and third-place Waltrip.

Bobby found himself a half-lap back at the finish. But it was the closest he had come to victory on a superspeedway.

Once the Winston Cup Grand National teams returned to Talladega, none of them could know the week would occur as it did.

Bobby gained some satisfaction in watching brother Donnie go to victory lane, even though Bobby could muster only a seventh-place finish for himself. Donnie was forced to call a relief driver due to a sour stomach and heat exhaustion.

During a caution period, Donnie quickly gulped a warm soft drink, which proved to be a mistake. He later radioed to his crew he was beginning to feel sick.

Moments later, a call went out over the public address system for Waltrip to go to Donnie's pit.

During the next-to-last caution period of the day, Waltrip assisted Donnie out of the Ellington Chevrolet and quickly strapped himself into the car. A blown engine had sent Waltrip's DiGard Chevrolet to the garage on lap 106 and he had no reason to stay. He was making preparations to leave the speedway when he heard the call.

Several cars were found to have large fuel tanks during inspection on pole day and the car owners of each were fined $200 by NASCAR. They were Hoss Ellington, Junior Johnson, DiGard Racing Co., Bud Moore and M.C. Anderson.

On Aug. 22, the song being played by Bobby's Matador for the return trip to Michigan was a sour one. The seventh engine of the year went up in smoke and relegated the team to a 26th-place finish.

A faulty clutch sent Bobby to the sidelines at Bristol on Aug. 28 after only 15 laps. Of the 29 cars to start the event, Bobby was officially listed in 28th place.

A fierce battle developed among Donnie, Pearson and Petty in the Southern 500 on Sept. 5 at Darlington Raceway. It was one of the most prestigious races of the year, but for Bobby, it was just another race. After 21 laps, the eighth engine expired.

Pearson emerged the winner by 2.5 seconds over Donnie with Buddy Baker third, Petty fourth and Yarborough fifth.

Bobby salvaged a sixth at Richmond on Sept. 11, a ninth at Dover on Sept. 18, and a 23rd-place finish at Martinsville due to a faulty rear end gear.

But his luck changed a bit at North Wilkesboro on Oct. 2 with a fourth-place finish, three laps behind race winner Waltrip.

The National 500 at Charlotte Motor Speedway resulted in another lost engine, which gave Bobby a 26th-place finish. But that was not the only problem experienced during the 334-lap event. On lap 186, Petty slowed dramatically with a mechanical problem, which triggered a multicar accident involving Bobby, Yarborough and Pearson.

Eleven laps after the crash, Bobby parked the Matador when its engine fell silent.

Again, Bobby enjoyed a victory of sorts in watching his brother Donnie dominate the American 500 at Rockingham in the Ellington Chevrolet.

The younger Allison led 374 of the 492 laps and virtually drove away from the competition. In the end, Bobby finished sixth, four laps down to his brother.

Donnie held the lead with 12 laps remaining at Atlanta International Raceway on Nov. 6 — a race abbreviated due to rain. But on the slick surface, Waltrip passed for the lead coming off turn two and went on to victory.

Bobby finished ninth, again several laps off the pace. But still, it was an encouraging effort.

In the final event of the year at Ontario, Calif., on Nov. 20, Bobby posted a seventh-place finish and watched Yarborough win his second consecutive championship.

It had been one of the most frustrating years of Bobby's career, and the future did not look much brighter. Finally, adversity may have won out. His career looked to be just a notation in the record books.

Neither Bobby or the Matador could survive another year of NASCAR Winston Cup Grand National competition at the rate both were struggling.

CHAPTER EIGHTEEN
A Return To Bud Moore

Bobby finally found his way to the recliner in his den after a long day of working at his shop in Hueytown. The winter chill made his bones hurt at the joints.

Being able to sit down and rest felt good to him, for throughout the 1977 NASCAR Winston Cup Grand National season, there was not much rest to be had. He fought constantly with a sour American Motors Matador as well as a sour stomach. Even though he said little about his mysterious illness to anyone, the nausea had begun the second day of practice for the Daytona 500 some nine months before.

He had just returned from Disney World in Orlando, Fla., where he'd contributed to the celebration of his parents' 50th wedding anniversary. While at one of the evening affairs, however, sickness overcame him. So much so that he asked his friend, Chuck Stallings, to fly him home to Alabama. Once there, Bobby spent five days in Caraway Hospital in Birmingham. Tests were performed and a diagnosis was delivered. Fatigue was deemed to be the problem, but Bobby didn't readily accept that answer. He was positive there was something more that the doctors had not discovered.

With the close of the season near, there were many worries that had crossed his mind for weeks. The fact that his major sponsors had not called to discuss financial arrangements for the upcoming season, along with the non-competitiveness of the Matador, made him more than nervous.

Bobby closed his eyes in an attempt to ward off the tremendous nausea he was experiencing. But suddenly the telephone rang on the table beside him and he reached for it.

"Yeah, Hello," he said.

"Hey, Bobby. This is Bud Moore. Look, I know you've been doing lousy and I've been doing lousy and I think we ought to see if we can get together."

Bobby shifted in his chair and perked up just a bit to the sound of Moore's words.

"Yeah, I hear what you're saying," Bobby replied.

"Come and see me and let's talk, say first of the week."

Bobby boarded his Aerostar and headed for Spartanburg, S.C., the location of Moore's shop. Once there, the two men sat in a modest but adequate wood-paneled office and talked about the possibility of their union for 1978.

"I feel like I've got real good equipment," Moore said. "But I can't seem to get that last little bit to get us a win. I'll admit we've had some reliability problems at times, but we're working all that out."

"I feel like we can," Bobby said. "I'll try to help you on the chassis and see if we can improve the handling of the car. I feel like I can get along with your people well enough.

"But Bud, I've got to tell you, I'm sick. I don't know what's wrong, but I have spells of real nausea at times."

"Don't worry about that," Moore said. "You just drive. Whether it's five laps or 500, you just do the best you can. We'll get someone else to drive for you if you have to get out."

"OK, let's do it," Bobby replied.

"Fine," Moore said. "We're planning to go to Daytona in a couple of weeks to test. I'll give you a call."

Two weeks later, Bobby drove through the tunnel gate of the Daytona International Speedway feeling optimistic. It was one emotion that had been missing for the better part of two years, since his 1976 and '77 seasons were nothing encouraging.

After a change into his driver's uniform and a round of "good mornings" to the crew, he sat down in Moore's Ford Thunderbird, fired the engine and backed out of the garage area. Only two warm-up laps at reduced speed had been completed when the engine blew.

While coasting down the backstretch, second thoughts concerning his teaming with Moore weighed heavily on his mind. Over the past two seasons, Moore had experienced a lot of engine trouble.

Bobby brought the car to a halt, removed his helmet and climbed out the driver's side opening.

"Don't worry, Bobby," Moore said. "We'll fix it and get it going again."

"Don't hurry," Bobby said. "I'm going back to the hotel to lay down. I'm not feeling so good."

During the short drive to the motel, he questioned himself even further about his decision to drive for Moore. He felt an emptiness deep inside at the thought of another long Winston Cup Grand National season filled with heartaches and disappointment.

The next morning, he returned to the track after a restless night. The car sat idle in the garage area, readied and waiting for its driver. With a fresh engine, it was time to see what the Thunderbird could do.

Once he took to the track and brought the car up to speed, Bobby's times were respectable, but not outstanding. A series of chassis adjustments increased the speeds slightly. Handling seemed to be the car's biggest asset.

The team's first outing at Riverside, Calif., on Jan. 22 further confirmed Bobby's worst fears. After only 40 of 119 laps, the engine blew, forcing a 30th-place finish.

From behind the controls of the Aerostar, the return trip to Alabama was a very long one for Bobby.

At Daytona for the 500, nearly a month later, Bobby posted a decent qualifying effort but still was required to compete in one of the two 125-mile qualifying races traditionally held on the Thursday prior to the race on Sunday. Steady rains brought out a multitude of colored tarpaulins, as activities were halted until Friday.

After NASCAR officials spent the morning drying the track surface with service trucks, the first of the two 125-mile qualifiers rolled off the line. Bobby started the Ford seventh and eventually found himself in the lead. But on lap 24 of the 50-lap race, Buddy Baker, driving the M.C. Anderson Oldsmobile, tried to go under Bobby's Ford and slid up the race track into him. Both cars were placed on the wreckers and hauled back to the garage area.

While he rode back to the garage in the driver's seat of his mangled race car, a bad spell of the nausea returned and once back at the transporter, he slipped his jacket over his driver's uniform and with a wave of his hand, returned to the motel west of the speedway. After a hot shower, he immediately fell into bed.

Saturday, as the sun rose over the second turn, Moore's crew was in the garage area working on the damaged frame on the left side of the race car.

"I'll be in Marvin Panch's camper if anybody needs me," Bobby announced to the crew. Feeling very ill, he found a place on a sofa there and attempted to sleep throughout the day.

By late afternoon, he returned with one thought in mind: To tell the crew he was going back to Alabama and that his racing was over.

Once through the garage gate, he noticed Moore's blue and white Ford under a sheet of shiny fresh paint. The brush strokes of the navy blue lettering were not yet dry to the touch. Under its hood sat a brand-new engine. There were a few minor dents in the body from the crash, but the frame had been straightened almost to perfection.

Bobby stared at the new creation briefly and said to himself, "If those guys can work that hard to get me a good race car, I can pull my belt just one more notch and drive it in the race."

The last practice session before the next day's race began with its normal fast paced changing of chassis combinations. Crew chiefs directed their respective crew members during spring changes, turns of wedge bolts and mounting of tires on hubs. Miraculously, Moore's Ford was part of such activity.

The pageantry of the Daytona 500 began early. Even the fans with cardboard signs requesting tickets came out early and were part of the fanfare.

The weather was cool and overcast come race time, which was no surprise, since nasty conditions had prevailed throughout Speed Weeks.

Due to his accident in the 125-mile qualifier, Bobby's battle-scarred Ford sat on the grid in 33rd, well back from where it was accustomed to starting.

As the green flag waved, the field began to experience problems, starting with Bobby's brother Donnie, who left the race after nine laps with body damage to his Hoss Ellington Chevrolet. Richard Petty, Darrell Waltrip and David Pearson crashed on the 60th lap when Petty's right front tire exploded, taking out all three of the leaders. A.J. Foyt creamed Lennie Pond's Oldsmobile when he hit the brakes for the blown engine suffered by Benny Parsons. Foyt encountered a series of flips before coming to rest on the infield grass.

Ironically, the traditional showdown in the closing laps was staged between Bobby and Baker, the two who had crashed so violently two days earlier. With 11 laps remaining, Bobby caught Baker low in the trioval to take the lead. Baker slammed his fist on the steering wheel in frustration as he realized that his engine was beginning to sour. Six laps later, the engine finally erupted in a plume of smoke, leaving Bobby to hold off Cale Yarborough for the victory.

Unknown to everyone in attendance that day, however, Bobby was in the midst of one of the toughest battles of his life. The nausea had been evident throughout the race, but while waving to the crowd on the cool-down lap, the worst spell of all suddenly came over him. All indications were he would be a very sick winner in victory lane.

Allison thought to himself, "OK, B.A., you've got to put on the best act of your life when you get in there to victory lane. You can't let anyone know you feel bad."

As he rolled to a stop amid a battery of cameras and announcers poised to catch his every word, he felt weak. The screen net came down as he wiped his grimy face with a white towel and a sponsor's cap was placed on his head before he was able to step from the car. After the flashbulbs and interviews finally concluded, one could have given him an Oscar for his performance.

"I'm so tickled I can't see straight," Bobby said from victory lane. "I've been coming here since I was a little boy and after 21 years of trying, it's really a thrill to win this race."

He averaged 159.730 mph for a payday of $56,300 in front a crowd 140,000 strong.

There were other wins with Moore in 1978, four more to be exact — at Atlanta, Dover, Del., Charlotte and Ontario, Calif.

Bobby experienced a carbon copy of the same physical symptoms while en route to victory lane in Atlanta. His sickness was enhanced when his crew moved the car while in victory lane at the request of some photographers. As they did so, the front spoiler on the Thunderbird caught Allison's heels and sliced them, filling his shoes with blood. No one except Judy knew of the incident and the tremendous pain her husband was suffering.

With the successes realized by season's end, the decision to team with Moore did not prove to be so unwise after all.

The nausea persisted and with Bobby's condition becoming progressively worse, more rigorous testing was completed at the Mayo Clinic in Rochester Minn. Bobby soon found himself on the road to recovery, due in part to a strange occurrence which took place during a conference with his doctor after the testing at the clinic.

Bobby sat alone for a few moments and then a specialist stepped into the room. He moved his 5-foot 8-inch, 350-pound frame around the desk and plopped into the chair.

"Now, Mr. Allison, I've been assigned to your case and quite frankly, I've looked over your records and my opinion is that I think you should quit racing," the doctor said.

"What makes you think that?" Bobby asked.

"You've been at it so long that I think your body is just tired out and your best bet is to quit racing."

"That's not exactly my idea," Bobby replied.

"Let me tell you something," the doctor said. "I hate being a doctor and I'm tired of hearing people's problems. There's my wife and all the credit card bills and those stupid little brats that I've got to take time off for to take to Little League, of all things. If you think you've got it rough, you ought to look at me and see how the other half lives. Then you wouldn't think you've got it so bad."

"Hey, hold on a minute," Bobby said. "We're a little mixed up here, don't you think? You're the one who needs the help. I'm fine. I'll see you later!"

With that, the nausea became more tolerable and eventually dissipated. As he suspected, something else — a hiatal hernia — was the cause of his illness.

The 1979 NASCAR Winston Cup Grand National season dawned like any other with the first race of the season being held at Riverside, Calf. Waltrip dominated the race, while engine problems once again halted Bobby's efforts. That started the year on a bad note.

When the competitors reached Daytona for the Daytona 500 on Feb. 18, Bobby found himself embroiled in controversy and the name "Allison" dominated the headlines.

Nearly everyone figured Waltrip to be the favorite because of his strength in the season opener. But Baker placed Harry Ranier's Oldsmobile on the pole with a record speed of 196.049 mph. Donnie placed the Hoss Ellington Chevrolet in the No. 2 spot and raised a few eyebrows with his performance.

The race began under gray, rainy skies which halted the start for a little more than 10 minutes.

Once the engines were fired, Baker led the first 15 laps, giving way to Donnie for six laps and Yarborough for two laps. There would be many lead changes before the day was complete.

On lap 31, both Bobby and Donnie Allison and Yarborough got into an altercation in turn two and spun. When all three machines were fired and back in the running order, Donnie was on the lead lap, while Bobby and Cale were down two laps.

Meanwhile, Waltrip watched the race from the point, ahead of Petty, Benny Parsons, Geoff Bodine, Neil Bonnett, rookie sensation Dale Earnhardt and Dave Watson.

Yarborough made up his laps while Donnie proved to be the class of the field. Bobby, however, did not make up his lost laps and was not in contention for the win.

On a restart with 22 laps remaining, Donnie and Yarborough hooked up in a tight draft and sped away from the field.

Only a couple of laps remained when Bobby received a call on the radio from his pits. He looked up in his rear view mirror about the time he heard the words being spoken in his ears.

"Bobby, the leaders are coming up on you so drop low and give them plenty of racing room."

"I certainly intend to do just that," Bobby said calmly into his microphone, reasoning he was out of the hunt.

Donnie and Yarborough whizzed by and took the white flag. With that, the two came off the second turn and headed down the backstretch. Yarborough dropped to the inside and started a classic slingshot move.

Donnie, being the leader, held his line. Other drivers had tried the move earlier in the week and gotten away with it. But Yarborough turned into Donnie, as Yarborough's left-side wheels were on the grass. As a result, they bumped once . . . then twice.

With the third bump, Yarborough turned his wheels right and sent both cars into the third-turn wall. They spun wildly to a halt in the infield grass.

Bobby witnessed the incident from ahead and felt a deep sadness at the sight of his brother's car crashing headfirst into the wall. Being concerned for Donnie, Bobby took the checkered flag then drove to a stop a few yards from the demolished racers.

"You want a ride back to the garage?" yelled Bobby to Donnie, who stood near his car, clearly dejected.

But before Bobby received an answer, Yarborough's voice boomed, "Why did you try to wreck me?"

Yarborough was walking toward the two brothers and began yelling profanities at Bobby, who sat strapped in his Ford, trying his best to ignore Yarborough.

He had lowered the window net earlier to speak to Donnie when he felt a hard impact to his face. Yarborough had reached in and hit him with his helmet.

Bobby sat dazed for a moment and fought to contain his composure. As he looked down and noticed the blood that had covered his uniform, only one thought filled his mind: "If I don't get out and address this right now, I'll have to run from Cale Yarborough for the rest of my life."

At that second, he pulled the joint buckle to the seat belts and crawled out the driver's side opening.

The three drivers engaged in a shoving match with Yarborough landing a solid kick to Bobby's thigh. But as the second kick was thrown, Bobby grabbed Yarborough's heel and uniform collar, eventually forcing him to the ground.

Safety workers on the scene then helped to separate them and broke up the fight.

Each of the three drivers returned to the garage area buzzing with reporters. Petty, who had inherited the lead after the Donnie-Yarborough altercation, was in victory lane celebrating his sixth Daytona 500 triumph. The Allisons and Yarborough attempted brief summations of the physical altercation in the infield grass.

Finally, exasperated with the entire incident, Bobby said to a crew member standing close by, "Get me some guards and keep these reporters away from me. I've said all I'm going to say about it."

With that, he worked his way through the crowd to the team's transporter.

Videotapes were reviewed by NASCAR officials minutes after the race had concluded. All three drivers were fined $6,000 from NASCAR for the incident, with Donnie being placed on six months' probation because he "acted in a manner contrary to the best interest of the sport" for forcing Yarborough into the grass.

A statement was issued from the Allisons' Hueytown home through their secretary, stating, "Donnie and Bobby are shocked at the amount of their fines and equally as shocked at the unfairness of the whole thing. They have requested a full-scale hearing (with NASCAR) and legal counsel is considering further action."

The Allisons received their wish, as a hearing was conducted in a privately owned hotel at the intersection of Highways 19 and 41 in Atlanta. The race at Atlanta International Raceway was set to take place the next weekend.

When Bobby and Donnie stepped into the rented meeting room, Lance Childress, NASCAR's national field director, sat in the far corner, Bill Gazaway, NASCAR's technical director and Les Richter, president of Riverside International Raceway — acting as mediator — sat at various places.

Metal tables and chairs filled the spacious room, insuring that no one had to sit close to the other. Yarborough was not present.

Richter began the meeting by saying, "It's unfortunate that we have to meet under these circumstances, but it must be done for the good of your relationship and the good of our fine sport."

"What are you suggesting, Les, that we were out to set him up," Bobby said.

"Something like that," Richter said.

"How could we be teaming up on poor ol' Cale Yarborough," Bobby said. "I wasn't even racing for the win. I was two laps down, The films show I wasn't blocking Cale. You've already established that."

"But it was Mr. Yarborough against the two of you," Richter said.

"I was obviously faster than Cale throughout the entire race," Donnie said. "I was just racing for the win like I do every week. I can't see where I did anything wrong. I was in the lead and holding my line."

"Gentlemen, gentlemen," interrupted Richter. "The point is that one car forced another car into the grass and both of you ended up in the wall. There was some unsportsmanlike conduct on the race track and certainly off the race track."

"OK, when I got hit, maybe I shouldn't have hit back," Bobby offered. "But if it was your brother, you would have gotten involved."

"Here's the way we're going to play this," said Richter. "We're going to give you back $1,000 dollars per race for the next five races — provided that you all conduct yourselves in a professional manner. The other $1,000 will go into the point fund. Any questions?

"Thank you, gentlemen."

It would not be Bobby's last encounter with NASCAR.

As the 1980 NASCAR Winston Cup Grand National season began, one fact seemed to be coming to light from the previous season. Bobby's Moore-prepared Ford seemed to be below competitive standards. There were several impressive outings, but a win did not come until May 18 at Dover, Del. Bobby took the lead with 12 of the 500 laps remaining and rolled to victory lane.

"This is a great victory today, but it could have been better," Bobby said. "A Ford is capable of winning only at Atlanta, Charlotte, Dover and Rockingham. We still need two Chevys for the other tracks."

By the July 4 Firecracker 400, Bobby's words were even stronger from victory lane there, hinting to the media his days with Moore were numbered.

"We're still not as strong as the General Motors cars," Bobby stated during the post-race interview. "I'm not knocking Bud Moore.

Bud has done a lot for me and I've done a lot for him. But at this point, we're 180 degrees apart."

Moore campaigned Ford products since he emerged on the circuit almost from its beginning and wasn't about to spend tens of thousands of dollars to convert to something else.

No one in the press box that day had any inclination Allison had met with another car owner and had tentatively agreed to a three-year contract starting with the 1981 season — driving General Motors equipment.

CHAPTER NINETEEN
The Controversial LeMans

After a week of perfect conditions, inclement weather played havoc with the season opener at Riverside International Raceway on Jan. 15, 1981.

Sunday morning dawned with rain falling over the majority of Southern California. Rains had stopped or postponed the event two of the last three years, causing teams a week's delay. But with the new downsized cars set to go into effect at Daytona a little over a month away, construction was still ongoing and crews needed precious time to finish. A few selected teams were allowed to enter those cars in the race at Riverside to test their performance and report their findings.

With that, NASCAR officials huddled along with RIR president Les Richter and decided to run the race if at all possible.

Once the rain ceased and the track was dried, drivers reported to their cars and the field finally rolled off the line 40 minutes later than the scheduled 11 a.m. starting time.

This was Bobby's debut in the Harry Ranier Racing 1977 Chevrolet Monte Carlo. The move to General Motors cars had been prevalent in his mind for the past three years. But his first race back in a General Motors product was the final appearance for the full-sized body styles in Winston Cup Grand National racing.

Bobby and Darrell Waltrip (in Junior Johnson's Chevrolet) were sent out ahead of the field to test the 2.62-mile track surface to see if it was dry enough to race.

On that fast test lap around the speedway, Bobby detected a problem and radioed back to the crew chief.

"I've got a pretty bad vibration in the driveshaft when I get up to speed," Bobby said. "I've got to pit."

"I'm running this pit and I say you can't pit," the crew chief argued.

"I've got to pit," Bobby returned.

"There's not a thing wrong with that drive shaft. Don't pit," the crew chief said firmly.

"If I don't pit right now, this car will not make another lap," Bobby said. "I've got to pit."

A crewman crawled underneath the car, confirmed a problem with the driveshaft and made repairs.

From there, it was an afternoon of catch-up, but on lap 52 of the scheduled 119 laps, Bobby moved into the lead. He eventually held off Terry Labonte, in Billy Hagan's Chevrolet, for the win.

While Bobby sprayed champagne in victory lane, the crew chief remained at the truck and did not join the celebration.

Remarkably, Bobby drove with a very sore right hand which had been crushed in an accident at Rockingham, N.C., in October of 1980 and jammed again while working on an engine for a Sportsman car.

"Sure it hurts, but winning is a good painkiller," Bobby said with a grin during the post-race interview in the press box.

Bobby stated his top priority for the 1981 season was to win the coveted Winston Cup championship.

"I want to put all the effort I can into winning the championship," Bobby said after capturing his 62nd win. "To do that, I'm going to cut down my short-track activity. And too, I'm going to a lot of races with my son Davey."

Even though his intentions were good, too many commitments kept Bobby busier than ever.

The younger Allison was 19 at the time and was seriously looking at his own racing career. Bobby wanted to work with his son as much as possible to prepare him for the tough elite circuit.

Immediately after the completion of the 1980 NASCAR Winston Cup Grand National season, all teams began preparing for the major overhaul of their race cars, required by NASCAR. For many years, the competitors used the larger body styles, but Detroit automakers had several smaller versions on the market and tossed the gauntlet down for NASCAR to meet the challenge by utilizing these same cars.

There were several driver changes during the winter months, including Bobby, who joined Kentucky businessman and long-time friend Harry Ranier. After being quite unsatisfied with Ford products, he was now driving General Motors equipment once again.

But the downsized cars posed many problems, as they had never been tested on the high-banked ovals until Bobby and a few other drivers took them to Daytona in December. With the larger Monte Carlo now parked after the win at Riverside, Bobby placed hope in an Oldsmobile Cutlass Supreme.

"The car is not handling well at all," Bobby said to a group of reporters. "After two days of testing, all we did was get the car from horrible to bad. I had hoped to do some drafting with Darrell, but right now I don't even want the seagulls out there with me."

There were several other drivers who echoed Allison's comments.

"The new cars are giving us a lot of problems — a lot of new things to think about," Waltrip said of his Junior Johnson-owned Buick Regal. "Detroit is going broke building these little critters and I don't put much faith in them. The small cars are just as fast but have poor handling characteristics."

David Pearson took a Chevrolet owned by Joel Halpern to Daytona on Dec. 12 and posted a very shaky speed of 192 mph.

"We've had the same problems the others had," Pearson said. "The car is loose in the corner. It's a fast car, but it doesn't handle good."

On Dec. 20, Richard Petty tested a Dodge Mirada (as 15,000 fans watched after the news leaked), but had unfavorable results. He was eight miles per hour slower than any of the GM models. He later brought a Buick Regal to Daytona with much more favorable results.

Added Dale Earnhardt, "I was nervous as hell during those tests. The cars aren't stable enough to run in a pack."

Cale Yarborough, in his first year with car owner M.C. Anderson after eight successful seasons with Johnson, said, "We need a lot more spoiler to keep these cars steady. I'd hate to see what happens when a bunch of cars go out there and try to draft."

Additional test sessions were scheduled at Daytona by most of the top NASCAR teams. The only major organization that did not was Bobby and Ranier, who chose to test at Talladega instead.

There was a special reason why.

Davey had been looking for a personal car and discovered the sleek Pontiac Grand LeMans in a brochure given to him by a salesman at a dealership in Alabama.

Recognizing its potential, he showed the brochure to Bobby and suggested using it in Winston Cup Grand National competition.

After studying the rules and car eligibility, Bobby thought the car would be very close to the Pontiac Grand Prix, but perhaps had more potential.

While testing the Oldsmobile at Daytona, Bobby, Ranier and Waddell Wilson found a dealership with a LeMans in stock. After studying the car closely, a call was placed to Mike Laughlin, owner of a stock car building firm in Spartanburg, S.C. He was given an order to begin construction. But on the work order were the words "Sportsman Car" with a fictitious Midwestern United States address.

The four men, Bobby, Ranier, Wilson and Laughlin, knew that Davey had stumbled into a potential gold mine and were very careful not to let their secret out.

Feeling the car would be outlawed by NASCAR, Bobby paid for the car out of his own pocket and felt at best it would be able to compete in only one race.

The basic car was picked up from Laughlin's shop and finished at Ranier's shop in Charlotte, N.C.

En route to Daytona for Speed Weeks, Bobby and Wilson traveled to Talladega, a superspeedway very similar to Daytona, to test the LeMans. The results were much more favorable with speeds in the 197-199 mph range. Word already had leaked that Bobby was burning up the track "with something that looked funny."

"We didn't start on the car until after the (Jan. 11) race at Riverside," said Ranier of the LeMans. "After testing the Oldsmobile at Daytona in December, we knew we had to do something."

As teams began to roll into Daytona in February for Speed Weeks, Bobby possessed the only LeMans in the garage area. And from the minute the car was unloaded, controversy surfaced.

Bill Gazaway, technical director for NASCAR, cornered Allison and Wilson as they entered the garage gate.

"What's that?" asked Gazaway. "You can't run that thing here."

"It's a Pontiac LeMans and the rule book says we can run a Pontiac LeMans," Wilson said.

"Well, we don't have templates for it, so just take it through inspection." said Gazaway. "But you won't get a sticker (indicating it had passed inspection) until we make some templates for it."

"Fine," Wilson said with a smile.

Bobby was allowed to practice the car and turned faster times than anyone else.

While Bobby was blistering the Daytona International Speedway, NASCAR officials thumbed through the pages of the rule book to see if the Pontiac LeMans was listed as one of the cars eligible for competition. NASCAR had to scramble to find one, because it had nothing by which to measure the car.

Soon, two of the Pontiacs were sent over to the speedway from a local car dealership for measurement purposes, so NASCAR could make the templates overnight.

In essence, Ranier Racing had caught everyone by surprise. That sent the competitors in the garage area, reporters and fans buzzing.

In response to continuous questions, Gazaway said, "The LeMans was on the eligibility list for over a year. All the rest of them got outfoxed. And you're going to have a heck of a time getting any one of them to admit it."

In one of many impromptu gatherings with the press, Bobby defended the LeMans by saying, "The LeMans has been in the rule book all along. Everyone got the '81 rules when we got ours. I really expected to see others (LeMans) here.

"I don't know why anybody else didn't come up with it. I sure wasn't going to call anybody and tell them."

After the templates were made, NASCAR scored some points in the controversy when the Pontiac didn't fit, forcing body work to be done on the rear quarter panels and height of the rear end.

But according to information from NASCAR, the car was legal for competition. Ironically, four separate mailings of specification sheets from NASCAR in 1979 and 1980 listed the LeMans but no one noticed it, except Davey Allison.

"The car is more stable due to the sloped back window," Bobby said. "We sacrifice a little in the frontal area to the other GM cars. The Buick has a narrower nose, but we'll take the stability the LeMans gives us."

That stability helped Bobby capture the pole position for the Daytona 500 at a speed of 194.624 mph, besting Waltrip, who posted a speed of 194.506 mph in a Buick.

Bobby's thrashing of the field was no surprise and was probably put best by Buddy Baker, driver of the Hoss Ellington Oldsmobile.

"It was Bobby Allison against the entire world out there today," Baker said.

Seven cars started the annual Busch Clash, a special non-points race for pole position winners. Bobby shot to the front after two laps and was pulling away when he thought he cut a tire, forcing a pit stop. It was later determined by Goodyear, Bobby did not cut a tire, but rather, the unfamiliar cars gave a false indication. He ultimately finished sixth.

Bobby's ability to totally dominate was evident among drivers and NASCAR officials alike. There were strong hints of a rule change specifically aimed at the LeMans to slow it down in order to reduce its advantage.

Next on the Speed Weeks agenda was the 125-mile qualifying races. But Bobby voiced his dislike for them during a press conference in the infield media center during an announcement to introduce Ranier Racing's new sponsor, Tuf-Lon International of Houston, Texas, a manufacturer of engine additives.

"I've never liked the qualifying races," Bobby said. "They're risky and potentially dangerous. If I win one, it doesn't count (as a Winston Cup Grand National victory) and I resent that.

"I could take the green flag and then drive into the garage area, but I won't do that. We're kind of caught between a rock and a hard place because this year, the 125s will be a learning thing for the new cars and the drivers."

Three days after qualifications and the Busch Clash, NASCAR ordered the spoilers on all cars to be enlarged from 216 to 250 square inches.

But the 125-mile qualifying races staged on Thursday proved the spoiler change did little to remedy the problem. Bobby led all but 17 laps of the first 125-miler and took the checkered flag under caution.

During that race, however, drivers John Anderson and Connie Saylor were involved in separate frightening accidents which sent the cars dancing and twirling on their front ends and then hydroplaning on their rooftops.

Waltrip won the second race in a highly competitive affair that saw 25 lead changes in 50 laps. Ironically, there were no serious accidents in that race.

In post-race interviews, Waltrip said, "If I can hold on to No. 28 (Bobby), I'll be all right."

To that, Bobby responded, "If you take Darrell out tonight and preach to him that he hasn't got a chance and I've got him beat, it might help."

At the completion of the races, the drivers gathered in the driver's lounge and viewed video tapes of the first race; the race in which Anderson and Saylor had spectacular accidents. No one could recall a time when cars behaved in such a manner at high speeds.

On Friday before the Daytona 500, NASCAR made a second spoiler enlargement from 250 to 276 square inches in an attempt to further increase stability of the cars for the safety of the drivers.

Starting on the pole in the 500, Bobby looked strong from the drop of the green flag. At his crew chief's direction, he dropped back just a bit, so not to show the competition or NASCAR the speed the LeMans possessed.

On lap 140 of the 200-lap race, Bobby was brushed by Buddy Baker which placed tire marks on the driver's side of Bobby's car, which was running third. With that, Bobby keyed the radio button in disgust.

"Listen to me," Bobby said. "We can sit here and get wrecked or we can go and win this race. I guarantee you the car I'm in will get outlawed after this race either way, so why not go to the front and win with it while we can?"

"All right, take it to the front," the crew chief responded. Bobby placed the LeMans in the lead for a total of 117 laps. Only Neil Bonnett's Ford Thunderbird was able to stay with Bobby. Baker and Earnhardt could pass but could not hold the lead.

Even though he had the dominant car, the race came down to fuel mileage. Halfway through lap 175, Bobby's engine began to sputter as he entered the trioval. He dropped into the pits for fuel and tires after traveling the entire distance of the race track out of gas. The race was all but lost. Bobby's only hope was that Richard Petty could not complete the remaining laps with the fuel in his Buick.

But Petty did go the distance and won his seventh Daytona 500. Bobby had to settle for second.

Back in the garage area, Bobby emerged from his Pontiac and fielded questions from reporters.

"It was hard to determine what kind of (fuel) mileage we were getting. It was the only time we went all the way on fuel. We just ran out sooner than we expected," he said.

"We had a good shot at winning, but you don't have it won until the checkered flag goes down."

At Richmond, Va., on Feb. 22, Bobby didn't fare quite as well as he did in Daytona. During the first lap of the first practice session, the throttle hung wide open and sent him through the fourth-turn wall, totally destroying the Pontiac he had used at Daytona.

Even though the car was a superspeedway car, Ranier decided to stick to his plan to fight NASCAR and run the LeMans. But at the time, it was the only car of that make the team owned. There was the Oldsmobile Cutlass Supreme tested at Daytona, but if NASCAR knew the car still existed, the LeMans would have been outlawed on the spot, citing the fact that Ranier had something else to race.

As a result, Ranier worked out an arrangement with Butch Lindley to start his Chevrolet to accumulate Winston Cup Grand National points. Lindley took over the wheel on lap 153, but left the race with engine problems on lap 276 of the 400-lap race.

Waltrip emerged victorious after gaining the lead over Ricky Rudd (in the DiGard Racing Buick) with 46 laps remaining.

Bobby found himself third in the point standings behind Petty and Earnhardt going into Rockingham, N.C. Again, Waltrip emerged with his second win of the year, but amid controversy.

Many felt Waltrip carried a large gas tank, but post-race inspection proved otherwise. Dick Beaty, NASCAR's director of Winston Cup Grand National racing, checked the fuel tank of the Johnson-owned Buick. The tests showed the car held 20.6 gallons before the race and 20.1 gallons after the race.

Few were convinced the car was legal.

Bobby finished sixth in the final standings and moved into second in points, 66 behind Petty.

Once in Atlanta for the March 15 Coca Cola 500, the controversy surrounding the Pontiac reached the boiling point.

Immersed in what had been a season long disagreement with NASCAR, Bobby and the Ranier team did not even attempt to qualify their LeMans.

Rather, they spent the day testing several different rear end spoilers in an attempt to reach some sort of compromise with the sanctioning body.

The specification given the team called for a spoiler one and one-half inches in height, which was two inches shorter than what was currently legal on the other models. The larger the spoiler, the more traction was increased, thus, producing a more stable car at speed. The one and one-half inches allowed the LeMans gave the car a decisive disadvantage.

NASCAR surmised the spoiler given to the LeMans would make it equal with the other cars since the car possessed the sloped rear window.

"We came here, took one lap with that one and one-half inch spoiler and I knew there was absolutely no way I could race with it," Bobby fumed to reporters. "We've worked with them, we did everything NASCAR wanted us to do. They (NASCAR) have offered us the two-inch spoiler but there is no way we can be competitive or reasonably safe for our own sakes or for others with a spoiler less than three and one-half inches.

"I have given up a lot for racing, but I wouldn't give up my life."

The controversy swirled around the garage area all day.

Ranier threatened to boycott the race by pulling his entry, going so far as to seek legal assistance on the matter.

The night before the Coca-Cola 500, Ranier asked Bobby to fly him to Montgomery, Ala., to meet with a Federal Court Judge seeking an injunction against the start of the event. But at midnight, the decision was made not to grant the order.

The next option was to simply boycott the race, but that move carried great consequences.

To load up and leave the speedway would cause Bobby to be virtually eliminated from a Winston Cup Grand National championship bid as well as remove the team from the coveted Winners Circle program.

While propped up against his car in the garage area, Bobby talked with reporters again, saying, "I am aware of what would happen. But I didn't join the Ranier team just to run in the top-10 — and that's what NASCAR says we can do with the two and one-half inch spoiler. Anyone who joins a team and is content just to run in the top-10 cheats himself, his sponsor, his car owner, his mechanics, his wife and children.

"So to tell me to make concessions just so I can run in the top-10 is something that just comes out of nowhere."

Ranier voiced his opinion by saying, "I don't want anything more than anyone else, all I want is the same thing. I want my car to race safely. This whole thing is just a bad joke and it's on us."

Bobby had the final comment, noting with his wry humor, "I'll put on a Petty T-shirt, get a can of beer and watch the race from the top of a truck in the infield."

Bobby refused to qualify on Thursday (Mar. 12) and Friday (March 13) and finally loaded his car on the trailer, threatening to go home. Fans, however, voiced their desire to see him race by scrawling out "We Want Bobby" in graffiti on walls and buildings.

Bobby met a final time with Ranier and decided to oblige — but he wasn't happy.

The final verdict came from NASCAR: "The spoiler height would be two and one-half inches and no more."

Bobby qualified on March 14 at a speed of 161.229 mph using the spoiler mandated by NASCAR. It was good enough for only the 30th position.

"It is actually pitiful," Bobby said, "but we will do the best we can. Our group is too honest, too sincere and too dedicated to winning the Winston Cup Grand National championship not to do everything in our power to achieve that goal. Our speed is not competitive. But maybe that is where they (NASCAR) want us. We're not happy, but we'll play the game."

Bobby ultimately finished fourth in the race, but his hands were bloodied from fighting with a car that was loose in every turn on every lap.

Privately, Ranier had agreed with Bobby that after Daytona, the team would need another type of car to race but did not want anyone to know that decision had been reached. He was determined to ride out the LeMans controversy to the end.

"We're committed to the Pontiac LeMans just as others are committed to Buicks, Oldsmobiles, Pontiacs, Fords, whatever. We feel that we are right, and we will continue to press the issue to get a fair deal. We didn't make the rules, but it is unreal that we're not allowed to go by them as they were originally written."

Bobby continued with Ranier's Pontiac at Bristol, Tenn., and finished third and then took a second at North Wilkesboro, N.C., and a ninth at Darlington, S.C. The frustration of fruitless attempts to make the LeMans competitive on the superspeedways came to a halt at the 1.366-mile South Carolina oval.

The crew worked feverishly to build a different make of car — and did get one completed — but was still forced to take the LeMans to Nashville, Tenn., and Martinsville, Va., where the finishes were 13th and third, respectively.

However, between those races, there was a moment of glory. Bobby scored the team's second victory of the season and first with a downsized car — a Buick Regal — at Talladega, Ala.

There was adversity to overcome in the form of a broken windshield, a dented rear end and a cut tire. But the win came at the line over Baker and Waltrip.

There was also a second at Dover, Del., added to the list on May 17. Bobby was ranked No. 1 in points by 168 over Ricky Rudd. Rookie Jody Ridley scored the Dover win.

Next came the World 600 at Charlotte Motor Speedway on May 24. By late afternoon, the day had turned bittersweet for the entire

Allison family.

Bobby drove a flawless race in a Buick Regal with sponsorship from Hardee's fast food chain. He passed Harry Gant with 70 laps remaining. The race was marred by several accidents — one of which sent Donnie to the hospital with serious injuries on lap 146. As Donnie entered turn four, he lost control and was hit in the passenger side by Dick Brooks, who suffered a separated shoulder as a result.

Bobby's younger brother by two years was removed from his car unconscious and had suffered several fractured ribs, a bruised right lung, a broken left knee and a broken right shoulder.

After a lengthy period of time for treatment in the infield medical center, Donnie was taken to Charlotte Memorial Hospital, where he was listed in "unsatisfactory but stable condition" in the intensive care unit.

When asked about his brother's accident during the hurried post-race press conference, Bobby said, "Donnie looked like he was hurt in the car. The car was torn up and he was slumped over. I knew it took them (rescue workers) quite a while to get him out."

Throughout the remainder of the race, Bobby had kept in close touch with his crew chief concerning his brother's condition.

"Naturally, I was very concerned," Bobby continued in post-race interviews. "I've raced side by side with my brother for 23 or 24 years now. I feel we've had the best brother relationship in professional sports. I know he'd be alarmed to see me like that, and I was alarmed to see him, but I felt obligated to do my best.

"We are going to support the family. I've got that airplane, and it can make a trip to Alabama two or three times tonight to move people around, if necessary."

Soon after, Bobby left the press box and entered an awaiting police car to take him to the hospital where his brother had been admitted.

Even though alert and talking the next day, Donnie's recovery period extended several months.

After posting a third in Texas on June 7 and blowing an engine at Riverside, Calif., on June 14, Bobby returned to victory lane at Michigan International Speedway on June 21.

It had been a dismal day for the Ranier Buick, as Bobby could seemingly hang on to the lead cars but did not have the strength to pass or hold the lead for very long.

With less than four laps remaining, Kyle Petty's Buick erupted an engine in turn two and sent many contenders spinning.

Bobby threaded his way through the damaged cars and found himself in the lead behind the pace car. At that point, the crew chief gave the order for Bobby to pit for fresh tires.

After the crew chief ended his transmission on the radio, Bobby quickly responded by saying to his crew chief, "We just won the race. I can't come in. If I do, I'll lose the lead."

"Look, I'm not getting into this with you again," the crew chief said. "I'm running this pit and I said pit."

"We just won the race," Bobby shot back.

"I said pit and I mean pit right now," the crew chief returned.

"There's two laps to go," Bobby said. "It's gonna take a week to clean up this mess."

Ignoring the order, Bobby remained behind the pace car and took the checkered flag under caution.

Rumors persisted Bobby would move to another team for the 1982 season. Several names cropped up. They were: Richard Childress, J.D. Stacy and Bill Gardner. When asked indeed if he had talked with those owners, Bobby responded, "You're not even caught up with 'em all yet."

Thirteen races passed before Bobby won the season finale at Riverside. He finished second for the NASCAR Winston Cup Grand National championship to Waltrip. Bobby lost the points lead with a 10th-place finish at Martinsville on Sept. 27 while Waltrip was victorious.

Going into the final race, Ranier and the crew knew Bobby would not be back in 1982. Friction was evident throughout the weekend.

Before the race began, the crew chief installed a rev limiter on his engine — a precaution against engine failure, often employed on road courses.

But the rev limiter was set much lower in rpms (revolutions per minute) than usual, requiring Bobby to shift three to four times more per lap to compensate for the low setting.

Knowing Bobby would tamper with the device, the crew chief mounted it on the passenger side of the car where it could not be reached from the driver's seat.

Bobby had tough competition from drivers Joe Ruttman and Terry Labonte and the rev limiter proved to be a hindrance as well as a drain of needed power.

With 15 laps to go, a caution was displayed and Bobby had his last conversation with his crew chief on the radio.

"It seems like every time the wheels turn on this car the rev limiter kicks in," Bobby said. "I'm going to pit. When I get in the pits, you do something about this rev limiter. Take a pair of pliers and cut the wires to this thing because if you don't, I'm going to loosen my seat belts and rip the wires off of it myself."

Reluctantly, the crew chief reached in and clipped the wires and Bobby went on to win the race.

As a result of yet another confrontation, the crew chief again refused to go to victory lane.

When asked to comment on his loss of the championship, Bobby said, "I would like to win the championship and I'm going to try a few more years. But I've had too many good times in racing to pout over something like this."

Bobby left Riverside and Ranier Racing a winner. He had been part of many teams during his 20-year career and he was about to join another one. Some believed it was owned by a man engaged in questionable business dealings. Many doubted Bobby's judgment.

But in order to further his career, Bobby took a chance. The team he was about to join seemed to have what he needed, so, for 1982, Bobby really had no choice.

CHAPTER TWENTY
Taking A Chance For The Championship

Twice earlier in his career, Bobby had been approached with an offer to drive for a Charlotte, N.C.-based team. But better judgment told him to seek employment elsewhere. The principal owners of the organization were considered untrustworthy by the racing fraternity, which took its evidence from past business dealings.

Known as DiGard Racing Co., and owned by Bill and Jim Gardner, it was one of the most controversial teams in the history of NASCAR. When word of Bobby's negotiations to be its driver surfaced, many could not understand his reasoning. Many drivers felt working for the Gardner brothers was professional suicide.

Former DiGard driver Darrell Waltrip had been involved in a legal dispute with the Gardners for many months in 1979 and 1980. Much of his tenure with the team, which began in 1975, was shadowed by unrest. In order to join Junior Johnson's organization at the start of the 1981 season, Waltrip had to resort to buying his contract from Gardner. No money figure was ever disclosed, but hearsay placed the amount Waltrip paid at over $500,000.

After Waltrip departed, Gardner hired Ricky Rudd, a young and talented newcomer, for 1981. His employ there proved to be the break Rudd needed, as his own operation was in danger of folding due to a lack of money. Rudd admitted he, too, had second thoughts about going with Gardner, but at the time, he felt he didn't have a choice.

During the closing months of the '81 season, Rudd requested to be released from his contract. Gardner granted his wish without any legal threats, feeling he could get a more experienced driver. By doing so, the move would help keep his current sponsor, Stokley Van Camp and its Gatorade label, with him a few more years. Gardner's unwritten policy was to spend other people's money and not his own, whenever possible.

Having left Harry Ranier, Bobby was becoming anxious over a ride for the 1982 season. Many complications and delays forced rewrites of the initial contracts with Gardner. During one of the final negotiation sessions, Bobby and his advisors became quite frustrated with the shallowness of the wording contained within the 86-page document and decided to seek a Winston Cup Grand National ride elsewhere. When Gardner saw them pack their briefcases and walk to the door to leave, different, more suitable contracts were soon presented and Bobby was named the team's driver.

"I was in a situation where I had to take Bill Gardner in order to have Gary Nelson and Robert Yates. I knew I had to compromise my own feelings and principles and everything else. But here were two guys (Nelson and Yates) who were really as determined as I was to go compete week after week against the big engines, the left-side tires (which were often illegally mounted on the right side of the cars), big gas tanks, the lightweight cars and still try to win the championship. The only way Bobby Allison could win a championship was to run a legal car against cars that obviously were allowed certain privileges.

"I had car owners that I had raced for before Bill Gardner who grew tired of the lopsided scrutiny. Consequently, I felt there was not a possibility of winning the championship with those people and I moved on."

Once at Daytona for Speed Weeks '82, the Buick Regal surfaced as the prominent choice of the majority of race teams and many were in the garage area. But the one prepared by Nelson (for Bobby) surfaced as the fastest. During winter testing and practice, it proved to be the class of the field among the entrants for the 500.

Teams rolled into the garage area on Feb. 4 and unloaded their cars and equipment, but almost immediately, drivers and crew members alike were buzzing over Bobby's Buick. The race car was sleek and polished in the standard of a NASCAR Winston Cup Grand National machine. But to many, there was something strange about its overall appearance.

A couple of days passed when Joe Gazaway, a NASCAR official, stopped at the rear of the car while it sat idle in the garage area. After some silent inspection, Gazaway walked over to Nelson with an announcement.

"This rear bumper is too high," Gazaway said. "You boys are going to have to lower it."

"But, Joe, we went through inspection and no one said a word about it," Nelson responded. "We won the Busch Clash with it that way and it was fine then. Why is it not legal now?"

"I'm looking at it and I say it's too high," Gazaway responded. "You've got to lower it a couple of inches."

Nelson continued his protest but to no avail. Joe Gazaway had a reputation among crew chiefs to find the fastest car and then bug its team with a series of changes right up to race time.

Under Nelson's direction, the DiGard crew had prepared the car beautifully. Without the customary big fender wells and bulges over the tires, it was fast simply because of the aerodynamic body. Where most cars would have enough clearance to place one's fist between the tires and fender, Nelson's car would not allow the space for even a finger. The body was legal, just much more aerodynamic than all its counterparts.

Gazaway ordered the bumper to be lowered or the car would not pass inspection and the team's entry would be pulled from the 500 starting lineup.

The DiGard crew cut the bumper loose and lowered it, which was a difficult job to complete in the garage area. The bumper was not placed on the car as well as it would have been at the shop under less strenuous circumstances.

On the fourth lap of the 500, Bobby was involved in a battle with Cale Yarborough in the M.C. Anderson-owned Buick.

Bobby was low with Yarborough just above as the two veterans exited turn four. Contact was made with the front of Yarborough's car, causing the rear bumper of Bobby's car to be pulled off. The long piece of steel bounced into the paths of Joe Millikan, Lake Speed, Geoff Bodine and three other cars. All continued to race.

Immediately, charges were placed by Yarborough's crew chief, Tim Brewer, stating the bumper was reaffixed in such a way to come off intentionally to make the DiGard Buick lighter and faster.

In response to the accusations, Nelson said, "There's no way in the world I would do something like that. When you start thinking of risking a man's life to win a race, then I'll get out of racing."

Bobby recovered from the incident with Yarborough and went on to lead 147 of 200 laps to record his second career Daytona 500 victory.

He gambled in the end and elected to forego his final pit stop. As a result, the car was silent as he coasted under the checkered flag. It was out of gas, but it was 22.87 seconds ahead of Yarborough.

Yarborough was not happy about the bumper incident.

"Allison cut me off," Yarborough said. "Suddenly, his bumper came off. It didn't take much of a lick to tear it off. I wasn't born this morning. We tested here over the winter and found the car would run better with the bumper off."

Concerning Brewer's statement about the bumper being rigged to come off intentionally, Bobby said, "His statements are not the most sensible statements I ever heard. Actually, my car ran looser after it came off. People always grumble when they get beat.

"I may have moved up too quickly on Cale and cut him close. If I did, that wasn't very sporting, but losing the bumper didn't help me run any faster. In fact, I felt it was a disadvantage.

"Maybe we didn't have it fastened on tight enough. Part of it was the mount, obviously. But I never have put anything on a car that would fall off."

The victory was worth $307,600 which included being placed on the 1982 Winner's Circle program, a NASCAR plan which awarded bonus appearance money to winning race teams, provided they compete in all events. It was a nice payday for Gardner. But Bobby's pay was no more than just a figure on a piece of paper, as he would receive no money for winning the most prestigious race on the circuit. There were many deals and promises behind the scenes to make up the payment, but none would ever become reality.

"What really happened was Bill Gardner spent a lot of my money on his other activities. He was constantly bargaining with me behind the scenes to get my money. One of his ploys was if I would sign the extension on the contract then I would get paid for Daytona 1982 and some of the other events we did well in way back then.

"I've never received all of the pay I was due when I drove for Bill Gardner."

Nelson took a Chevrolet Monte Carlo to Richmond Fairgrounds Raceway for the second race of the year. With the Daytona 500 victory behind him, Bobby was the favorite to win the race.

But problems struck during a Feb. 20 practice session. While traveling through turn one, the throttle hung wide open and sent

Bobby through the first-turn guardrail and a fence. He landed in front of the grandstand. The car was almost a total wreck.

Bobby went through the guardrail at the other end of the race track for the same reason while driving for Harry Ranier the year before.

The crew winced at the sight of the extensive damage upon the car's arrival back in the garage area. Nevertheless, they elected to fix the mangled machine instead of resorting to a backup car.

Nelson huddled with the crew and work began immediately. The front structure of the car was badly damaged as well as all the body parts in front of the steering wheel. That included the firewall, oil reservoir and the radiator.

Several hours passed before work ceased a few minutes past midnight. The crew returned at 4:30 on the morning of the Feb. 21 race.

Bob Rodgers and Glen Wood, owners of two rival teams not challenging for the NASCAR Winston Cup Grand National championship, offered to turn their cars over to Bobby for the race. Their drivers, Tom Sneva and Neil Bonnett, agreed to step out if Bobby chose to accept either offer.

Bobby thanked both team owners but opted to use parts from another DiGard car because the team had been experimenting with a certain chassis setup and felt staying with its car would provide the best overall results.

Dave Marcis won the race to record his first victory in six years. A hard rain fell just after the leaders pitted on lap 249 of the 250 laps that were ultimately completed, leaving Marcis in the lead when the event was red-flagged. Bobby finished eighth and held a seven-point lead over Terry Labonte in the early point standings.

At Bristol (Tenn.) International Raceway, on March 14, Bobby struggled throughout the 500-lap event, but managed a fifth-place finish, one lap down to winner Darrell Waltrip in Junior Johnson's Buick. Disappointingly, he led no laps, which hurt his championship bid.

The team suffered a blown engine at Atlanta on March 21. Waltrip once again went to victory lane, while Bobby fell to 22nd after leading a total of 17 laps. He encountered problems, however, on lap 242 of the 287-lap event, shortened by 41 laps due to rain.

Bobby lost 43 points to Labonte. It was the first of several weak engines to go under the hood of the DiGard cars, which proved to be Bobby's nemesis throughout the season.

Activities at North Carolina Motor Speedway in Rockingham, N.C., were to be held on Feb. 28. But inclement weather in the form of ice and snow postponed the event and another rainout on March 7 set the stage for the race to be held on March 28.

As a result, the weather situation created a bit of controversy.

As was NASCAR procedure, the field was determined in the first and second day time trials on Feb. 25 and 26, with Benny Parsons of Ellerbe, N.C., winning his first-ever pole position at his "home track" with a speed of 147.577 mph.

NASCAR rules stated that all cars must be impounded and start a race on the tires on which they qualified. But the rule was waived as two races had yet to be run after the second Rockingham rainout.

To further complicate matters, a sealant dubbed "Bear Grease" was laid to repair cracks in the track's surface. The result was the equivalent of driving on ice, which made for a long afternoon for all the drivers.

Bobby dirt-tracked his way around the 1.017-mile speedway and finished fourth in the 500-mile event behind race winner Yarborough, but lost another 10 points to Labonte. He led 14 laps until his tires faded slightly at the end.

Another blown engine sent Bobby to the sidelines in the Rebel 500 at Darlington, S.C., on April 4, which translated into a drop to third place in the point standings. Dale Earnhardt drove Bud Moore's Ford to victory to score his first triumph since 1980.

At North Wilkesboro, N.C., the DiGard Monte Carlo did not perform well, as crew chief Nelson admitted the team missed the chassis setup for the race. Bobby finished eighth, one lap down to race winner Waltrip.

With three laps remaining in the race, Allison and Labonte made contact in turn three.

The right side of Labonte's Billy Hagan-owned Chevrolet was severely damaged and his right-front tire was blown, forcing him to tour the track on the rim. His slower speed made it appear that Labonte could not keep up with the pace car and several cars passed him. As a result, there was considerable debate over Labonte's finishing position. After a two-hour meeting with NASCAR, he was moved from fourth to second in the final order.

Labonte continued to lead the point standings by 69 over Parsons. Ironically, neither of the leaders had won a race to this point of the season.

The engine problems continued at Martinsville, Va., causing a

17th-place finish and a further drop in the points. It was as if the team had been plagued by some invisible being, set to strike at any unsuspecting moment. Yates massaged his engines carefully, but his tweaking seemed no match for the demon living there. The results were beginning to grate on the entire team.

"The engine problems were a real disappointment because we had already lost a few of them by the time we got to Talladega. Usually, the cars handled and drove exceptionally well. But the engines left something to be desired. Nobody could really put their finger on what was making them break."

At Alabama International Motor Speedway on May 2, Bobby suffered mechanical problems and finished six laps behind race winner Waltrip. The event came down to a very close finish among the lead pack consisting of Waltrip, Labonte, Parsons and Kyle Petty, in his first competitive run for Petty Enterprises.

The one bright spot of the day came when Donnie returned to racing for the first time since his near-fatal accident at Charlotte on May 24, 1981. He finished a strong sixth in his comeback attempt in the Bob Rodgers Buick.

"It was great to see Donnie get back to racing. He had a tough recovery period after such a hard hit there at Charlotte. I just felt that at some point in time, he would get back to doing what he loved most."

Waltrip virtually sailed alone for a victory in the May 8 Cracker Barrel Country Store 420 at Nashville International Raceway. He led 419 of the 420 scheduled laps and sent his competition packing up for another race.

The race marked a first for Bobby and crew chief Nelson. Neither of the two veterans had ever used power steering on a race car.

Use of the device required some testing during an actual race and with Nashville being a short fairgrounds race track, it provided just enough laps to get Bobby adjusted to it. He finished sixth, four laps down to Waltrip.

Once the team returned to Charlotte, they studied the new steering mechanism further and made some changes.

Going into the May 16 Mason-Dixon 500 at Dover, Del., Waltrip had already driven Johnson's Buick to five victories as well as four pole positions. As if to flaunt his might, Waltrip toured the one-mile facility on May 15 to a record-setting 139.308 mph for his fifth pole position.

But it was Bobby who put a stop to Waltrip's early-season reign.

Bobby's fortunes turned with a three-lap victory over Marcis in the May 16 Mason-Dixon 500 at Dover Downs International Raceway.

With the power steering problems resolved, Bobby was able to lead 486 laps of the 500-lap event. His only competition for the win came from Waltrip and Earnhardt. But Waltrip exited the event late in the race with a blown engine and Earnhardt spun midway through the race.

Two firsts had been accomplished once the crew met Bobby in victory lane; it was the first victory in NASCAR history for a car equipped with power steering and the first downsized Chevrolet Monte Carlo to win.

Bobby wiped his face with a shop cloth and took a few swallows of Gatorade before he emerged from the driver's seat.

"The guys went to work this past week and I can't say enough about how it paid off," Bobby said. "We've had some problems at times this season, but everyone is willing to shoulder part of the blame for the problems — including me.

"We didn't have any problems today. But we were embarrassed, downright embarrassed, last week at Nashville."

On lap 442 of the 500-lap race, Waltrip coasted silently to the garage area, ending his hope for a sixth victory for the year. Upon further examination, Johnson noted one of the cylinder heads had broken.

For the World 600 on May 30, Bobby fell a lap down to leaders Bonnett and Bill Elliott but managed to score a third-place finish. But by June 6, his luck changed again. Leaving Charlotte, Labonte led in points by 66 over Waltrip.

Rain storms plagued activities at Pocono (Pa.) International Raceway and throughout the 200-lap event, dark clouds hovered over the speedway.

Thinking the race would be red-flagged with 41 laps remaining, Bobby elected to stay on the race track, foregoing a badly needed pit stop for tires and fuel.

The rain never got hard enough to warrant a red flag condition and just three laps later the engine in Bobby's Buick fell silent.

Bobby's car was in danger of coming to a stop on the race track. But in his rearview mirror, he saw Marcis fast approaching and waved to him for a push.

Marcis gently placed his car's front end to Bobby's rear end and pushed him back to the pits. There, Bobby received fuel and tires to go the distance.

His closest rival was Tim Richmond, who also pitted for tires and fuel, but Bobby did not lose a lap and was back in the lead and stayed there. Bobby logged his 69th NASCAR Winston Cup victory after leading the final 30 laps. The victory was assured when the seventh caution flag of the day was displayed with four laps remaining.

Marcis received a great deal of criticism for pushing Bobby's Buick, especially from Richmond's crew chief, Robert Harrington. Both Marcis and Richmond were sponsored by J. D. Stacy.

"Why would he do that?" Harrington asked some nearby reporters. "To me, he took a win away from us. We can go home feeling like Dave Marcis took a race away from us. I don't know why he would do that to a team owned by the man who sponsors him."

The lead changed 44 times with 11 drivers heading the field at one point or another.

At Riverside International Raceway on June 13, the nightmare that plagued Bobby's championship hopes returned once again. Engine problems sidelined both the Chevrolet driven by Bobby and the Buick driven by Waltrip. Bobby slowed on lap 47 while Waltrip only completed 28 of the scheduled 95 laps.

Labonte, still searching for his first victory of the year, was passed in the closing laps by Richmond, who scored his first ever Winston Cup Grand National victory.

As a result, Labonte's lead in the point standings increased to 144 points over Bobby and 210 over Waltrip.

While at Riverside, Marcis was informed his sponsor, J.D. Stacy, would not be associated with his team after the June 20 race at Michigan. The decision came after Marcis assisted Bobby at Pocono.

There was another top-five finish at Michigan and then the DiGard Buick returned to victory lane.

It meant a sweep of races at Daytona, both in February and July. Bobby mastered a very hot day and survived a four-car crash near the end of the 200-lap event to score his fourth victory of the year.

Bobby, although equipped with a superb car, admitted the win was not an easy one. In fact, the outcome might well have been different if it had not been for the four-car accident. The impact threatened to send Harry Gant's Buick into the grandstands after contact with Richmond and Richard Petty on lap 136 of the 160-lap event.

"It was really quite alarming," Bobby said of the accident after witnessing it through his rearview mirror. "I could see two cars get together. They were two of the strongest cars and I certainly couldn't sell the others short."

Following the accident, Bobby's only real challenge came from Elliott, driver of the Harry Melling-owned Ford. Elliott had lost at Charlotte by a few feet to Bonnett and a car length to Bobby at Daytona.

Elliott was found in the garage area dousing himself with cool water after suffering from the Florida heat.

"I really don't know if I could catch Bobby or not," Elliott said. "His car was superior in the corners. On the last restart (on lap 141, following the four-car accident) I tried to hang on him in the draft the best I could."

Bobby's sweep of Daytona was only the fourth in the speedway's history. Glenn "Fireball" Roberts swept events at Daytona in 1962, while Cale Yarborough and Lee Roy Yarbrough accomplished the feat in 1968 and 1969, respectively.

"It's a great feeling and I'm really happy," Bobby said. "When we finished up our last practice session yesterday (July 3), the car felt like it would go anywhere I wanted it to go. We had changed our spring setup drastically from the way we had it here in February and it worked perfectly."

Labonte experienced engine problems in his Buick and ultimately finished 27th.

"I wish that would have happened last week," Bobby chortled of Labonte's fortune, citing that the Texas native received a $25,000 bonus from R.J. Reynolds Tobacco Co., the series sponsor, for leading the series standings at the halfway point. "The way to win a championship is to race hard and race to win. You do that, and the points will come your way."

Leaving Daytona, Bobby held a 35-point lead over Labonte and a 186 point lead over Waltrip.

Waltrip countered Bobby's lead with a victory at Nashville on July 10. Bobby suffered through another dismal run and a series of pit stops to lumber to a 19th-place finish. With that, Labonte retook the lead in the point standings by 29 points.

On the return to Pocono, Waltrip had a victory in the Mountain Dew 500 in hand until a dwindling fuel supply cost him the lead. Several miscalculations were made by other teams, including Waltrip's Junior Johnson crew. With no choice but to pit with four laps remaining, Waltrip dropped off turn four and went to the pits for a splash of fuel.

Bobby inherited the lead and went on to capture his 70th career Winston Cup Grand National victory.

"Gary (Nelson) said we were going to make it and I believed him," Bobby said. "We were not concerned about running out of fuel. We were geared up to race, but we felt whoever led (the last few laps) was going to run out of fuel."

But Waltrip had another thought in mind.

"I didn't even think about running out of gas, but we started running out on lap 197 (of 200 laps)," Waltrip said. "It was too late then to stop for fuel."

The win enabled Bobby to move within 14 points of Labonte with Waltrip 148 back in third.

For the first time all season, Nelson elected to take a Pontiac LeMans to Talladega on Aug. 1.

The car performed nicely, but with NASCAR's rules dealing with the rear spoiler, it continued to be rendered non-competitive. With the slightly smaller spoiler, Bobby fought with the handling characteristics throughout the race and could only muster a 10th-place finish.

For the sixth time during 1982, Bobby visited victory lane with his win at Michigan International Speedway over Petty.

But Petty forced Bobby to work for the victory. Petty staged a come-from-behind effort in the final 15 laps and erased a 10-second deficit.

On the white flag lap, Bobby dropped low down the backstretch in hopes of breaking any draft between the two cars. Bobby held on for the victory.

"He (Petty) was coming on strong," Bobby said. "He was running more consistent laps than I was, so I tried to throw him something he might not expect. It must have worked because we got to the finish line first."

After a strong second-place finish to Waltrip at Bristol on Aug. 28, Bobby found himself ahead in the point standings by 65 over Labonte. Waltrip's eighth victory of the season helped to close the gap between him and Labonte ever so slightly.

The Southern 500 on Sept. 6 proved to be a day of caution flags, as 14 waved during the 367-lap event at Darlington, S.C.

Bobby led for 88 laps but cut a tire and hit the second turn wall, requiring suspension repairs that kept him behind the wall for an extended period of time.

Yarborough emerged victorious over Earnhardt and Petty for his fifth career Southern 500 win.

Bobby left the famous South Carolina speedway with a 115-point lead over Labonte and a 132-point lead over Waltrip, who blew his engine on lap 240.

Back at Richmond Fairgrounds Raceway, Bobby returned to championship form with a victory over Tim Richmond after a pass on lap 327 of 400 and held the lead the rest of the way. For the first time during the season, Bobby could take a slight sigh of relief as far as his bid for the title was concerned. Leaving Richmond, he held a 147-point advantage over Waltrip with only seven races remaining. But there were still races to be completed and anything could happen.

Sure enough, Bobby's slight feeling of security did not last.

Waltrip edged Kyle Petty for the victory at Dover the next week, which cut a sizable chunk out of Bobby's points lead. After fighting an incurable water leak all day, the DiGard Buick finished 10th, 13 laps down. As a result, Waltrip gained ground by 46 points.

Bobby began to feel the championship slide from his fingers after the 400-lap event at North Wilkesboro on Oct. 3. Waltrip once again went on to victory, while Bobby suffered a blown engine and completed only 141 laps. His lead was now just 15 points and everyone at DiGard began to feel the pressure.

"Even though we were having so many engine failures, I contin-ued to have confidence in Robert Yates. I knew Robert was working as hard as he could on those engines, but things kept happening that were out of his control."

Once at Charlotte on Oct. 10, Bobby dominated by leading 280 of the 334-lap race. With eight laps remaining he lost yet another engine, but managed to increase the points lead he held to 37 over Waltrip. On lap 238, Waltrip's Buick was involved in a 10-car crash in turn four, which also eliminated several other contenders.

The worst occurred once again at Martinsville, Va. Bobby slowed down the backstretch after a puff of smoke blew from the headers. As he sat on pit road, his crew lifted the hood and could only stare at their third-straight sour engine. The result was a loss of the points lead to Waltrip by 37.

At Rockingham on Oct. 31, Waltrip scored his 12th win of the year. But Bobby led the most laps and finished second. By doing so, he tied Waltrip in race points (180) and kept from losing ground.

Waltrip wasn't happy with NASCAR's points system.

"I drove 500 hard miles and won the race, and I don't pick up anything in the point race," Waltrip said. "There needs to be a bonus for winning the race. There is not enough emphasis on winning — and that is what the sport is all about. They're giving bonus points for leading a race under the yellow flag (referring to Bobby) but no bonus for winning the race."

Bobby seemed to have the race well in hand until problems occurred with only 42 laps left to complete. He had just finished a 12.7-second pit stop and hustled off of pit road toward turn one. He spun on the apron and collided with the inside guardrail. Waltrip passed him and went on to win by 9.5 seconds.

Of the accident, Bobby told reporters, "We had the best car, the best engine, the best everything. Then I spun off pit road and lost the race." Dejected over the day's events, he changed out of his driver's uniform and quickly left the speedway.

Going into the next to last race of the year at Atlanta on Nov. 7, Bobby knew he wasn't out of the championship hunt. The team took extra precautions while making preparations on the car at their Charlotte shops. It was determined to win the final two races of the year.

They left Atlanta victorious, as Bobby managed to pass Waltrip for the win with 24 laps to go, chopping Waltrip's points lead to 22.

Bobby outran Waltrip and Gant in a 10-lap dash after Petty spun and hit the third-turn wall on lap 313. Petty led 54 laps and looked to be on the verge of ending a 38-race losing streak before he crashed.

But Bobby found himself on the point and held it for the win.

"I beat Waltrip out of the pits and figured I'd have enough power to stay in front," Bobby said from the press box. "This tightens up the points race. We're going to Riverside to win and hope things turn out for the best."

Both Bobby and Waltrip entered the gates of Riverside International Raceway convinced each would emerge as 1982 NASCAR Winston Cup Grand National champion.

Each driver suffered mechanical problems and misfortune. For Bobby, there were two flats and stripped lug nuts that put him a lap behind. He struggled throughout the day and was unable to make up the lap. He ultimately finished 16th.

Waltrip suffered gear box problems but not enough to cost him the championship, winning over Bobby by 72 points. The final race rundown showed Waltrip in third behind race winner Richmond and second-place Rudd.

With the season completed, Bobby flew back to Alabama to rest and regroup during the winter months. He would, once again, be with DiGard for the upcoming season, along with Nelson and Yates. The '82 season had shown his team's potential. All he could hope for was that 1983 would be his year to win the title.

Seventeen days after the race at Riverside, Bobby lost a very close friend. Country music singer and part-time race driver Marty Robbins died of a heart attack in a Nashville, Tenn., hospital on Dec. 8, 1982.

The loss saddened Bobby.

But 1983, and its promise, beckoned.

CHAPTER TWENTY-ONE
The Champion

By the time snow flakes first began to fall and lightly accumulate on the bare trees around the DiGard Racing Co. shops, the 1982 NASCAR Winston Cup Grand National season had been finished for nearly three weeks.

Disappointingly, only 72 points had separated Bobby from winning the championship. Five times now, he had been the bridesmaid, only to see someone come from behind and take the coveted prize away. The thought Waltrip bested the team for the second straight year was annoying.

Team members began preparing for the '83 season in the usual fashion — like gangbusters. After some careful analysis, changes were being made, all for the cause of securing the championship.

With all testing for Speed Weeks complete, it was once again time to head south to Daytona for the 500. But Speed Weeks turned out to be anything but good.

Before the two-week span concluded, Bill and Jim Gardner were the proud owners of two crashed race cars.

Bobby destroyed the team's primary Chevrolet Monte Carlo during the fourth lap of the 50-lap Busch Clash on Feb. 14. The backup car was lost in a crash during practice two days later.

The fact equipment had been lost robbed the team of much of its preparedness.

Crew members were dispatched back to the shop to retrieve the team's only other Chevrolet Monte Carlo, the car Gary Nelson had readied for the short tracks.

A flat tire sent Bobby back to 17th in the second 125-mile qualifying race. However, his qualifying speed put him in 35th in the starting lineup for the 500.

Even though he was not a factor early in the 500, Bobby ran as high as third until a flat tire forced a ninth-place finish behind race winner Cale Yarborough, who wheeled the same "controversial" Pontiac LeMans Bobby drove for Harry Ranier's team in 1981.

Yarborough's victory was something of a surprise, as he flipped a Chevrolet Monte Carlo in turn three after posting a speed of 200.533 mph during qualifying. He had gone 0.33-mph faster than the lap Benny Parsons turned at Alabama International Motor Speedway in a Ranier car the previous August.

The car was badly damaged and as a result, the Ranier team was forced to switch to a backup car, dropping Yarborough to the rear of the field. That made his speed "unofficial."

Once the race concluded, every member of the DiGard Racing crew was anxious to leave Daytona after two terrible weeks.

As with any race, the Feb. 27 Richmond 400 marked a new beginning for the team.

There was no better way to forget the trials of Daytona than with a win. That's exactly what happened in the state capitol of Virginia. The Richmond 400 marked the first victory for the team in '83.

Had there been a few more laps remaining in the 400-lap event at the 0.542-mile Richmond Fairgrounds Raceway, Dale Earnhardt easily could have been victorious.

Bobby had nearly a lap on Earnhardt when he was forced to pit for fuel with only 16 laps remaining. Once Bobby's Chevrolet roared out of the pits, Earnhardt had closed the gap to four seconds. As the two cars flashed under the line, Earnhardt was pressing hard on Bobby's rear bumper, but came up short.

Bobby emerged from the Monte Carlo in victory lane with a familiar red shop rag in hand and a wide smile.

"I knew I had to have that last pit stop for fuel," Bobby said immediately. "We had counted the laps and knew we had to stop."

Bobby admitted he adopted a different driving line than Earnhardt in the closing laps which proved to be the key to his victory.

"I was running good enough through turns one and two but not three and four," Bobby said in the press box later. "I glimpsed behind me and saw where Dale was strong and that made me change my line between three and four. When I did that, I think I helped myself just enough because it would have taken Dale three more laps to catch me."

The second backup car Bobby ran in the Daytona 500 was

dubbed, "No. 22-C." The car Bobby wheeled to victory at Richmond was dubbed "No. 22-D."

The March 13 Carolina 500 at North Carolina Motor Speedway in Rockingham, N.C., was a race of beginnings and endings.

Bobby went into the 500-mile race with career earnings of $3,998,546 and the $10,695 paid for his 10th-place finish pushed him over the $4 million dollar mark.

The only other driver to surpass $4 million in earnings was Richard Petty.

Before the start of the race, Bill Gardner announced the team would be switching to Buick Regals starting with the March 20 Coca-Cola 500 at Atlanta International Raceway.

But a blown engine marred Bobby's efforts in Atlanta, relegating him to a 25th-place finish.

It did not prove to be a good race for anyone. Rains hampered qualifying activities on March 17 and delayed the race from March 19 to March 27. Almost on cue, heavy rains began to pelt the speedway just after country music singer Lee Greenwood hit the last note of the National Anthem.

On April 10 at Darlington (S.C) Raceway, Bobby salvaged an eighth-place finish behind race winner Harry Gant, who inherited the lead when Waltrip's Junior Johnson-owned Chevrolet began to puff smoke.

Bobby put the newly-built Buick out front for 22 laps, but simply was not strong enough to challenge for the lead.

There was a second-place finish for the DiGard team at North Wilkesboro (N.C) Speedway on April 7.

Waltrip was able to hold on to win at the track the Johnson team considers "home."

At the end, Bobby trailed Waltrip by over eight seconds. To win at North Wilkesboro, one must beat Johnson's cars, which usually dominated each race there in the early 1980s.

"If we could have had one more caution flag at the end, I might could have caught Darrell," Bobby said during post-race interviews. "But that would have been the only way. He was really dialed in today and he ran a great race. Nobody could touch him.

"We were the best of the out-of-town cars. Junior and those guys are hard to beat here."

At Martinsville, Va., on April 24, Waltrip began to look like championship material again after a disappointing start to the year.

Waltrip and Johnson used a savvy "gamble" that paid off handsomely.

With 15 laps to go, Neil Bonnet's Rahmoc Racing Chevrolet blew its engine, setting up the final caution flag of the day.

Bobby was the leader at the time of the caution and was being closely challenged by Waltrip, Gant, Ricky Rudd and Joe Ruttman.

As Bobby led the train of cars toward pit road, Waltrip cut hard right, then quickly left, and did not cut on to pit road. That left him in the lead for the final 13 circuits.

Bobby managed to salvage a third-place finish.

Petty scored his second win of the season at Talladega, Ala., on May 1. Bobby was forced to settle for 10th, two laps off the pace, due to a series of cut tires and minor mechanical problems.

A spectacular end-over-end crash by Phil Parsons on lap 73 caused great concern for the Lake Norman, N.C., driver. It appeared that Waltrip's Chevrolet suffered a blown right front tire, sending his car out of control, making contact with Parsons' Pontiac.

A total of nine cars was involved, including those of Yarborough, A.J. Foyt, Kyle Petty, David Pearson and Tim Richmond.

Parsons hit the outside wall hard and then began a series of rolls and flips in mid-air before coming to rest on the grass at the base of the high-banked second turn.

Miraculously, he received only bruises and a minor fracture of the right shoulder blade. Kyle Petty received a sprained shoulder and bruises.

At Nashville, Tenn., on May 7, it was another showdown between Bobby and Waltrip — at least in the opening laps.

By the halfway point, Waltrip had two laps on the field at his home track, except for the cars driven by Bobby and Gant.

Bobby managed to secure a second-place finish, but felt great disappointment in not winning the race. For the first time, the event had been named in memory of longtime friend Marty Robbins, who died the past December of complications after open heart surgery.

During the victory lane ceremonies, Ronnie Robbins, the son of the country music singer, presented Waltrip with Robbins' driver's uniform and copies of some gold record albums.

Bobby returned to victory lane on May 17 at Dover, Del., in the Mason-Dixon 500. The win proved to be a morale boost for the DiGard team in their quest for the championship.

During recent weeks, Waltrip had gained considerable ground in the points race and looked to be gaining strength for the future.

The Franklin, Tenn., driver had three victories on the short tracks and looked unstoppable there. Bobby and Nelson had already discussed the need for better performances on tracks less than a mile in distance and hoped to be where Waltrip was at this point of the season.

Waltrip was a scant fender ahead of Bobby's Buick at Dover Downs International Speedway when a torrential downpour hit the area with five laps remaining. When the red flag was displayed, Bobby had moved in front for the win.

"I knew we had 'em covered," Bobby said wearily. "I could see the rain coming so I knew I had to be in front. I knew that Darrell knew he couldn't beat me when we came down to the caution flag on the last lap."

The win put Bobby on top of the Winston Cup Grand National point standings.

"Darrell has had us covered the last few weeks. But one of their guys was telling us what they were doing, so Gary has had our guys make the proper adjustments," Bobby said.

"And boy, it really worked."

When Bobby made the statement, the press box began to buzz.

"You're saying someone on Junior's crew is telling you everything they're doing?" asked an unidentified journalist.

"I can't really say any more about it," Bobby responded.

"Looking back on '83, we knew Darrell and Junior were dropping lead weights out of their cars. That's how they were gaining on us.

"When the weight fell out, that constituted something falling off the car and NASCAR looked at it as just a piece of sheet metal. To them, it was no big deal."

Five days before the race, Darlington Raceway President Barney Wallace, a longtime friend to Bobby who was an original investor in the speedway, died after a long bout with cancer.

Waltrip returned to victory lane at Bristol, Tenn., on May 21 to record yet another short-track victory. But Bobby's was the only car in the lead lap when the race concluded.

For the second straight week, Bobby was again on top in the points race.

The World 600 at Charlotte Motor Speedway was seemingly Bobby's for the asking — until he was collected in another driver's misfortune.

On lap 343 of the 400-lap event, Bobby found himself racing hard with Bill Elliott for the lead. Bobby was pulling away just a bit when the engine in Sterling Marlin's Chevrolet expired, sending parts and oil over the racing surface in the dogleg area of the 1.5-mile speedway.

Both Bobby and Elliott spun over the trioval grass toward pit road.

That left Neil Bonnett in the Wood Brothers Ford in position to take his first victory of the season.

"I was called while I was running down the backstretch and told the lead cars had wrecked," Bonnett said. "I really didn't realize what had happened at first. I was really surprised to see who it was."

Bobby settled for a third-place finish while Elliott followed in 17th.

But due to lap leader awards, Bobby's total winnings for the race amounted to $66,925 — nearly $16,000 more than Bonnett. Bobby held a 190-point lead in the standings over Richard Petty

At Riverside, Calif., on June 5, Bobby finished a disappointing 23rd due to handling problems. Ricky Rudd scored his first career Winston Cup Grand National victory while driving for former driver Richard Childress. It was also Childress' first win as a car owner.

Race track humorists accused Bobby of starting his own diamond mine after the Van Scoy Diamond Mines 500 at Pocono, Pa. It marked Bobby's second consecutive victory in the event and his second $5,000 diamond ring in addition to his $31,100 winner's share of the purse.

He led 143 of the 200-lap event, going into the lead for good on lap 156.

Eleven different drivers swapped the lead for a total of 22 times. But it was a combination of superior gas mileage and quick pit work that clinched the victory for Bobby.

With 13 laps remaining, Tim Richmond pulled into the pits for a splash of fuel. Two laps later, Richard Petty followed suit.

Bobby made his stop on lap 194 and three seconds later, was back on the track. All that was required was just enough fuel in the tank to insure the victory.

His margin of victory — 9.6 seconds over Waltrip — was a healthy one.

"We pitted three laps after them (Richmond and Petty) and we were getting better gas mileage," Bobby said. "We could have finished without the stop, but with the advantage we had it would have been foolish to take a chance.

"Robert Yates worked a lot on fuel specifics, such as how much gas it takes to produce each horsepower the engine puts out. Plus a lot of guys don't get all the gas out of the tank."

With the win, Bobby increased the points lead he was holding since the Dover, Del., race in May to 163 more than Bill Elliott and Petty, who were tied at 2,000 each.

The victory was also the 76th of Bobby's career, which tied him with Cale Yarborough for third on the all-time victory list.

Bobby's return to Michigan International Speedway on June 19 didn't begin very well, to say the least.

Shortly before starting positions were determined, Bobby found himself involved in a five-car accident along with Richmond, Ron Bouchard, Terry Labonte and Dave Marcis.

The melee was triggered when Labonte spun his Chevrolet and Bouchard spun to avoid him.

Both Bobby and Richmond elected to go to the high side, but Richmond hit Bobby hard in the rear, causing the two cars to lose control.

Granted, it was not the best way to begin a race weekend. But ironically, two drivers involved in the crash during the practice session went on to record their best-ever MIS finishes, while the other three managed to finish in the top-five.

Race winner Yarborough was loose for a time early in the event. His Ranier Racing crew worked feverishly to dial in the Chevrolet.

The race marked the first time a Daytona 500 and Indianapolis 500 winner started in the same field at Michigan. Yarborough began the race in ninth; Tom Sneva in 32nd.

Yarborough stalked his prey until lap 158, then led for the first time.

Two pieces of metal on the backstretch set up the final caution period from laps 175-178. Bobby pitted for left-side tires only, while Yarborough and Waltrip took on four tires.

Both Bobby and Yarborough were set for the duration and elected not to pit when Kyle Petty spun on the backstretch.

During that final caution period, Yarborough conveyed to television viewers via an in-car camera the time had come to mash the gas and put his ride out front.

"I pushed it to the limit because I know anything can happen when there's a whole lot of people running close at the end and I wanted to get as much of a lead as I could," Yarborough said later.

Bobby and the DiGard crew assumed Yarborough would have to make one final pit stop for fuel. But the final caution periods altered his strategy.

"We were drafting Cale, and I was right where I wanted to be," Bobby said, describing the final 50 laps. "We figured he'd have to stop for gas, and we were going for broke. The next two cautions messed up our strategy. As it turned out, he was just stronger than we were."

Bobby barely nipped Richmond for second, while Waltrip did the same with Labonte for fourth.

Buddy Baker ended a 33-race winless streak in the Firecracker 400 on July 4 at Daytona Beach, Fla. He drove the Wood Brothers Ford as Harold Kinder dropped the white flag to indicate the final lap. As he exited turn four, the engine fell silent, out of fuel. Had it been a close race, Baker would not have had a chance.

Morgan Shepherd turned some heads with his second-place finish in the J.D. Stacy Buick, while David Pearson brought his Chevrolet home third.

Labonte and Bouchard were in the fray until dry gas tanks forced them to the pits and out of contention.

"Toward the end, I was running behind Terry and that was where I wanted to stay until I felt like it was time to make my move," Baker said. "I was leading in the Daytona 500 and you saw what happened. Cale got by me and so did Bill Elliott. I wound up third because I was stupid. There was no way that was going to happen again. If a paper bag had been leading this race, I was going to run behind it."

Baker's plan was to use the slingshot move ever so popular at Daytona. But there was no need when Labonte fell from contention.

"I was right behind Terry when he ran out of gas and I had to cut to get around him," Baker said. "I barely made it, but I almost didn't. In fact, I'm not so sure I didn't hit the wall."

Shy of the halfway point at the 79-lap mark, Dick Brooks cut a tire on the backstretch and spun out between turns three and four.

It left Bobby's Buick and Richard Petty's Pontiac with nowhere to go but into Brooks' Ford.

As a result, Petty went to the garage with severe frame damage. Bobby sustained damage but was able to continue to a 14th-place finish and thus lose a minimal amount of points.

On Friday, July 3, Bobby and Judy met Jim Gardner, Robert Yates and Gary Nelson in a conference room in the offices of the International Speedway Corporation based at DIS. The occasion was the signing of a new contract.

At the signing, Bobby was halfway through his original three-year contract.

Still, the paychecks were slow in coming, usually behind by months.

"The three-year extension was a maneuver on the part of Bill Gardner to tie me up and tie up sponsors and the entire racing picture.

"What really happened was Bill Gardner had spent a lot of my money on his other activities. He was constantly bargaining with me behind the scenes to get my money. I thought I could get some of the money I was owed from 1982."

At Nashville, Tenn., on July 16, it was a Bouchard/Earnhardt show. Bouchard grabbed the pole at 103.020 mph — a first in his career — and earned himself a spot in the 1984 Busch Clash.

Earnhardt, on the other hand, led 212 of the race's 420 laps and unseated Darrell Waltrip, the heavy favorite at his home track.

It was a competitive race with only four cautions for 25 laps. Bobby swapped the lead 12 times with Earnhardt, Waltrip, Bonnett and Marcis.

Bobby eventually finished fourth and maintained a comfortable 202-point lead over Waltrip — 2,629 to 2,427.

There was no loss or gain for Bobby in the points race on the return trip to Pocono, Pa., on July 24. Nor was there for Waltrip.

Waltrip finished second to race winner Richmond and gained 170 points, plus five points for leading a lap. Bobby finished third, gaining 165 points as well as five points for leading a lap and five more for leading the most laps.

The event was a test of patience and pit strategies. There were several strong contenders for the victory as well as two red-flag periods due to rain.

Following the second delay, only 45 of the 200 laps were left to complete.

Richmond took the lead from Waltrip on lap 133 and when the yellow was displayed for huge rain drops on the competitors windshields, Bobby, Gant, Waltrip and Bonnett pitted, leaving Richmond on the track until lap 145.

When the green flag once again was displayed, Bobby shot into the lead, but was passed by Gant on lap 160. From there, it was a mighty exchange at the point. Waltrip led laps 161 to 164, Gant 165-169 and Richmond took over again through lap 174.

The showdown between Richmond and Waltrip began to take shape with Bobby and Gant watching intently behind in case of a slip by the two frontrunners.

Waltrip pitted on lap 187 for fuel only. Richmond made his stop on lap 191. But Richmond returned to the track and passed Waltrip, who was third behind Elliott and Marcis.

Richmond took the lead two laps later and held it for the distance.

After the race, Richmond said, "Joe (Mattioli, president of the speedway) and Pocono are the reasons I'm in Winston Cup racing. That is why this win is so special. I couldn't be happier."

Richmond began his racing career in Indy Cars, but it was Mattioli who lined him up with his first Winston Cup stock car ride, that of car owner D.K. Ulrich.

As soon as the engines died in the garage area at Talladega, Ala., on July 31 the roar of controversy arose. And Bobby found himself right in the middle of it.

Because he was fighting for the championship, Bobby was accused of placing his lapped DiGard Buick between race winner Earnhardt and second-place finisher Waltrip as the cars whizzed through the third and fourth turns on the final lap.

It was said the move was done to keep Waltrip from gaining any ground on Earnhardt and possibly winning the race. Bobby did not want Waltrip, who stood second in the points, to further intensify the season-long battle.

As the cars roared down the backstretch, Earnhardt made his move on Waltrip. It was an ideal place to be at Talladega, since the draft and slingshot played such an important role on the fast, high-banked track.

Earnhardt dashed to the low side of Waltrip and took the lead as the cars headed into turn three.

Bobby came with them, but he was two laps down in ninth position and not a part of the final outcome. He kept his Buick on Earnhardt's rear until the pack entered turn four.

Waltrip managed to move up before the checkered flag flew but simply ran out of time.

Even so, Earnhardt was determined to make his move on Waltrip on the backstretch.

"Normally, when you do that, you leave the other guy plenty of time to get back around you," Earnhardt said. "But I saw the slower cars of Kyle Petty and Bobby Hillin ahead and I knew they would be a factor when I got to the trioval. I figured they might give Darrell some problems there, so I went ahead and made my pass."

Waltrip wasn't happy with Bobby's last-lap move.

"We ran up on a slower car (Allison's) and that won the race for

Dale," Waltrip charged. "I am thankful for the second-place finish, however, since it picked up some points for us in the standings."

Asked about the incident, Bobby said, "I made a clean pass on Darrell and what I did probably helped him. Being as he didn't win, he's probably using that as an excuse.

"We were busting our hump for ourselves. We had to make sure we weren't losing position. NASCAR wouldn't tell us if we were running competitively with the No. 98 (Joe Ruttman) or the No. 47 (Ron Bouchard) so we had to look out for ourselves. There was money and points at stake."

An Allison did win at Talladega International Motor Speedway during the weekend, however. Davey managed to log his second ARCA (Automobile Racing Club of America) 200 while driving a Pontiac Ventura.

Just three days after the race, Waltrip announced he had agreed to drive Johnson's cars for another three years, despite a two-car team in the works for 1984. Bonnett was hired to drive for the second team.

Of the 37 cars that started the 400-mile event at Brooklyn, Mich., only seven competitors fell out of the event and Bobby was one of them. On lap 137 of the 200 laps which made up the distance, Bobby coasted down pit road and turned left into the garage area.

With Waltrip finishing second behind eventual winner Yarborough, the 170-point lead Bobby was enjoying was cut to 61 (3,013 to 2,952 for Waltrip).

"The oil pressure just went zip," Bobby said to a group of reporters that had gathered outside his garage stall.

Waltrip gained even more ground with a victory at Bristol, Tenn., on Aug. 27.

Bobby posted a third-place finish, but received criticism for pitting during the final caution. It translated into a loss of 20 points.

On lap 411 of the 500-lap event, Bonnett crashed while racing with Ronnie Thomas and the final caution flag was displayed.

Race leader Earnhardt pitted for tires and was followed by Bobby and Waltrip. It was Waltrip's crew which produced a lightning fast pit stop and returned him to the track first. Earnhardt followed with Bobby in third.

Then to complicate the scenario, heavy rains fell unmercifully. On lap 419 the event was red-flagged and eventually called official.

Waltrip gained 175 points for winning, plus gained 10 additional points for leading one lap and leading the most laps (215).

Bobby, on the other hand, never led a lap and received only 165 for this third-place finish. If he had remained on the track during the last yellow caution period, he would have earned rather than lost 20 points.

But Bobby didn't see the incident as a mistake.

"We were still racing for the win," he said. "If we are going to ride around and just pick up five bonus points, then we are giving up the rest.

"What we were gambling on is we'd have a better pit stop than the others and be leading the race on new tires."

Bobby got back on track with his fourth career victory in the Southern 500 at Darlington (S.C.) Raceway on Sept. 5. With the win, he became the oldest driver to ever win the Labor Day Classic. He was 46 on Dec. 3, 1982. When Buck Baker won the Southern 500 in 1964, he was 45.

Members of the media began to prod Bobby about his new title of "Grandfather." His youngest son, Clifford, was father to Leslie Kay Allison, born just over two months before.

"Hey, how about keeping that quiet, OK?" Bobby said with a smile. "But I reckon it's time to brag. I've got a little nine-week-old granddaughter and she's a little tiny thing. It's a new experience for me, but she can already say one word. It's 'Grandpa.'"

Bobby led 118 of the 367 laps over the 1.366-mile course. The 97-degree heat took its toll on many of the drivers before race's end. Bobby admitted the heat was a concern for him, even though he had a reputation of being able to withstand hot temperatures.

"I guess it was as hot here as any time it's been over the past few years," Bobby said. "I was really conscious of it, especially during the first five laps. I was worried I might not make it. But Gary Nelson talked to me on the radio and he offers a lot of encouragement, which helped put me at ease. I figured I would pace myself."

Close to the halfway point of the race, Nelson retrieved an air chisel and cut a hole in the car's roof to improve air circulation.

"Don't tell (Bill) Gazaway (NASCAR director of competition) about it," Bobby said jokingly in the post-race interview. "We cut a hole in the roof because we used a car that had a different roll cage. There was a roll bar where the small vent window usually is and it actually blocked air from coming into the car."

NASCAR officials made the DiGard crew patch the hole on a later pit stop. A few days after the race, NASCAR confirmed Nelson had been fined for the incident.

Including Allison, nine drivers led the event 17 times. But Bobby took the lead for the final time on lap 342 when his closest challenger, Elliott, relinquished the lead for a 7.1-second stop for gas.

"Our car was set up excellent," Bobby said. "We didn't make a single change all day. We didn't add bite or anything."

The heat was a factor for Elliott.

"I got so hot and tired out there I wasn't able to challenge Bobby," Elliott said. "I made a mistake with almost 80 laps to go when I didn't pass Labonte to get to Bobby. I could have made a run at him.

"I was just holding on out there. It was the first time I've ever wanted to get out of a race car and I started thinking about it with 50 laps to go."

Bobby's good fortune continued at Richmond, Va., on Sept. 11.

It was basically a two-car race between him and Ricky Rudd. Allison led three times for 210 laps while Rudd held the point twice for 135 laps.

Late in the event, Rudd had the Richard Childress-owned Chevrolet in second and was using the high groove to catch Bobby. That fact was first reported by Jim Gardner, who was in the press box acting as spotter for the team.

Gardner radioed the information to Bobby over the two-way radio and Bobby adjusted accordingly.

In the end, Bobby crossed the line 0.86-second ahead of Rudd to claim his second consecutive victory in as many starts.

More important to Bobby was the fact he once again had padded his points lead over Waltrip in the duel for the Winston Cup Grand National championship. By finishing two positions ahead of Waltrip, Bobby picked up 15 more points and his lead stood at 71 points (3,548 to 3,477).

On the points battle, Bobby said, "If we win the race, it doesn't matter where Darrell finishes. If we don't, then it is important to know where he is.

"Part of our game plan is to have a better record on the short tracks and I think we have done that. Our record shows it."

In eight short-track events, Bobby had compiled two wins, three seconds, two thirds and one fourth.

Further ramifications surfaced over the hole cut in the roof at Darlington. NASCAR Winston Cup Director Dick Beaty confirmed that the DiGard team had been fined an additional $500 for the incident

When asked if cutting the hole was justified, Nelson said, "It was done in the interest of safety. Drivers were dropping like flies out there."

The sixth victory of the season at Dover, Del., on Sept. 18 prompted Bobby to compare DiGard Racing to the Green Bay Packers National Football League team.

"We run Vince Lombardi-style of racing," Bobby said, referring to the late Green Bay head coach. "We do our best every week, but no tricks. Maybe we use a few little tricks, but no big ones."

When Bobby took the lead away from Geoff Bodine on lap 476 of the 500-lap event, he accomplished the following: He led 195 laps, the most of anyone, and picked up an additional 10 Winston Cup points. He also increased his point standings lead to 101 over Waltrip, who ran into a series of mechanical difficulties.

The win also placed him in third on the all-time win list behind Richard Petty (197) and David Pearson (105).

Even though Bobby held a healthy lead over Waltrip in points, there was still room to be cautious.

"I've been behind 101 points lots of times," Bobby said. "They're (Johnson and Waltrip) tough and we can't let our guard down any. You always worry about Darrell or anyone else in Junior's cars."

After Rudd's total dominance at Martinsville, Va., on Sept. 25, Bobby managed to lead 48 laps and finish in the next best spot. He gained only five points over Waltrip, who finished third.

On Oct. 2, Waltrip gained renewed hope for the championship. He passed Bobby with 21 laps remaining to score his sixth victory of the year and pulled himself to 91 points behind Bobby.

Bobby finished seventh in the lead lap at Charlotte Motor Speedway in the 500-mile fall event on Oct. 9. Waltrip, however, managed to post a second-place finish behind Richard Petty and found himself only 67 points away from the points lead.

Petty's 198th career win was tarnished by serious rules infractions. His engine was oversized at 381.983 cubic inches, exceeding the maximum 358 cubic inch limit. There were also left-side tires on the right side of the car.

Petty was fined $35,000 and lost 104 Winston Cup points.

Waltrip felt the win should have been taken from Petty, but NASCAR stuck to its policy of allowing the fans to know who won the race before they leave a particular race track.

Bobby was a bit disappointed with his finish. Before the race began, he felt the car would perform much better than it did.

"We never could get it right all day," Bobby said. "We lost six places and whatever points that is, that's what we lost today, unfortunately. It was pretty incredible (to see Petty win.) His car ran good."

At the time the statement was made, Bobby had no idea Petty's Pontiac was illegal.

Going into Rockingham, N.C., for the next race on Oct. 30, Bobby was leading the point standings, followed by Waltrip, Elliott, Petty and Gant. Bobby held a 67-point lead.

But misfortune struck. When Labonte rolled into victory lane after a hard-fought battle with Rudd, Bobby only held a 27-point lead — 4,349 to 4,322.

On lap 114, a right-front tire exploded on the DiGard Racing Buick while Bobby held the point. The car was momentarily uncontrollable and struck the fourth-turn guardrail and as a result, heavy damage occurred to the right front, which led to extensive work behind the DiGard pits.

A total of 43 laps passed before Bobby was able to return to the track. He was 16th in the final finishing order after being greatly helped by attrition.

Waltrip was unfortunate, also. But his situation was less serious. He was involved in a crash with Yarborough in turn one on lap 10. But he still managed a fifth place finish, three laps down to Labonte.

For the first time in months, the championship looked to be slipping away from Bobby — for the third straight year.

Bobby appeared headed for his seventh win of the season at Atlanta on Nov. 6 after leading the most laps — 128 of 328. But during a late-race caution, he routinely came down pit road. In the process, he ran over a piece of debris. A tire blew.

Swerving, the car's right front glanced off the pit road wall. Fortunately, the crew was able to make repairs without losing a lap. The magic chassis setup was lost, but a third-place finish was salvaged.

"I guess it was a stroke of luck," Bobby said of the pit road crash. "It probably cost us the race, but it could have happened on the track and I'd have been in real trouble. I'm lucky the tire blew where it did."

Waltrip struggled to finish ninth and fell 64 points in back of Bobby. With one race to go, a few smiles could be detected on the faces of the DiGard crew. But they were cautious about claiming the title. Anything could happen in the final race at Riverside, Calif.

Nearly three weeks passed before teams arrived at Riverside International Raceway. There was great fanfare surrounding the championship and both Bobby and Waltrip were caught up in hectic schedules. There were countless newspaper, radio and television interviews to grant amid concentration on the job at hand — driving the race car.

All Bobby had to do was finish 13th or better to win the championship, no matter what Waltrip did.

When it came time to qualify, Bobby's time was good enough to place the DiGard Buick in sixth. Waltrip started everyone buzzing by placing Johnson's Chevrolet in the pole position.

Finally, Bobby sat behind the wheel of his Buick waiting for the command to fire the engine. All preparation had been finished. Only 119 laps separated him from his first championship after nearly two decades of trying.

The strategy decided upon before the race was to be conservative, something Bobby had never been used to. But more emphasis was placed on winning the war instead of the battle.

As the cars rolled off the line, the excitement was building. But dark clouds were looming up above and they threatened to open. That already had dictated strategies for the race.

Nelson busied himself glancing over the equipment positioned in the DiGard pits to insure all was in its proper place. The sounds of air wrenches being tested whistled loudly and grated slightly on everyone's nerves.

Just after Harold Kinder displayed the green flag, Bobby's voice cracked over the two-way radio.

"Gary, I think I've got a tire going down," Bobby said after moving ahead to fifth position.

"OK, next time by, bring it in," Nelson said. "We can't take a chance of getting caught out on the end of the track,"

Bobby's pit stop under green dropped him back to 27th in the running order.

Two laps later, Bobby radioed again.

"Gary, I've got another one going down."

"Let's do it again, Bobby," Nelson said, shaking his head back and forth. "We'll be ready when you get here."

Another stop was completed and Bobby found himself a lap down. They had not planned to race hard, but with ground lost to flat tires, it was now a must.

Nelson began to think something wasn't quite right. Flat tires two years in a row were more than coincidence, especially since DiGard Racing was involved in championship battles both years.

The problems were not over.

The race shaped up accordingly: Waltrip led the first 32 laps; Rudd, laps 33-34; Bobby, lap 35; Petty, laps 36-45; Benny Parsons, laps 46-74; Richmond, 75-87. The event was red flagged on lap 87 for rain but Parsons reassumed the lead on lap 88, followed by Earnhardt from laps 89-92. Richmond took lap 93, and Waltrip led lap 94; Richmond laps 95-111; Parsons, 112-114; Elliott, 115-119.

During one of his pit stops, Bobby received a full tank of gas only to feel the car jerk and sputter 10 laps later.

"Gary, I'm out of fuel," Bobby said disgustedly.

"Bobby, you can't be," Nelson said. "I show you've got at least a half a tank. I'm sure of my numbers."

"Well, it's spitting and cutting out pretty bad."

As Bobby exited the pits for a third time, the car needed only 10 gallons in its 22-gallon tank.

Approximately 20 laps later, Bobby radioed that he was out of fuel again. But the team received a break when the dark clouds overhead finally let loose and caused a caution.

Once the race resumed, Bobby nursed his ill ride to a ninth-place finish, in the lead lap with race winner Elliott, who scored his first career victory.

Waltrip's sixth-place finish was academic. Bobby had won his first NASCAR Winston Cup Grand National championship.

Still on the track, Bobby dropped the screen net and raised his hand in celebration. The 24,000 in attendance cheered wildly as a salute to the newest champion.

As he rolled to a stop in victory lane alongside of Elliott's Ford Thunderbird, Judy Allison reached inside the car and greeted him with a hug and kiss.

"I've worked hard for a long, long time," Bobby said as crew members sprayed beer and champagne unmercifully. "My wife Judy has worked with me. This is something I've wanted for my entire career and today I'm going to celebrate it. I just thank God for it."

The celebration continued for the next two hours. It marked being the best and the release of the pressure and stress that had built since the start of the season.

Bobby received a hero's welcome when he departed the plane at Birmingham International Airport and again when he arrived at Hueytown. He flew home commercial, as the engine in his own plane blew on Tuesday, Nov. 15 en route to Riverside, Calif.

As his feet touched the tarmac, Bobby studied the faces of the hundred or so people who had gathered, along with camera crews from two Alabama television stations. There were banners, signs and cheers everywhere.

There was a large banner stretched across the driveway which read "Welcome to Miller Time" — the slogan of Bobby's sponsor —and another which read, "1983 National Champion."

When Bobby stepped through the front door of his home, there were decorations everywhere and on his bed was a sign which read "1983 Grand National champion sleeps here."

Congratulatory comments from those who lived in Hueytown were heard by the Allisons for many weeks.

One week passed before some crew members returned to the shop. With the season over, many took some time off to rest.

When Nelson arrived, the car had been unloaded from the transporter but untouched. During that brief time off, Nelson was concerned about the fuel problem which arose at Riverside and wanted to get to the bottom of it.

With the assistance of Elvin Rector, a member of the team, Nelson loosened the fittings leading to the fuel filter, located atop the fuel cell. Still under pressure, gas poured out — but a foreign substance was obviously in the liquid. A quick taste of the mixture proved sugar had been placed in the tank. Nelson speculated it was placed there by way of a fuel can since standard procedure was to never leave the car unsupervised.

Once the fuel cell had been taken apart, a massive amount of sugar was discovered. At that point, Nelson placed his tools on a nearby work bench and placed a call to Dick Beaty, NASCAR's Winston Cup director.

Beaty, a Charlotte resident, came over to the shop to investigate the situation. He, too, agreed the fuel contained sugar.

Further inspection of the tires Bobby used at the start of the race revealed what was speculated to be bullet holes, possibly of a .22 caliber.

Both men agreed to keep their findings quiet, as not to disrupt the NASCAR Winston Cup Awards banquet scheduled for a few weeks away at the Waldorf-Astoria hotel in New York.

But word of the incident did get out.

Rector did mention the incident in passing to his girl friend, who mentioned it to someone whose husband worked in the media.

When the Allisons, Nelson and the DiGard team arrived in New York on Dec. 6, 1983, the topic of conversation was the sugar incident.

The week before he left for the NASCAR Awards Banquet, Bobby received a call from The White House, requesting his presence at a State Dinner.

But upon entering the Washington, D.C., apartment of Mike Curb to change for the dinner, he discovered he was given two left shoes along with his tuxedo before leaving New York.

Bobby borrowed a pair from Curb's closet. But they were much too small and caused him great pain throughout the evening visit with President and Mrs. Reagan.

On Dec. 8, a glittering affair took place at the Waldorf Astoria and was called the most festive NASCAR Awards Banquet ever. It was embellished by a telephone call to Bobby from the President and not long after, Vice President George Bush stopped by en route to Argentina to extend his congratulations.

The evening was capped by a special recording made by the country music group "Alabama" who sang the rewritten lyrics to its hit, "My Home's In Alabama" to praise Bobby for his first championship. More than a few in attendance were moved to tears.

The night belonged to Bobby, who was accorded all the tributes and rewards befitting his championship.

The day after the banquet, Bobby said, "It's the biggest of any one thing I've ever accomplished. But it's also that I'm on par with the Pearsons, Yarboroughs, Pettys and Jarretts. I've never won a championship, but now my name is in the record book with those guys."

Bobby would have a new title in 1984, that of "Reigning Champion."

Unknown to those sipping champagne on center stage during that gala evening in New York, the end to Bobby Allison's glory days was very near.

CHAPTER TWENTY-TWO
Continued Turmoil For The Reigning Champion

Between November of 1983 and February of 1984, Bobby's personal services schedule was busier than at any other time during his NASCAR career. But that was understandable, as every reigning champion has many demands placed on his time.

Bobby never openly expressed the slightest feeling of fatigue during the preseason shuffles to radio stations, autograph sessions and charity appearances, as the adrenaline kept him at a sharp level. There was an unmistakable confidence in his smile as well as his overall appearance. On occasion, a newspaper reporter would tag along and attempt to record the champion's day. But soon, he would become tired and cut back stops or either quit the tour all together.

Obtaining a championship proved hard work, but Bobby had longed for the chance to defend a title for the majority of his career and to finally have it under his belt was special to him. No matter what was accomplished in the days, months or years ahead, Bobby's name would always be etched in the NASCAR record book among "Winston Cup champions."

Before the season could even get started, Bobby became deeply disturbed over one particular deal instigated by Bill Gardner. Robert Yates was placed in a position of building engines for DiGard Racing as well as one of Allison's chief rivals over the years — Richard Petty — who was now driving for car owner Mike Curb, former Lt. Governor of California.

One engine failure was too many and for Bobby, the odds against producing flawless engines increased dramatically when the first powerplant was shipped to Curb's Kannapolis, N.C., shop.

Expressing his displeasure about the situation to Gardner got Bobby nowhere. Yates did not want to provide the engines but, according to his contract, was obliged to do so.

Bobby was cautious of the new engine arrangement. But at least the season began much like 1983 with a victory in the second 125-mile qualifying race which helped to determine the starting line-up for the Daytona 500 scheduled for Feb. 19. Unlike '83, no cars were destroyed before the 500 in practice sessions or non-points races.

The Busch Clash did not include Bobby, however, as he did not win a pole position in 1983. But still, that did not dampen the spirits of the crew. It was the 500 that was so important.

Disappointment struck with a faulty camshaft, which forced Bobby to finish 34th behind eventual winner Cale Yarborough, who scored his second consecutive Daytona 500 win after a slingshot move on Darrell Waltrip.

It was during the Busch Clash that Speed Weeks' most dramatic scenario unfolded. Ricky Rudd and Jody Ridley made contact coming off turn four which sent Rudd, in the Bud Moore Engineering Ford, into a series of flips into the grass separating the trioval from pit road. Many spectators in attendance as well as those watching the 15-minute telecast on CBS Sports felt the crash was one of the worst ever witnessed.

Fortunately, Rudd escaped with severe bruises, battered ribs and swollen eyes. It could have been far worse and as fate would have it, Rudd finished seventh in the 500.

Dressed in heating balms, ace bandages and a special "flak" jacket, Rudd came to the next race, at Richmond, Va., on Feb. 26, and left with a victory. It was a spectacular comeback and anyone of lesser mental and physical strength very likely would not have finished without a relief driver.

For the second consecutive week, Bobby experienced engine problems and finished 30th in the 32-car field and was 26th in the

Winston Cup point standings.

But on March 4, Bobby moved into 12th in the points with a victory at North Carolina Motor Speedway in Rockingham, N.C.

Surprisingly, the sun made an appearance, which was uncharacteristic for the spring event. It proved to be a positive note for Bobby's season, which appeared to have storm clouds just ahead.

Due to broken camshafts in both the Daytona 500 and Richmond 400, the battle between Bobby and Waltrip for another title had not yet materialized, which was somewhat of a surprise. Everyone expected the '84 season to be much like the fourth round of a prize fight, as the two had gone head-to-head the previous three years.

Bobby started 15th and initially felt the qualifying position could be a problem, knowing how quickly the leaders can overtake a car in the middle of the pack at the 1.017-mile facility.

"We knew we were at a disadvantage starting so far back," Bobby said. "There was a lot of traffic and good running cars ahead of us. But Gary Nelson and I talked a bit and he'd ask me how the car was running and I'd try to relate that to him. He would plan his adjustment accordingly."

The surprise of the day came at the hands of Dick Brooks, who led five times for 169 laps in the underfinanced Junie Donlavey Ford.

But his day ended when he and Bobby got together on lap 358 as the two cars exited turn two. Brooks sustained heavy damage and after extensive repairs, lasted until lap 384.

Bobby took command when he passed race leader Terry Labonte in the first turn on lap 437 of the 492-lap event and never really looked back.

Bobby came close to being involved in an accident on lap 374 involving seven cars. The race was red-flagged for 34 minutes so repairs could be made to the third-turn guardrail.

At Atlanta International Raceway on March 18, Bobby's Buick was the only car able to run with leaders Benny Parsons, Yarborough and Dale Earnhardt.

The order was reversed once the checkered flag fell, as Parsons emerged victorious for his 21st career win, followed by Earnhardt and Yarborough.

Bobby finished fifth just behind Richard Petty, one lap down at the end.

A faulty rear end plagued Bobby's efforts at Bristol, Tenn., on April 1 after he had lapped the field. Ultimately, he finished 19th.

As Bobby dropped from the lead, Waltrip placed the Junior

Johnson-owned Chevrolet into the lead and went on for the win.

Further mechanical problems sent Bobby to a 22nd-place finish at North Wilkesboro, N.C., on April 8 and a 20th at Darlington, S.C., on April 15 after an early-race altercation.

"I haven't seen anything like it (his damaged race car) since the Modified days," Bobby joked to reporters.

But the DiGard Racing team briefly returned to championship form with fourth-place finishes at Martinsville, Va., on April 29 and Talladega, Ala., on May 6.

Bobby found himself involved in a three-car crash at Nashville, Tenn., on May 12 which helped to set up a controversial finish between teammates Waltrip and Neil Bonnett.

While Allison, Kyle Petty and Rusty Wallace were spinning wildly on the backstretch during the next-to-last lap, leaders Bonnett and Waltrip were headed back to the start-finish line where the caution flag and the white flag (to indicate the final lap) were waving from the flagstand.

Waltrip made the move around Bobby's stalled Buick as did Bonnett, who nearly hit the outside retaining wall in doing so. But he went on to barely edge Waltrip by two feet at the checkered flag.

Richard Petty scored his 199th career victory at Dover, Del., on May 20. Bobby settled for a 12th-place finish, eight laps down to Petty, after suffering handling problem with his Buick. The engine in Petty's Pontiac was a Yates engine and was built in the same building where Bobby's Buick had been readied for the race.

Bobby scored his second victory of the year in the World 600 at Charlotte Motor Speedway on May 27. The win marked a series of career accomplishments.

His victory in the World 600 was his 600th career start. The win was No. 81 of Bobby's career, which placed him in third on the all-time winners' list in NASCAR Winston Cup Grand National competition.

Also, his winnings of $88,500 made him only the second driver to win more than $5 million in a career.

"Awwwright!" Bobby said when informed of his financial status. "Now, don't any of ya'll tell the IRS.

"This win means a lot. Our team has had a lot of problems this year. That's no secret.

"But it was especially tough this week. We were involved in a couple of wrecks last week at Dover and Nashville the week before. We used the same car in both races."

Bobby ran a good race throughout the 400-lap event at the 1.5-mile speedway and stayed solidly in contention. He took the lead for the first time on lap 22 and never ran lower than third. By lap 221, when the first caution appeared, only Yarborough, Bobby and Earnhardt were on the lead lap.

When Yarborough's Chevrolet erupted an engine with 17 laps to go, Bobby was right there to inherit the lead.

Bobby got a tremendous advantage during a long caution-free stretch of racing because his Buick was getting excellent gas mileage.

He first pitted his Buick on lap 67 and ran 123 miles, which meant he was getting 5.59 miles on a gallon of fuel. By comparison, other drivers were getting 4.45 miles per gallon. NASCAR rules dictate that cars could carry a maximum of 22 gallons of fuel.

Better mileage numbers prompted many — including NASCAR officials — to suspect Allison's gas tank was illegal.

Although no protests were filed, NASCAR conducted a lengthy post-race inspection and concentrated on such areas as door panels, roll bars, dashboard, all enclosure material at the dashboard and lines leading to the fuel pump and radiator.

"Bobby's car simply gets good gas mileage," said Winston Cup Director Dick Beaty after the inspection produced no illegal maneuverings.

Nelson's logic was simple; use as much of the area allotted to him by the rule book as possible.

NASCAR's standard procedure called for removing the fuel cell and measuring the dimensions from the outside, which were nine inches tall, 33 inches long and 17 inches wide.

The rubber bladder was 10 inches by 34 inches by 18 inches — an inch larger. Because the bladder would wrinkle as fuel was burned, the fuel cell usually only held 19 gallons.

After discovering the error, Nelson's cars held exactly 22 gallons. The fuel cells in the cars of the other competitors held 20 or 21, thus giving Bobby better fuel mileage.

Bobby logged a strong third-place finish at Riverside, Calif., on June 3 behind race winner Labonte in the Hagan Enterprises Chevrolet.

After a late caution flag in the Pocono (Pa.) 500 on June 10, Bobby finished seventh to race winner Yarborough. But he could have possibly been in a better position to win had a scoring error not occurred.

The yellow flag was brought out on lap 154 for a stalled race car in turn three. Nearly three laps passed before the NASCAR pace car picked up a leader — the Pontiac driven by Bob Riley, the only driver who did not make a pit stop.

Both Bobby and Earnhardt were placed a lap down by mistake and were never reinstated into the lead lap.

When the green flag waved after the final caution period of the day at Brooklyn, Mich., on June 17, there were nine cars in the lead lap battling for the win — including Bobby's Buick.

But Bill Elliott got a good jump on his fellow competitors and went on to win the 200-lap race. Bobby ultimately finished sixth.

On July 4 at Daytona International Speedway for the 400-mile event, Bobby was able to see a friend he had met the previous November — President Ronald Reagan.

Bobby posted a strong run, but had to settle for a fourth-place finish behind Petty (who scored his 200th career win), second place Harry Gant and third-place Yarborough. Yarborough had driven down pit road on the last lap, thinking the race was over. In fact, he and Petty had battled furiously to the start-finish line to begin the final caution period with just two laps left. Petty nipped Yarborough for the win. Had Yarborough not driven down pit road, he would have finished second instead of third.

Petty's win was especially disheartening for Bobby, as another Yates engine rolled into victory lane with his long-time rival.

To make matters worse, Yates was forced to go to the Curb transporter to retrieve the engine on July 3, as he had not been paid for that powerplant as well as any others that had been built and used.

Rather than cause a scene in the garage area, it was decided to let Petty use the engine.

Many questions were being asked by the team's sponsor as to where their money was being spent.

The corporate spies continued to ask questions about costs of various items. For example, Nelson was told to inform them a team show car cost $80,000, just in case anyone asked. In all actuality, the cost was closer to half that amount.

In efforts not to say the wrong thing to the wrong person at the wrong time, tremendous tension formed within the personalities of the team.

On July 14 at Nashville International Raceway, Elliott, Earnhardt, Bobby, Waltrip, Rudd, Ron Bouchard and Geoff Bodine led various times throughout the 420-lap event.

But it was Bodine who led the most laps in the Rick Hendrick-owned Chevrolet — a total of 327 laps and went on to score his second win of the year. Bobby managed a fifth-place finish.

After crashing in the opening laps at Pocono on July 22, Bobby was relegated to 28th with 128 laps to his credit.

Bobby scored another fourth-place finish at Talladega, Ala., on July 29. At the end, however, there were several positions determined by photo finish, including Bobby's, as race winner Earnhardt had to hold off a ten-car lead draft when the field took the white flag to signal one lap remaining.

Waltrip scored a victory at Brooklyn, Mich., when race leader Elliott fell off the pace. He was out of fuel with only seven laps remaining.

Bobby's Buick was never a factor in the race and finished a disappointing 11th, two laps back.

Labonte returned to victory lane at Bristol on Aug. 25 after crashing his Chevrolet twice.

But to secure the win on the final lap, Labonte held off Bobby by 1.44 seconds as the two cars crossed the line.

For the first time in the history of NASCAR racing, the Southern 500 was held at Darlington, S.C., on Sunday instead of the traditional Labor Day Monday.

Bobby limped home 10th, due to near-terminal engine problems, behind winner Harry Gant, who started from the pole and led 277 of the 367 scheduled laps.

But the top-10 finish did move the DiGard team into fifth in the point standings — but only briefly.

A 25th-place finish at Richmond Fairgrounds Raceway on Sept. 9 dropped Bobby back to eighth place in points. Again, the cause was engine problems.

The race at Dover added more disappointment in the form of injury.

As Bobby drove through the third turn on lap 120 of the 500-lap event, a tire sent him out of control, forcing a hard crash into the fourth-turn wall. The result was a broken collarbone and cracked right shoulder blade.

After being checked in the infield care center, he was transported to the Dover, Del. hospital. The doctor checked Bobby and made plans for the following day.

"I have you scheduled for surgery tomorrow to repair the break in your shoulder," the doctor said in a matter-of-fact tone of voice.

"We'll get started first thing in the morning."

"I don't think so," Bobby said. "I'm going back to Hueytown. I'll take care of my shoulder there."

"How do you plan to travel?" the doctor asked.

"I'm going to fly," Bobby said.

"You can't fly," the doctor said. "You've got a bruised lung and it will never stand the pressure of high altitude."

"I'll take my chances," Bobby said, and checked himself out of the hospital.

Once in the air, the physician's prediction came true. Soon, Bobby found himself in great pain and only able to muster a voice just over a whisper.

"Take this thing down a bit," Bobby said, pointing in that direction with his right index finger.

"We can't take it down," said the pilot. "If we do, we won't have enough fuel to get home."

"We can buy more fuel," Bobby said painfully. "Take it down."

Soon, the aircraft was landed in Knoxville, Tenn. for re-fueling.

Even though he continued to nurse his injuries and had his right arm secured in a sling, Bobby boarded his Aerostar and prepared to fly to Martinsville, Va., for the Sept. 23 event there.

Flying alone, he concluded the preflight checks and took off.

But to fly the aircraft was no easy task, as most all of the functions had to be made with his left arm. Soon, the airplane's wheels left the ground and Bobby was airborne.

About 20 minutes into the flight, the warning lights flashed and buzzers sounded, indicating a problem with the right engine.

Bobby quickly turned around and headed southwest back to Bessemer Airport.

To have an engine shut down would not cause great concern to an experienced pilot who had the capability to use both arms. But having a severe shoulder injury meant landing the plane was going to be slightly difficult.

The wheels of the plane finally touched the ground abruptly but remained steady and straight, allowing Bobby to complete the landing successfully

Inspection indicated a faulty turbo, but repairs were completed in about 30 minutes. Soon, he returned to the air and was en route to Martinsville Speedway.

Prior to race time, an agreement was made with short-track veteran Butch Lindley to act as relief driver for Bobby after the first lap of the race was completed.

Bobby pulled to a stop and was quickly assisted out of the DiGard Buick as Lindley slid behind the wheel. A total of 185 laps was completed before rear end problems forced Lindley to finish 23rd behind race winner Waltrip.

Continuing to nurse his shoulder injury, Bobby completed 332 of 334 laps at Charlotte Motor Speedway on Oct. 7 and managed to log a 10th-place finish behind Elliott.

Meanwhile, the bills were still being forwarded to the team's sponsor — Miller Brewing Co. — in Milwaukee, Wis. Many unpaid bills found their way to Nelson's desk, too, and several times, such necessities as reservations for lodging would be turned down because of delinquent Digard Racing Co., bills still in the hotel's possession.

Being placed in a desperate situation, Nelson often would use his own personal charge card to secure rooms, only to have a past due notice for the bill come to his home after the receipts had been turned in.

All the while, the sponsor continued to pump thousands and thousands of dollars into the team, but no one knew exactly where the money was going.

Payroll checks were being cut much later than expected, including those for Bobby and Nelson.

Yet, that same month, Bill Gardner announced plans to build an elaborate industrial park, shops, and even a test track near the team's headquarters in Charlotte. Everything in the complex was to be state-of-the-art.

Even with uncertainty all around it, the team was legally bound to perform to its utmost.

Bobby led much of the event at North Wilkesboro on Oct. 14, but was passed by Waltrip on lap 269 and later was passed by Gant for second. Still, he was able to hold the third position in the final finishing order.

During a Sportsman race at Rockingham, N.C., on Oct. 19, Bobby reinjured his shoulder and called upon Bonnett to compete in the Winston Cup race the following day. Bonnett parked his Junior Johnson-owned Chevrolet on lap 169 after a crash and immediately went to Bobby's pit to offer relief. The result was a fifth place, one lap down to race winner Elliott, who edged Gant for the win.

Bobby returned at Atlanta, Ga., on Nov. 11 to finish fifth behind Earnhardt. Tragedy struck when rookie driver Terry Schoonover lost his life in a single-car accident on lap 122.

At the race's conclusion, it was determined the Winston Cup championship would come down to Labonte and Gant at Riverside, Calif. Neither driver finished at Atlanta due to mechanical problems, which left Labonte in the lead by 42 points.

Once at Riverside on Nov. 18, Bobby finished the year with a seventh-place finish behind race winner Bodine.

Labonte finished third, while Gant came home eighth, thus granting Labonte with his first Winston Cup championship by 65 points.

Bobby had hoped to successfully defend his title, but the many engine and mechanical problems dropped him from contention early in the season.

The prospects of winning races in 1985 looked very bleak and Bobby wasn't getting younger. With the level of competition increasing with each passing year, sponsors were paying closer attention to the statistics and performance charts.

His career was in deep trouble at the expense of mismanagement by someone he was legally bound to serve.

CHAPTER TWENTY-THREE
End Of The Nightmare

Bobby didn't want to admit to himself what he was feeling, but there was no escape from reality.

He may have hurt his career by staying with a team with suspicious management practices. He knew as much when he placed his name on the renewal contract. Several problems had surfaced during the first 18 months of the original contract.

Much had changed since those early days of 1982. The DiGard Racing Co. had become diseased right before his eyes. Now, it was like terminal cancer. It was slow, painful and uncertain.

Bobby had hoped for a multi-championship team such as what was experienced by Cale Yarborough and Junior Johnson in 1976, '77 and '78. But there was nothing he could do about rebuilding the team, and quite honestly, he wasn't sure he wanted to.

Lack of communication and financial problems at an all-time high were being talked about by those outside the team.

The enthusiasm of the championship year had been replaced with dissension and arguing among crew members. There was also a shortage of adequate parts. It was not the first time problems surfaced within the team. But this time, the future of the organization looked bleak.

"The team had simply disbanded as a unit. They were still on the payroll and employees of the business, but they no longer acted as a team. Gary Nelson seemed to want to go in another direction career-wise and so did Robert Yates. Pretty soon there was little effort toward

making and keeping the team successful.

"As a result of all that, I felt I was not being supported adequately by those who once would have put up with all of the uncertainty Bill Gardner kept brewing within the team.

"The championship had been won and every person on the team had lost that desire to win and be competitive. Their own personal objectives were now in the forefront."

Having signed the three-year extension the past July while at Daytona International Speedway, Bobby was subject to driving anything Gardner provided for him, regardless if his equipment was capable of winning.

To dissolve the contract was virtually impossible, as the stipulations for Bobby's employ were being met — barely.

But there were other surprises for Bobby to negotiate as well.

As he stepped through the gate at Daytona to start the season, Nelson approached him in the garage area.

"Bobby, I'd like for you to meet Paul Giltinan, a chassis engineer who has just joined the team," Nelson said. "He'll be in charge of our chassis setups this season."

"When did all this come about?" Bobby asked inquisitively

"Just yesterday," Nelson said. "Bill (Gardner) hired him. And he also hired Robin Pemberton. You know Robin, don't you? He worked for the Pettys last season. He's now your crew chief."

Once again, it was another poorly conceived, last-minute plan from upper management at DiGard.

Bobby had nothing against either Giltinan or Pemberton. But Nelson had been his crew chief since February 1982 and working with two new faces would take some adjusting.

"What's your function going to be with the team?" Bobby asked Nelson.

"I'm just going to be in the background a bit from now on," answered Nelson. "Bill has some special things he wants me to work on."

As Bobby expected, the entire 10-day session at Daytona International Speedway was a nightmare. There were mediocre performances during qualifying and races during Speed Weeks and then in the Daytona 500, he dropped out of the race with a faulty clutch on lap 82 and finished 33rd.

At Richmond, Va., on Feb. 24, the car was not up to capability and that forced a 16th-place finish. Bobby qualified fifth and led laps 111-117, but there was nothing more to his day.

As he changed out of his driver's uniform, he knew it would be a long season.

After only 262 of 492 laps at Rockingham, N.C., on March 3, Bobby's Buick lost another clutch, sending him back to 31st in the final finishing order.

Nelson had busied himself with a research and development program and also helped Pemberton at the race track. But still, Bobby could see a need to have Nelson in command once again on a full-time basis. In his eyes, the best research and development program could be done from the race car under him and not with a separate vehicle.

There was hope that a return to strength was forthcoming at Atlanta International Raceway on March 17, as a fifth-place finish was recorded there. But Bobby struggled all day with an ill-handling chassis and led only two laps under caution.

With a 13th at Bristol, Tenn., on April 6, Bobby considered himself a lucky man. Just past the halfway point, the steering wheel came off in his hands while at speed on the backstretch and for several hundred yards, he miraculously steered by placing his hands around the steering column's splines.

Once the car was brought to a halt on the track apron, Phil Parsons, then watching the race from the sidelines after the engine in his Chevrolet blew, retrieved the steering wheel from his car and handed it to Bobby.

Many of the crew members felt the steering wheel incident was just further proof of the bad equipment with which they were having to work.

There was a 10th at Darlington, S.C., on April 14 to mark a somewhat stimulating finish. Elliott continued to dominate the superspeedways with a win there. He would be hard to beat for the championship, even under the best conditions.

The DiGard short-track program was encouraging with a third-place finish at North Wilkesboro, N.C., on April 21 and a fourth at Martinsville, Va., on April 28.

At Talladega, Ala., on May 5, Elliott placed himself closer to the Winston Million bonus, given to a driver who could win three of four selected races — the Daytona 500, the Winston 500, the Coca-Cola 600 and the Southern 500 — in a single season. His victory was highlighted by an astonishing comeback, with which he made up two lost laps without the aid of a caution flag.

Bobby finished fourth to post his best superspeedway finish of the year.

The highlight of Bobby's weekend came while watching Davey drive a Buick Regal to victory in an ARCA event on May 4.

At Dover, Del., on May 19, Elliott was victorious again. But Bobby could only muster a 13th-place finish. No matter what the crew did to the team's cars, they simply would not perform consistently.

In order to successfully combat the powerhouse organizations such as Elliott's Melling Racing team or Earnhardt's RCR Enterprises team, new equipment was desperately needed. But with bills continuing to go unpaid by DiGard's management, there were no funds to make improvements. More accurately, there were no funds being spent for what the team had already used. Many speculated Gardner was using funds provided by Miller Brewing Co. to fund several of his businesses.

Nonetheless, Bobby was able to score a third-place finish at Charlotte Motor Speedway on May 26 in the World 600 and joined race winner Darrell Waltrip and second place Harry Gant as the only three drivers to finish in the lead lap.

At Riverside, Calif., on June 2, Bobby looked to be in line for his first victory of the year. But with only 16 laps to go, Terry Labonte passed him, as did Harry Gant, dropping Allison back to third.

The top-five finishes were returning. But confrontations among the team members were at an all-time high.

It was Gardner's usual manner to speak with his department heads, Allison, Nelson and engine builder Yates, individually, as not to have witnesses to what may or may not be said. With such a tactic, key players were pitted one against the other with no concrete policy on any given subject.

But prior to the June 5 Winston Cup race at Pocono, Pa., Gardner met with them as a group to discuss the team's situation.

In the meeting, Bobby quit as the team's driver, citing numerous obvious problems within the organization. Legally, he could not leave. Had he attempted to walk away, Gardner might well have enforced a contract buyout, as Waltrip was required to do at the end of the 1980 season.

Upon hearing Bobby express his desire to leave, Gardner quickly attempted to smooth the situation and allowed Bobby the right to return to setting up his own chassis, thus firing Giltinan.

Gardner also instructed Nelson to field a car from his research and development stable in order to find and correct the problems within his original team.

He didn't know it at the time, but Gardner had placed a hangman's noose around his own neck and never saw the rope pass before his eyes.

Bobby competed in the race at Pocono and finished ninth, two laps behind race winner Elliott, who continued his hot streak.

There was also a sixth-place finish at Brooklyn, Mich., on June 16 behind Elliott once again, who was seven for nine on the superspeedways after 14 races were completed.

The break Bobby had longed for came at Daytona Beach, Fla., on July 4.

Nelson busied himself with the research and development team, referred to as Gardner Racing Co., based in the small, but adequate, shop maintained by independent driver Greg Sacks in Welcome, N.C.

Sacks had purchased two Chevrolet Monte Carlos from Harry Ranier Racing when its driver, Yarborough, felt Fords would perform better on the superspeedways. The car in Sacks' possession was the car Yarborough drove to victory in the 1984 Daytona 500.

With Nelson's expertise and the funds to buy winning equipment, the car's chassis received the parts it needed to run competitively.

Sacks had Giltinan set up the chassis but it wouldn't handle until Bobby said, "Copy mine." Then, the car became a force to contend with. The Manituck, N.Y., native qualified ninth, while Bobby continued to struggle with the team's main entry, starting from the 27th position.

When he fired his engine, it seemed to run well at that point. But early in the race, it began to miss. Bobby drove directly to the garage area where he had one one of the mechanics remove the valve covers on the engine and immediately saw the problem. A lock nut had been left off a rocker arm adjuster and this allowed the adjustment on that valve to become loose. When Bobby saw that, he was convinced Gardner had gotten someone to loosen that nut which convinced him he should leave Digard Racing, Co. right then.

Sacks led on three occasions for 33 laps and scored a major upset victory. Bobby did not lead a lap and finished a dismal 18th.

But Bobby was content with the day's events. The moment Sacks took the green flag, Bobby's contract with Gardner was officially null and void. Running a second car was expressly forbidden in his contract and Gardner had done just that with Sacks.

Bobby quickly consulted his lawyers as well as a judge. By 10 a.m. on July 6, he was no longer obligated to Gardner in any way.

"The situation at DiGard was a miserable one in the latter years. I was constantly having to go to Bill Gardner to get paid for what he owed me. He was constantly working out deals with me behind the scenes.

"When the situation happened at Daytona, I was lucky to make the race and here's Sacks with a car much better than the one under me. I felt I was treated very unfairly in the deal. That proved to me that with the right equipment, the team could win. As it turned out, I happened to be the driver in the wrong equipment and saw Gardner's fielding of two cars as my way out. Had that not occurred, I could have easily had to fulfill the entire contract through 1987. I didn't see much way around it."

Finally, the nightmare was over. He would do what he had done so many times in the past — field his own equipment out of his Hueytown shops.

By 2 p.m. on July 6, Miller Brewing Co. contacted Allison and offered sponsorship for the remainder of the season. Further, permission was granted by Gardner to run the No. 22 on the roof and doors of Bobby's cars since a major promotion by the brewery centered on the number. Many speculated pressure was applied by the sponsor, who also continued to sponsor Sacks. Sacks became Bobby's replacement as DiGard's driver. Beginning with the event at Pocono, Pa., on July 19, DiGard's number became 77.

Bobby was a bit concerned about being back in business for himself. But at least he was in a professional circumstance once again.

A team was quickly assembled and a Buick was readied out of the family shop in Hueytown.

Once qualifying began at Pocono, Bobby circled the triangular speedway and took the 23rd starting spot.

Two days later, Elliott scored yet another victory while Bobby finished 12th, two laps off the pace. Still, it was not a bad finish for a team that had to be constructed virtually overnight.

But the return trip to Talladega, Ala., proved to be a disappointing effort. After qualifying a Chevrolet 38th in the 42-car field, Bobby logged a 27th-place finish, two laps in arrears to Yarborough, who had been struggling to get the new Fords on track.

Again, Davey brought Bobby great joy, this time with his first NASCAR Winston Cup start. Wheeling a Hoss Ellington Chevrolet, the 24-year-old driver finished a strong 10th.

At Michigan International Speedway on Aug. 11, Bobby wheeled a Ford Thunderbird but crashed on lap 85 of the 200-lap event and finished 36th in the 40-car field.

Another crash occurred on Aug. 24 at Bristol and an engine was lost at Darlington on Sept. 1, resulting in 22nd and 30th-place finishes, respectively. In those races, Earnhardt mastered Bristol, while Elliott drove his Ford to victory and captured the Winston Million bonus at Darlington.

On Sept. 8, Bobby crashed his Buick at Richmond Fairgrounds Raceway after 222 of 400 laps. The cause of the crash was a blown right-front tire, which happened as he exited turn two. It produced a 28th-place finish.

But because of the Richmond crash, an introduction was made that later proved to be valuable to Bobby.

The bright spot of the season came at Dover on Sept. 15, as Bobby finished a strong fourth behind eventual winner Gant, second-place Waltrip and third-place Rudd.

Bobby's Ford performed flawlessly and gave everyone on the team hope of a possible victory before season's end.

Earnhardt scored his fourth victory of the year at Martinsville on Sept. 22, while Bobby settled for 10th in a Buick rented from Stavola Brothers Racing. The rental was required as Bobby's short-track car had been damaged so severely at Richmond.

But at North Wilkesboro, the bad luck returned. Again in the Stavola Buick, Bobby only completed 36 of the 400 scheduled laps when his engine erupted, causing a last-place finish.

Gant again was victorious at the 0.625-mile Wilkes County track.

A return to Charlotte for the 500-mile event there produced a 14th-place finish behind Yarborough's Ranier Racing Ford.

With North Carolina Motor Speedway in Rockingham, N.C., just over a mile in length, Bobby felt the Stavola Buick would perform well. He once again decided to rent the car.

But a broken rear end forced another 38th-place finish.

Waltrip was victorious again and was staging yet another championship run. The title would be determined in the final race at Riverside, Calif.

Having been credited with 305 of the 328 laps that made up the 500-mile race at Atlanta International Raceway on Nov. 3, Bobby wheeled the Stavola Buick to a disappointing 26th-place finish.

Still, plans for 1986 called for Bobby's services to be provided to a team which had yet to be formed. The deal included an excellent sponsorship package. High-level meetings took place and ground for a shop was broken.

News of the operation was kept surprisingly quiet. Bobby was a key factor in the creation of the new entity.

As a result, Bobby's spirits were high when he thought of his future. Only one race remained to be completed to end the season and as far as Bobby was concerned, it could not come quickly enough.

Once at Riverside for the season finale on Nov. 17, Bobby walked away with a 17th-place finish, again with Stavola Racing.

Many people looked at Bobby's accomplishments for the year as nothing short of miraculous, considering the obstacles. He had answered a tough challenge with the cards stacked heavily against him.

Waltrip captured his third career championship, besting Elliott by only 20 points after the Dawsonville, Ga., driver experienced transmission problems at Riverside.

Bobby left Riverside knowing he had an excellent chance at scoring his second career championship in 1986.

After all, he was joining car owners who were serious racers with an unlimited financial arrangement. There was written proof the bills would be paid and their word would be rock solid.

Two months would pass before the steel beams and sheet metal for the new Winston Cup shop would begin to take shape. Bobby stood with his car owners, with shovel in hand, awaiting the press and photographers to arrive for the announcement. There was new ground to be broken.

CHAPTER TWENTY-FOUR
Two Drivers, Two Cars

Once in the Florida sun, the rays began to feel good on Bobby's face. The problems of the past year were far behind him and his outlook for the future was optimistic.

Sitting on the back of the Stavola Brothers Racing transporter, Bobby recalled a conversation that had taken place during the latter part of the 1985 season. Had that meeting not transpired, his NASCAR Winston Cup career would have been severely jeopardized.

While at Charlotte Motor Speedway for the 500-mile event in October of 1985, Bobby had been summoned by Bill and Mickey Stavola's public relations representative, Ed Brasefield. The two men with interests in aggregates and various real estate holdings in New Jersey wanted to offer Bobby a job with their race team for the 1986 Winston Cup season.

With his own equipment in very poor condition due to blown engines and accidents, Bobby had driven some of the Stavola cars almost out of necessity. At times, his efforts were impressive.

In 1985, the Stavolas purchased the fledgling race team owned by Bobby Hillin, a Texas native whose father was once heavily involved in Indy Car racing.

Before going with Stavola Racing, Hillin made some favorable impressions, showing he had talent, which was nurtured under the guidance of noted crew chief Harry Hyde.

Bobby entered through the front doors of the Stavola shops and sat in one of the smaller offices at Stavola Brothers Racing. The others would soon be arriving.

Soon, both Stavola brothers, along with Hillin and crew chief Ron Pureyear, entered the room and took a seat.

"As you all know, Bobby Allison is joining us for the 1986 season," Bill Stavola said. "We will eventually build an additional shop to house that operation but for now, we will make the necessary adjustments here.

"We are assembled to discuss our strategy for the season."

"Well, Bill," Bobby interrupted. "I think the best thing for us to do would be to put young Bobby (Hillin) in an ARCA (Automobile Racing Club of America) car and I will work with him and guide him and . . ."

Bill Stavola looked up from the paperwork he was reading and caught Bobby's eye.

"Bobby Hillin is our Winston Cup driver," Bill Stavola said. "You can drive for us, too, if you want to,"

Bobby quickly extended an apology to Hillin, which was graciously accepted. He sat quietly; a bit sheepish.

"What we have here are two equal teams with adequate sponsorship to back them," Bill Stavola said. "I trust both teams will work with one another to get one — or hopefully both — into victory lane."

Those in attendance openly agreed with the arrangement. The trouble was, most two-car operations were rarely equal in performance. One car usually fell behind the other, due in part to the fact one team usually received stronger, higher-quality parts than the other.

Many other points were covered during the two-hour meeting. But once it was adjourned, each person in the room dedicated himself to strong consistent performances. There was a round of handshakes.

As Bobby left the office and sat in his car, the thought of going to a two-car team would certainly raise questions from the media. After all, for many years he strongly and openly disagreed with a two-car situation and refused to have any part of one.

Bobby's mind returned to the sandwich and soft drink in his hands. Soon the sound of race engines, firing in the garage area, filled the air.

For the first time in decades of racing at Daytona, everyone was confused — and it had nothing to do with rules of competition. People were having a difficult time with the new division names NASCAR had assigned during the winter.

The Winston Cup Grand National division, NASCAR's elite

group, was now being referred to solely as the Winston Cup division after the cigarette brand, while the former Late Model Sportsman division was given the title of Busch Grand National Series, as it was sponsored by Anheuser-Busch, the prominent beer company.

It caused some head-scratching for the fans as well as the media — who were simply not geared to use product names in their material.

A prime example of the situation was the newspaper Grand National Scene, which covered primarily NASCAR's elite division. But with the name, readers were misled as to the paper's content. "Grand National" now referred to what was once known as "Late Model Sportsman." Even so, nearly two years would pass before the paper's name was changed to Winston Cup Scene.

At Daytona, what wasn't immediately obvious in the competition was the equality of the teams.

In the Daytona 500 of Feb. 16, Hillin drove his Buick to a fourth-place finish behind race winner Geoff Bodine, second-place Terry Labonte and third-place Darrell Waltrip, in the same lap with the leaders.

Bobby, however, didn't fare as well. His Buick fell by the wayside with a blown engine after only 21 laps, which dictated a last-place finish.

On Feb. 23, both Bobby and Hillin did well in a race that left two of the sport's most famous drivers feuding at the end.

Bobby drove through a track full of debris to a fourth-place finish after both Waltrip and Dale Earnhardt crashed on the back stretch during the last lap of the 400-lap event at Richmond, Va.

With Waltrip in the lead and Earnhardt trailing, Earnhardt's left front fender made contact with Waltrip's right rear, sending Waltrip hard into the wall.

Waltrip retaliated by slamming into Earnhardt in the first turn after both had crossed under the white flag.

While the two drivers were expressing their dislike for one another, Kyle Petty snaked his way through and took the Wood Brothers Ford to his first career victory.

Earnhardt was initially fined $5,000 by NASCAR and placed on a one-year probation. After appeal, however, the fine was reduced to $3,000 and the probation period was dropped.

At Atlanta International Speedway on March 16, Bobby finished ninth in the 42-car field, one lap down to longtime short-track veteran Morgan Shepherd, who scored an upset victory in an unsponsored car.

On April 6, Bobby found himself one lap down to Rusty Wallace in the 500-lap event at Bristol, Tenn.

There were good finishes in the early part of the season. But Bobby felt there could be more improvement as he and the team became more accustomed to one another. Under crew chief Jimmy Fennig's direction, the team could be a contender.

More proof of the team's strength came at Darlington, S.C., on April 13. There, Bobby was able to secure a third-place finish behind Earnhardt and Waltrip, even though a lap down at the end.

A sixth and an eighth at the next two short-track events at North Wilkesboro, N. C., and Martinsville, Va., prompted some members of the media to look upon Bobby as a driver with an outside shot at the Winston Cup title.

Once at Talladega, Ala., on May 4, there was no doubt.

Bobby logged his first victory in two years after outlasting Bill Elliott's Ford and outdistancing Earnhardt.

In the closing laps, Bobby had all four tires on the Stavola Racing Buick smoking as he sailed around the 2.66-mile Alabama International Motor Speedway.

Elliott had the race well under his command and led a total of 116 of the 188 laps. But a blown engine sent him to the sidelines with only 13 laps remaining.

With Bobby in the lead, Ron Bouchard, Earnhardt and Buddy Baker challenged hard for the point.

On the final lap, Earnhardt pushed his Richard Childress Racing Chevrolet out front by a few inches. But Bobby answered the challenge and took the lead away by driving around Earnhardt on the outside groove. He went on to win by 0.19-second.

"It's been a little too long for me," Bobby said from victory lane. "I've had a habit of letting things slip out of my grasp. I may be over the hill, but I'm enjoying what I'm doing."

Bobby was referring to his age, 47, which made him the oldest driver to win a Winston Cup event at the time.

The win, the first for Stavola Brothers Racing, consisted of a field where all participants qualified at over 200 mph.

Coming off the victory, his first since the 1984 World 600 at Charlotte Motor Speedway, Bobby gave a stellar performance at Dover, Del., on May 18 but fell just short to Geoff Bodine, who led the final 44 laps for the win.

Since the start of the season, Hillin had driven the other Stavola entry to three top-five finishes and three top-10s. Still, the issue of equality was not settled. Bobby's experience was far greater than Hillin's, which counted for some of the more impressive runs. Also, wrecks and mechanical failures had played a part in Hillin's record.

But thereafter, Bobby's finishes were not as impressive as they had been earlier.

He scored a 12th at Charlotte on May 25, a 13th at Long Pond, Pa., on June 18, an 11th at Brooklyn, Mich., and a 15th at Daytona Beach, Fla., on July 4.

On July 20, however, a fifth-place finish came upon the return trip to Pocono International Raceway in Long Pond, which eased some of the disappointment.

The tables seemed to turn a bit on the return to Talladega on July 27.

Hillin claimed his first career Winston Cup victory after holding off eight other cars in the lead lap by inches as they crossed the finish line. Some racing historians debated whether Hillin, 22, was the youngest winner of a Winston Cup event.

Bobby did not do nearly as well.

During the final lap of the race, Sterling Marlin hooked Bobby's bumper, which sent both competitors into the first-turn wall, along with Rick Wilson and Jim Sauter.

After going out of control, Bobby's Buick slammed hard against the outside concrete barrier and came to rest at the bottom of the apron.

The car was destroyed, but Bobby was not injured.

The final standings showed Bobby in 10th position, just three back from his son Davey, who had driven the Junior Johnson Chevrolet in place of Neil Bonnett, who had suffered a cracked collar bone and broken rib at Long Pond the week before.

Another string of mediocre finishes plagued Bobby through the better part of August. There was a 12th-place finish at Watkins Glen, N.Y., on Aug. 10, a 24th at Brooklyn, Mich., on Aug. 17, an eighth at Bristol, Tenn., on Aug. 23.

With six laps remaining in the Southern 500 at Darlington on Aug. 31, Bobby managed to take second place after Elliott hit the fourth-turn wall. But his Buick was not quite strong enough to overcome a 2.0-second lead held by eventual winner Tim Richmond, a winner for the fifth time during the season.

Bobby scored an eighth-place at Richmond on Sept. 7, but was forced to settle for 20th at Dover on Sept. 14. Tire and chassis problems plagued the team throughout the grueling 500-lap race at the one-mile facility that is often a test of endurance for the drivers.

More chassis problems bit the team at Martinsville on Sept. 21 and forced a 21st-place finish, followed by a 22nd-place finish at North Wilkesboro due to a broken axle.

At Charlotte on Oct. 5, the weekend could have been the worst of the year for the entire team.

Two broken A-frames on the right front of the Stavola Buick sent Bobby hard into the third-turn wall, ending his day after only 33 of 334 laps.

A blown engine left Bobby on the sidelines at North Carolina Motor Speedway in Rockingham, N.C., on Oct. 19, resulting in a 25th-place finish.

At Atlanta on Nov. 2, Bobby managed a 16th-place finish, four laps down to eventual winner Earnhardt, who captured his second Winston Cup title.

In the final race of the year, Bobby finished seventh at Riverside, Calif., which gave him a seventh-place finish in the final point standings.

The two-car operation didn't seem to be working as well as Bobby had hoped. He saw room for improvement in 1987 and was determined to address those concerns, beginning with off-season testing.

CHAPTER TWENTY-FIVE
And Now, It's Davey's Turn

At the start of the 1987 NASCAR Winston Cup season, Bobby found himself having mixed emotions over a situation very close to home.

Over the previous winter, there had been a great deal of speculation over the driver who would fill the vacancy on the team co-owned by Harry Ranier and J.T. Lundy.

Their driver, Cale Yarborough, announced at the end of the 1986 season he would be leaving the operation to form his own team.

Unknown to Bobby at the time, his aspiring and determined son Davey had his eye on the job.

By late fall, the ride was still open. Davey had countless short-track races to his credit. After three Winston Cup events with car owner Hoss Ellington in 1985 and a struggle with very limited sponsorship, Davey contacted Ranier and tossed his name into the hat.

Bobby had driven for Ranier in 1981 and during that year, Davey positioned himself as closely as he could in and around his father's race car in hopes of gaining every bit of information possible in an effort to further his Winston Cup aspirations.

On occasion, Ranier would take the younger Allison aside and ask him if he was ready for Winston Cup racing. The conversation would usually end with Davey saying no, and Ranier would agree. But Davey would always end the conversation with, "It won't be long."

A few years passed and Davey found himself enjoying several short-track victories around the Southeastern United States, due in no small part to a group of young helpers known as "The Peachfuzz Gang."

But the Winston Cup event at Talladega, Ala., on July 27, 1986 had made a great difference. It was the race in which Davey wheeled a Junior Johnson Chevrolet to a seventh-place finish in relief for an injured Neil Bonnett.

The stellar finish gave Davey something positive for his Winston Cup portfolio.

Many drivers dreamed of having the Ranier-Lundy job and during those months of uncertainty, the team's phone rang off the hook. Each applicant had a story to tell.

At the end of August, Davey called Ranier and asked to see him. A meeting was arranged within a few days.

This time, Ranier was convinced Davey was ready and an agreement was signed that day.

Immediately, Davey went back to Hueytown and met with his Dad.

"I've got the ride with Harry Ranier for next season," Davey said in between grins, as he was on Cloud Nine.

Bobby did not speak for a moment. Instead, extended a hand of congratulations. His eyes told how proud he was of his son.

"Davey, I really think you should finish the Busch Series races you've arranged," Bobby said. "After the season is completed, I think you should leave Bobby Allison Racing."

Davey agreed, since he knew the finances his Dad had with which to pay his employees was limited. At the time, the younger Allison had drawn a paycheck of $250 a week and even though his house payment was $500 a month, there were months when the bills were juggled a bit.

But those problems seemed to be in the past. Knowing he would join a first class ride at the Daytona 500 kept Davey's adrenaline pumping.

"Davey, I've got to tell you, I've got mixed emotions about the situation," Bobby said. "I'm not disappointed that you've got the ride. But there are certain situations that I went through. I just want you to keep your eyes open to that and be careful."

Davey knew what his father was referring to, as he had been around when Bobby had to deal with various personalities associated with the team. Being an outsider, Davey could look at those incidents from a different perspective.

After only a few minutes of talking, Bobby found himself overwhelmed with joy and excitement for his son.

At the Southern 500 at Darlington in September of 1986, the announcement of Davey's new assignment was made to the media. With the departure of Waddell Wilson, Joey Knuckles was hired as crew chief for the team.

Davey considered Knuckles a plus, as the two had grown up together and often played touch football in the infield of speedways as children.

When the 1987 season opened, Bobby was just a few stalls away from his son in the garage area at Daytona International Speedway. At times, he saw Davey climbing in and out of a sleek white, black and gold Ford Thunderbird. Bobby often found himself clicking the stopwatch on his son's efforts.

Davey knew the importance of performance and became the first rookie driver in the history of the Daytona 500 to start on the outside front row. He was beaten for the pole position by Bill Elliott, who posted a speed of 210.364 mph.

Bobby was busy helping fine-tune the efforts of Stavola Brothers Racing, but was outqualified by his son by four positions.

Neither of the Allisons led any of the 500 held on Feb. 15. But even though Davey found himself down several laps after losing a right-rear tire after a pit stop, he placed his Ford at the head of the field in an attempt to make up lost ground. He impressed the racing fraternity right away.

Bobby managed a third-place finish, while Davey settled for 27th.

Bobby struggled a bit at Rockingham. N.C., on March 1. Due to a chassis problem, he found himself six laps down to Dale Earnhardt at the checkered flag.

There was some pleasure gained in the fact Davey had won the pole at 146.989 mph and led the first 29 laps.

Earnhardt set the stage for the year early by winning again at Richmond, Va., after severely crashing his car in practice the day before the race.

Rather than return to the Midway, N.C., shop for another car, the Richard Childress team took the car to a local repair shop and miraculously rebuilt the battered machine.

Even so, Bobby's efforts gave him a ninth-place finish, one lap down at the end.

The chassis problems continued at Atlanta on March 15. There, Bobby could salvage only a 19th-place finish in the 41-car field, eight laps behind race winner Ricky Rudd, in the Bud Moore Ford.

Davey had driven unsponsored cars to that point in the season, but at Atlanta he carried the logos of Texaco to a fifth-place finish.

At Darlington, S.C., on March 29, Bobby received one of the worst scares of his career.

Davey spun his Ford in the third turn of the 1.366-mile speedway and was hit by his father's Buick.

Immediately, Davey's Ford broke through the guardrail at the bottom of the turn with the impact splitting the fuel cell. The car was suddenly engulfed in flames.

Bobby watched in horror from his rearview mirror. Before his car actually came to a halt, Bobby had dropped the screen net and was on foot, racing back to his son's burning machine.

Davey escaped unhurt and was talking with rescue workers when he was met by his Dad. For a long moment, the eyes of the two men met. Bobby wanted to say something but the words wouldn't come, as he was clearly concerned for his son's safety. Finally, some words broke through.

"I'm OK," Davey said, standing closely to his father. "Are you OK?"

Bobby could only offer a nod of his head, as seeing his son's smile sent a sigh of relief over him.

There was a 14th-place finish at North Wilkesboro, N.C., on April 5, a 23rd at Bristol, Tenn., on April 12 due to a crash and an eighth at Martinsville, Va., on April 26. Except for the third-place finish at Daytona, it had been a lackluster year to that point for Bobby.

At Talladega, Ala., on May 5, Bobby's performance in qualifying improved dramatically, as he found himself on the outside front row.

But before the 178-lap event at the 2.66-mile speedway came to an end, the day would have its terrifying, and satisfying, moments.

On lap 21, Bobby found himself in close company at the front of the field as he exited the fourth turn onto the front chute.

Without warning, his right rear tire exploded, sending his Buick airborne into the catch fence separating the track from a packed grandstand.

As his car began a series of spins in the air, the catch fence was caught by the rear of Bobby's car and dragged across the race track for several hundred yards.

Debris from the car as well as the bent and twisted fence posts covered the track, sending cars behind them spinning wildly to avoid Bobby's Buick, which had come to rest in the center of the racing surface.

A couple of spectators suffered incidents in the frightening crash.

James Townes of Union City, Tenn., suffered an eye injury and was treated at Eye Foundation Hospital in Birmingham, Ala. Kenneth Goldman was treated for a wound in his chest. At least three others were treated trackside and released.

The race was red-flagged for two hours, 38 minutes and 14 seconds for repairs to the catch fence.

Bobby had initially decided to return to Hueytown after the crash, but at Judy's request, they both stayed to support Davey. He was running well and appeared to have a chance at victory.

Once the event was given the green flag again, Davey truly was the class of the field and led 101 of the scheduled 188 laps, which was cut by 10 laps due to impending darkness.

At the checkered flag, he finished a scant 0.78-second ahead of Terry Labonte, Kyle Petty, Earnhardt and Bobby Hillin.

"When I looked up in the mirror and saw Dad going into the fence, it was an emotional low period of my life," Davey said. "I saw him head for the grandstand. I though he was going into it. When I saw him crawl out of the car, it lifted my heart back up to where it's supposed to be."

Both Bobby and Davey suffered blown engines in the 600-mile event at Charlotte Motor Speedway on May 24 and were obviously no match for the pace Kyle Petty set.

Bobby finished 22nd and was bettered by Davey by six positions.

On May 31, however, the Allisons staged a stellar battle between one another at Dover, Del.

For over 300 laps, the Allisons exchanged the lead and battled one another in close quarters until Bobby's engine expired on lap 359.

From there, Davey led all but two of the final 153 laps to log the second win of his career.

"It was a thrill to run with my Dad," Davey said. "I've learned a lot from him about this place. I've run some Sportsman races here and I've listened to what he's told me."

At Pocono International Raceway on June 14, Bobby finished sixth in the lead lap behind race winner Tim Richmond.

It was an emotional victory for the Ashland, Ohio native. For many months, Richmond had been sick with a mysterious disease, but he had been cleared by doctors to compete. He would later suffer the consequences of AIDS.

An eighth came at Riverside on June 21 for Bobby, again behind Richmond, who drove the Hendrick Motorsports Chevrolet around Phil Parsons with 10 laps remaining. The victory would be the last of Richmond's career.

A mechanical problem developed on Bobby's car at Michigan International Speedway on June 28, causing a disappointing 27th-place finish. But the 400-mile event at Daytona International Speedway, the next race, was much kinder.

With only two laps remaining, Bobby was able to muscle his way around Ken Schrader and then escape a terrible last-lap crash to get the win.

It was his 84th career victory.

For over most of the 160-lap event around the 2.5-mile high banked speedway, Bobby found himself a lap down. He restarted the race in 13th with five laps to go after a caution flag was displayed when Rick Wilson hit the wall four laps earlier. Unnoticed by virtually everyone in attendance was Bobby's move to the inside just ahead of the pack at the start-finish line in the race back to caution flag. Suddenly, he was once again on the lead lap.

Bobby led the pack out of turn four on the final lap. But Schrader's Ford spun out of control, taking the Chevrolet of Harry Gant with him.

Schrader's car made contact with Gant and slid over the racing surface on its roof. Schrader emerged from Junie Donlavey's Ford unhurt.

Bobby beat Buddy Baker to the finish line by 0.4-second.

"I think most of the crews realized we were back on the lead lap," Bobby said. "I saw my number wasn't on the scoreboard, but I knew where we stood. We were probably the only ones to change all four tires on the yellow flag pit stop. It made all the difference."

Another engine erupted and sent Bobby to the garage area at Brooklyn, Mich., in the next race. It resulted in a 27th-place finish.

At Talladega, Ala., on July 26, Davey came from behind and picked off his fellow drivers; stalking them down one by one. But he had to settle for second behind Elliott.

Upon arrival at Watkins Glen, N.Y., on Aug. 10, Davey tested his Ford and immediately consulted with his Dad. The son, not familiar with a road course, sought his father's knowledge.

After some consultations between the Allisons' pits, Davey finished a respectable 17th in the 40-car field.

Bobby, however, managed a ninth-place finish in the lead lap with winner Rusty Wallace in the Blue Max Racing Pontiac.

Earnhardt finished eighth and held a 473-point lead in the Winston Cup point standings.

Bobby logged a seventh at Brooklyn, Mich., on Aug. 16, followed by a 22nd at Bristol, Tenn., a 26th at Darlington, S.C., on Sept. 6 and a 12th at Richmond, Va., on Sept. 13, nine laps off the pace.

The mediocre finishes continued. On Sept. 20, Bobby found himself in seventh, two laps down, followed by an eighth at Martinsville on Sept. 2 and a 17th at North Wilkesboro on Oct. 4.

For the next outing, the Stavola Brothers crew provided a stellar car for activities at Charlotte Motor Speedway. That included a blistering speed as Bobby captured the pole position at 171.636 mph.

Bobby seemed en route to his second victory of the season by leading the event six times for 142 of the 334 laps. But as the checkered flag waved, he was second behind Elliott.

Bad luck returned to the team at North Carolina Motor Speedway in the form of another blown engine after only 135 of 492 laps.

Bobby was able to log top-five finishes in the final two races of the year at Riverside, Calif., on Nov. 8 and at Atlanta on Nov. 22.

Despite a year of mediocre finishes and several blown engines, Bobby managed to earn a ninth-place finish in the final Winston Cup standings.

Many changes were due to take place during the off-season, the biggest of which was a radical alteration in the Stavola Brothers team's colors for the 1988 season.

At times, new paint schemes and crisp new uniforms played a big part in boosting a team's confidence.

Bobby was optimistic. He anticipated good things once the team rolled into Daytona.

He had no way of knowing . . . .

CHAPTER TWENTY-SIX
Racing Together

During a scheduled week in January, those NASCAR Winston Cup teams campaigning the newly redesigned General Motors cars were given track time at Daytona International Speedway for testing.

Both Stavola Brothers race teams were present and each time Bobby and Hillin returned to the garage area for consultations with their respective crews, various adjustments were made.

Bobby and crew chief Fennig were very pleased with their Buick. So much so, there was time for making radical chassis changes and experimenting with some combinations not completely legal in the NASCAR rule book.

Soon, Bobby was driving the sleek new Buick at speeds bordering the 200 mph mark. Additionally, the car felt so good Bobby controlled the steering wheel with two fingers on his left hand.

Upon returning to the garage area, Bobby was asked to take Hillin's Buick out onto the track in hopes of getting the car dialed in, as the team and driver had been struggling with its chassis and could not turn very fast speeds.

Bobby took the car out and ran several laps. According to the stopwatches that clicked on pit road, he managed to surpass the 195 mph mark.

Upon returning to the garage stall, Hillin's crew made its way to the car. It wanted Bobby's thoughts on the mysterious and irritating chassis.

"Well, how was it?" asked a crew member.

Bobby stared at the gauges on the dashboard for a moment and slowly let his eyes meet those of the inquiring crew member.

"Give me a second to let the hair on the back of my neck settle down and I'll let you know," Bobby said. "I've got to tell you. I really admire Bobby Hillin for getting what he has out of this car so far."

After extensive work on Hillin's chassis, the Midland, Tex., driver started the Daytona 500 in ninth in the 42-car field, while Bobby found himself in third behind Ken Schrader and Davey Allison, who were on the front row. Bobby acquired his starting spot by winning the first of two 125-mile qualifiers.

On Saturday, Feb. 13, Bobby was victorious in the Goody's 300 NASCAR Busch Series event using a Piper Aircraft-sponsored car. He was thus tagged as the driver with the most momentum going into the Daytona 500.

The second 125-mile qualifier was won by Darrell Waltrip in a wire-to-wire victory.

Sunday dawned with a crispness in the air, similar to an early spring day. It was a perfect day for racing and one that would treat the race engines kindly.

Before the start, Bobby was interviewed for a national television audience. He was considered the favorite, having won virtually everything thrown at him during the week.

Finally, all drivers were strapped into their cars with window nets in place. Soon the roar of the cars as they rolled off pit road caused 140,000 fans to come to life.

Once the green flag waved over the 500, Bobby shot out into the lead and held it for the first lap and within a few laps, he and Waltrip quickly separated themselves from the others.

But they didn't stay away. Other leaders included Rusty Wallace, Lake Speed, Sterling Marlin, Ken Schrader, Phil Parsons and Harry Gant, just to name a few.

On lap 106, Richard Petty suffered a terrifying crash while exiting turn four.

His Pontiac was clipped by Phil Barkdoll's Chevrolet and as it swapped ends, A.J. Foyt made contact and lifted the car's rear into the air.

Petty barrel rolled several times before coming to rest in the center of the speedway. Only seconds passed before Brett Bodine found himself with nowhere to go — except into the front snout area of Petty's battered machine.

Petty was removed from the scene on a stretcher as everyone in attendance, as well as the national television audience, expected the worst. One noted journalist in the electronic media predicted Petty's career was over.

Surprisingly, he was not seriously injured. He suffered a badly sprained ankle and torn ligaments.

The main hull of Petty's car remained intact, which was a credit to its builder, Jay Hedgecock, a racer himself from High Point, N.C.

The car was later transported on a flatbed truck and used to promote safety at selected seminars on the subject.

Ironically, it was destroyed when a tree fell through a warehouse as Hurricane Hugo hit the Carolinas in September of 1990.

A total of 42 laps was run under caution in the 500 while repairs were made to the catch fence damaged during Petty's accident.

On lap 152, Bobby began to make his move for the front and snatched the lead away from Waltrip on lap 155.

Four laps later, Davey moved into second place and the trio of the Allisons and Waltrip opened up a 4.16-second margin.

On lap 162, Bobby gave way to his son when he pitted for gas and began a stream of green flag stops. Davey followed on lap 164. So did the rest of the leaders save Waltrip, who remained on the track until lap 176 and had built up a 36-second margin on the field. Waltrip spent 10 seconds in his pits getting fuel, foregoing new tires.

Gant brought out the sixth caution flag when he crashed in the second turn. After another series of pit stops, Parsons was the leader, followed by Davey, Waltrip and Bobby.

Before the lap was completed, Bobby had moved into the lead with Davey right behind him. Then, on lap 185, something gave way inside the inner workings of Waltrip's engine and he quickly faded, losing the five-car draft in the process.

Debris on the track brought out the seventh and final caution flag on lap 188. Two laps later, the race resumed with a tight five-car pack consisting of the Allisons, Buddy Baker, Parsons, and Terry Labonte. Waltrip hung on, a distant 11th.

On lap 192, Baker moved into second place in the third turn, but Davey quickly moved alongside him to retake the position. Caught outside the draft, Baker drifted to eighth place.

Just four laps from the finish of the 200-lap event, a 13-car draft was formed with Bobby holding the point. But the final challenge came from Davey. As their two lead cars exited turn four. Davey took the low groove and while he could pull alongside his famous Dad, he simply did not have the horsepower to pass.

As the two Alabama drivers crossed the finish line, Bobby had won his third career Daytona 500 by just two car lengths over Davey. It was the first father-and-son finish in NASCAR competition since Lee and Richard Petty took the two top spots in a 100-mile event at Heidelberg Speedway near Pittsburgh in July 10, 1960.

Davey pulled alongside his Dad on the cool-down lap and offered his congratulations. Bobby signaled to him with his left hand; a wave of one finger which said, "I'm still the master."

After victory lane ceremonies were completed, Davey joined his Dad in the press box for post-race interviews. Both fielded questions while Judy beamed proudly for her two men.

"It was really good to be in front," Bobby said. "It was a great feeling to look back and see somebody you think is the best coming up and know it is your own son. It is a very special feeling and it is hard to put in words."

Davey offered his thoughts. The love and admiration for his father became evident as he spoke.

"I've got mixed emotions," Davey said, concerning the finish. "I had a lot of dreams when I was growing up. And one of them was to be battling my Dad to the wire in a race. The only difference is I wanted to finish first."

When discussing the final lap, Davey offered, "I knew my best bet was to help Dad get away far enough so I could protect second place and make a move if I could. I knew he had been watching how I passed everyone earlier. He knew my car was working really well on the outside, so there was no way he would give up the outside line. That's why he was up there between turns three and four.

"So I tried to fake that I was going high and get under him. I knew if I was successful, the only way I was going to win was by a few inches."

Bobby grabbed the microphone and offered his version.

"I think the reason I went up front as often as I could was my impression my car was the best one left. Darrell was strong, but I felt I was stronger. Then something happened to him and he faded. So my impression was to get the lead and not get hung up with someone in a fairly good car and get the sheet metal bent up.

"I saw the nose of Davey's car out of the corner of my eye, but I thought I had enough suds to beat him."

Davey's stellar finish was somewhat of a miracle, to say the least. During the final practice session for the 500, Davey scraped the wall, causing great damage to his Ranier Racing Ford.

"It was a mess," Davey said, referring to his badly damaged racer. "Among other things, it bent the snout, broke the steering box and crunched in the right-side sheet metal. But the crew is a great bunch of guys who worked late into the night to fix the car. It proves how tough they are and I had complete confidence in the car. I think this proves this team is for real.

"We want to win the championship this year and being second in points to my Dad after the first race is a good way to start out.

"I just wonder what would have happened today if I hadn't wrecked the car."

"Son," quipped Bobby, "there are 29 more races this year to find out."

On Feb. 21, the tour moved to Richmond, Va., for the second event of the year. Both Bobby and Davey were clearly the sentimental favorites, as their close finish in the most prestigious event of the year was still fresh on everyone's mind.

But Bobby's Buick could only muster an 11th-place finish, one lap down to eventual winner Neil Bonnett, who made only his second start since his bone-crushing accident at Charlotte Motor Speedway the past October.

Davey crashed his Ford early in the going and only completed 276 of the 400 laps scheduled.

It was the last event held at the old 0.542-mile Richmond Fairgrounds Raceway. By the time the tour returned in the fall, a new 0.75-mile, D-shaped track would be constructed.

Bonnett's strength continued to surface at North Carolina Motor Speedway in Rockingham, N.C. on March 6. Coming from deep within the field, the Bessemer, Ala., driver steadily progressed and first led the 500-mile event on lap 122.

Both Bobby and Davey found themselves struggling to finish 22nd and ninth, respectively. Both were many laps down at the finish.

At Atlanta on March 20, Bobby posted another 11th place finish, but Davey didn't fare as well.

As Alan Kulwicki's engine blew on lap 29 of the 328-lap race, Davey's Ford was positioned directly behind it, and after slipping in his oil, plowed into the first turn wall. Eventually, he finished 40th in the 42-car field.

Davey's stock took a jump with a third-place finish at

Darlington, S.C., on March 27, as he was in the same lap with fellow race leaders Kulwicki and winner Lake Speed.

Bobby finished in ninth, two laps off the pace. For him, such finishes continued, each just a tick off the performances of the winners.

There was a fifth-place finish at Bristol, Tenn., on April 10, followed by a 20th at North Wilkesboro, N.C., and an eighth at Martinsville, Va.

Davey's record of finish for the three events were 29th, eighth and sixth, respectively, all off the lead lap.

But once back on a superspeedway, Bobby qualified his Buick in second at Alabama International Motor Speedway on May 1.

Phil Parsons held the lead the final 14 laps to record his first-ever victory. Throughout each lap, Bobby was on his bumper but did not possess the necessary strength to get around him.

Davey suffered another blown engine and was forced to settle for a 34th-place finish.

After being involved in a crash at Charlotte Motor Speedway on May 29, Bobby could salvage only a 17th in the final order.

Davey, however, fared better and finished fifth.

The finish was repeated for Davey at Dover, Del., on June 5, while Bobby settled for 10th.

At Riverside, Calif., both Allisons suffered problems, but each finished. At the checkered flag, Davey was 32nd but his father had improved that by 10 positions.

It would be the last race in which both Allisons would return together to the garage area.

A week later, the Winston Cup tour moved to Pocono International Raceway.

It would be the site of Bobby's worst racing accident.

CHAPTER TWENTY-SEVEN
The Recovery And Beyond

Judy Allison stood quietly for a moment, allowing the words spoken by Dr. Stevens to sink in.

"Very grave?" Judy asked again.

"I've examined him very closely," Dr. Stevens said. "He has a broken right shoulder blade, fractured ribs, a severely broken left leg and internal injuries. It's also my belief he has a brain injury. There is pressure building on his brain which at this point is lethal. We must drill a hole in his skull to relieve that pressure. If we don't do something right now, he could suffer permanent brain damage or worse."

Judy put her face in her hands and began to cry for a few moments. Her mind drifted back to the Daytona 500 five months before and thought of all the glory her husband enjoyed. It was as if a wonderful dream had come to life. But as she opened her eyes, the reality of her surroundings struck.

Judy rose from her seat and walked over to Dave and Millie Demerest, Bobby's cousins who had attended the race.

"Dave, what should I do?" Judy asked.

"Judy, you're the only one who can make that decision," Dave said. "No one can answer that but you."

Judy then turned to Ed Gossage, the public relations representative for Bobby's team sponsor, Miller Brewing Co., who had just arrived from the track. The question was posed to him as well.

"I agree with Dave," Gossage said. "It's not my decision to make, either. But maybe you should listen to the doctor."

After a brief moment of silence, Judy turned to Dr. Stevens with her decision.

"I know he wouldn't want to live if he had to be a vegetable," Judy said. "I feel like this is something we need to do. Where are the papers? I'll sign them."

Dr. Stevens flipped the silver clipboard open and produced an ink pen from his pocket. Quickly, all the places marked with an "X" had been scribbled upon.

As Dr. Stevens turned to leave, he said, "I will do everything I can to bring your husband back the way he was."

Immediately after Judy secured the necessary paperwork, preparations for surgery began.

While Dr. Stevens and his assistants scrubbed for surgery, the area on Bobby's head where the drilling would take place was shaved clean. Initially, Bobby's heart and blood pressure ratings on the monitors were satisfactory. Once Dr. Stevens felt comfortable with those readings, drilling at the rear of his skull was performed and an external tube was inserted for drainage.

Near the end of the procedure, the monitors began to dance and Bobby was in trouble, as his heart rate and blood pressure took a nose dive.

Soon, the monitors displayed a straight line. There was no activity.

Dr. Stevens hit Bobby's chest hard with his fist and began CPR. Although Bobby's life seemed lost, Dr. Stevens did not give up hope.

"Listen here you old son-of-a-bitch," Stevens said, "you've got to make it cause you've got to make both of us look good."

Work continued and soon, the monitor activity resumed, increased and stabilized once again.

Dr. Stevens met the family in a waiting room just outside of the Intensive Care Unit.

Meanwhile, Davey arrived at the hospital. Upon seeing his mother, he embraced her and the two walked back into the waiting room to have some time alone. Davey's emotional state seemed to be a mixture of calm and turmoil, almost to the extremes of each. But that was understandable. His father was critically injured and there was nothing he could do to help him — aside from praying God would ease the pain of his injuries.

Soon, members of Bobby's race team came by as well as others in the racing community, including team public relations representative Tom Roberts and his wife Joannie. They had helped with the

sponsorship responsibilities at the track. Once the victory lane celebration with race winner Geoff Bodine concluded, however, Roberts
elected to go to the hospital to assist Gossage in handling the rush of
reporters and fans searching out information on Bobby's condition.

Judy, Davey, the Demerests, Gossage, and the Robertses were
moved to a waiting room outside the Intensive Care Unit, where
Bobby was taken after a brief stay in recovery after surgery.

Once secured in ICU, his severely broken left leg was placed in
traction and tubes were placed down his throat for feeding and medication purposes. A neck brace was also in place for precautionary
measures, along with a breathing apparatus strapped over his nos-
trils.

On occasion, Davey would move around the floor but with that,
another problem developed. Each time the elevator doors would open,
fans wearing T-shirts bearing the Allison name would be inside, each
looking for Davey or some other members of the family. Finally,
Gossage was forced to hide the younger Allison in a small private
waiting room.

Nine hours after the accident, many rumors were beginning to
surface all over the country. Some reports that were broadcast
announced he had died of the injuries received in the crash.

Hospital security called and informed Gossage there were six
remote TV satellite trucks in the parking lot ready to set up to broadcast information back to their respective stations.

Basic stand-ups were being done with information already
known for hours.

There was an early attempt to give information to the media but
it failed miserably. Just minutes after arriving at the hospital,
Gossage talked Judy into issuing a statement on her husband's condition.

After drafting the quarter-page statement, Gossage called the
number he had gotten off the phone in the press box and a reporter
answered. After reading the statement over the phone, the reporter
said, "We can't use this. There's nothing there."

The statement listed injuries as a broken leg and fractured ribs,
but said nothing about the head trauma.

Later, it was discovered the paper on which the reporter recorded Gossage's statement was thrown in a nearby trash can and never
shown to anyone.

The track had issued its own statement about Bobby's injuries,
some of which were totally false.

"This stuff really bugs me," Davey said to Gossage. "Dad doesn't have a bruised heart, but everyone is reporting he does. You've got to fix it. Everybody at home says you're not telling them the truth."

"Davey, we issued a statement and gave it to the track but it wasn't used," Gossage said. "I can't retract what somebody else writes."

The two men became quite irritated with one another and a shouting match ensued. But later on, Davey apologized and said, "you can't control what they write or what they broadcast."

"Davey, there's all kinds of rumors floating around," Gossage said. "You need to talk to your Mom and determine the best way to handle them. My advice is to tell the truth."

"I'll talk to Mom about that in the morning and we'll decide something," Davey said.

As the hour approached 10:30 p.m., Judy, Gossage and Roberts decided to talk about the race team and how to help it continue. There were contractual obligations concerning sponsorships that had to be met, as well as commitments to the Winner's Circle program, which required a team to run all the races in order to receive the bonus money from NASCAR.

Almost immediately into the conversation, the name Mike Alexander surfaced as a possible replacement driver while Bobby was recovering from his injuries. If Bobby were able to once again drive a race car, it would happen quite some time in the future.

By midnight, Gossage and Roberts elected to return to their hotel rooms in nearby Scranton, Pa., while Judy, Davey and Millie Demerest chose to stay at the hospital. Davey chose a small waiting room while Judy and Mrs. Demerest shared a conference room nearby. Before turning in, Judy discussed her husband's condition with a very pleasant nurse who had just come on duty.

"If Bobby wakes up and sees these tubes, he might think things are really bad and start ripping them out," Judy said. "I just want to make you aware he might try that."

"I understand," said the nurse. "I'll be aware of that and check on him."

At approximately 4 a.m. on June 20, Davey jumped up from his makeshift bed on the sofa in the waiting room and walked into the hallway. Once there, he met his mother but the two had not communicated since just after midnight.

"Did you get the same feeling I got?" Davey asked his mother.

"Yes," Judy responded.

"Do you want to see Dad?" Davey asked.

"Yes."

At that moment, the pretty young nurse came down the hallway to check on her special patient.

As the three entered the room, they could not believe their eyes. Bobby had flipped himself over face down in the bed and the breather hose was on the floor.

But his left leg continued to be in traction, even though a great strain was placed upon it because he was nearly on his stomach.

Later that morning, Davey met with Gossage to talk about how to handle the news media.

It was decided the hospital could only give conditions. Each morning, Gossage and Judy would meet to discuss the situation. The news media would not be told for three to five days, a move to keep false stories saying Bobby had taken a "turn for the worst."

Finally, Gossage faced the media and tried to field as many questions as possible. This was eventually done on a daily basis.

The generosity of Stuart Millar, owner of Piper Aircraft, was outstanding. He allowed the use of his Piper Cheyenne 400 to transport family members to and from Alabama to visit Bobby.

By Thursday, June 23, Davey had stayed at the hospital until the very last minute before it was time to fly to Michigan International Speedway for qualifying for the next race. It was tough on Davey to leave, but obligations had to be met. Even though he had not spoken to him, Davey knew that was what his father would want him to do — take care of the job at hand.

While en route to MIS, several drivers stopped by the hospital to visit — such as Dale Earnhardt, Rusty Wallace, Richard Petty and Buddy Baker, to name a few. Each offered words of encouragement to Bobby and those family members who had been continuously by his side.

During visits from others, Bobby would wear a racing cap to help promote a more normal look since the shaved area where the external tube was inserted was highly visible.

Later that afternoon, a television and VCR were wheeled into the room on a cart and placed where Bobby could get a good view.

The husband of a nurse who worked in the ICU unit had taped the crash off his satellite dish and offered it to Dr. Stevens for review.

Dr. Stevens played the tape and for a few moments Bobby watched intently. But soon, his attention drifted away. The tape was played again and again, but Bobby acted uninterested.

The next day, Judy gave Bobby some news.

"They've decided to put Mike Alexander in the car at Michigan this coming weekend," Judy said.

With that, Bobby quickly jerked his body into a knot — with the leg still in traction — using his right arm and leg as if he were trying to protect himself from being harmed.

Judy stood in amazement and quickly contacted Dr. Stevens with the news.

After a brief discussion, both Judy and Dr. Stevens were convinced Bobby was not unhappy with the team's decision on a driver, but rather, he was reacting to the bone-crushing accident he had suffered. Judy's words seemed to trigger something.

By Saturday, June 25, Bobby began to recognize family and friends and communicate with hand signals, as tubes that remained down his throat did not allow him to speak.

Using his right hand, Bobby would hold up one finger for "yes" and two fingers for "no."

On Sunday, June 26, the Winston Cup circuit staged its first race since Pocono at Michigan International Speedway.

In an effort to familiarize Bobby with stock car racing, a television was moved back into his hospital room so he could watch the race. On the rear of Michael Waltrip's Pontiac were the words "Hurry Back Bobby" in large red letters. Buttons with the same message were also distributed throughout the garage area to show support for a longtime friend.

Davey qualified the Ranier Racing Ford in third position and by the 22nd circuit, he had gained the lead. He held the point for a total of 44 laps. To that, Bobby managed a smile through the tubes between his lips.

But on lap 70, Davey's engine expired and gave him a 35th-place finish. Once Bobby saw his son's black and white machine roll slowly into the garage area, the smile turned to a sort of pout with his bottom lip.

Alexander wheeled Bobby's Buick to a 10th-place finish, one lap off the pace to winner Rusty Wallace.

Four days later, Bobby underwent four hours of surgery to repair fractures of the left leg. He suffered a broken fibia, a broken tibia and a severely broken femur, the worst of the three.

In order to repair those fractures, doctors inserted a steel rod through the bones.

Also, the external tube inserted the night of the accident was replaced with a ventriculoperitoneal tube which was capable of draining fluid from his skull into his abdominal cavity. The fluid would then be absorbed by his body.

Bobby often faded in and out of consciousness after the surgery, partly due to being sedated to ease the pain of the broken leg.

By July 1, doctors elected to remove the tubes Bobby had been forced to tolerate for weeks. They also removed the IVs. He was soon able to eat solid foods, such as spaghetti noodles.

There were times when Bobby would talk with Judy. They would have good conversations. But it all depended on how well his schedule of X-rays, optical, vocal and breathing therapy went.

It was a time when Bobby was seemingly having to start over. He was having to learn how to talk and manage, almost like a child. But it was Judy's strong faith in him as well as her religious strength which allowed her to help him tirelessly.

On July 4, Judy pushed Bobby around the Lehigh Valley Medical Center in a wheelchair. It was the first time he had been able to leave his room since the accident.

On July 14, the same day he was removed from the pain-killing morphine, Bobby began physical therapy. Still, because of the strong doses of medication, he would continue to drift in and out of consciousness from time to time.

During his first physical therapy session, Bobby was strapped to a tilt table, which enables a patient to become aware of motion and gravity. The first reading was at 80 degrees, the second at 85 degrees and third on July 18 at 50 degrees, which offers a sense of being upright.

On Tuesday, July 19, Bobby was able to stand in a stooped position with the use of parallel bars. By July 20, he was nearly standing and afterward, he showed his greatest sign of improvement by asking for a "barley pop" — a Miller beer. By July 21, he was standing.

Throughout the early physical therapy, Bobby continued to wear the neck brace and the open-air cast on his left leg.

There were a couple of distinguished visitors who dropped by to give Bobby their respects. They were actor Paul Newman and Indy Car driver Mario Andretti.

"Now listen, here, Bobby," Andretti said, "I know you are a strong person and you can overcome this. You can't give up. You've got to keep working at it."

Andretti's hour-long visit was a pep talk for Bobby. The two had been friends since the year Andretti won the Daytona 500 while driving for Holman-Moody. Later that year, Bobby also drove cars for the organization under the direction of former driver Fred Lorenzen.

There was another highly respected friend who dropped by as well. He was Rags Carter, a Modified driver who campaigned at all of the South Florida tracks long before Bobby began his Winston Cup racing career. Every day, he would check to see if Judy had everything she needed.

The progress continued for 30 days and was the basis for Bobby's condition being upgraded from guarded to satisfactory.

On Aug. 21, Bobby sat quietly in his wheelchair at the door of his room at Lehigh Medical Center. Finally, 62 days after being admitted in grave condition and clinging to life, the decision was made: He was going home to Alabama.

There were many well-wishes from those doctors and nurses who worked at the hospital. Several gave handshakes, others offered hugs and still others shed tears. Not only was he a patient; he had become a member of their family. His leaving was an example that a miracle had been performed. Bobby promised each one he would be back to visit.

The same day, Davey won his first race of the year in the second event of the season at Michigan International Speedway.

Davey grabbed the lead 23 laps from the finish and held the point for the win over Rusty Wallace.

"It was a long time coming, but I knew we were going to win," Davey said. "I want to dedicate this win to my Dad — and all the working people who support Winston Cup racing in the United States. This race is for them."

It had been decided that the day for Bobby's departure from the hospital should be the same as a race, to allow the least amount of publicity possible. It came on the same day as the year's second race at Talladega, where the reporters congregated. During the broadcast of the 500-mile event at the 2.66-mile speedway, however, Ken Squier announced the good news to a national television audience.

Bobby was moved to Lakeshore Rehabilitation Hospital in Birmingham, Ala., and would continue physical therapy at the Birmingham Police Academy.

Three weeks after being admitted to Lakeshore, Bobby awoke one morning very unsure of his surroundings.

When he opened his eyes, he was staring up at the ceiling. But the room was strange and totally foreign to him.

"When they brought me home I was conscious but I still wasn't all there. I woke up saying to myself, 'Where am I and what has gone wrong?' But more than anything, I'm saying to myself, 'Why do I hurt so bad?'

"I was laying there in bed trying to get my bearings but I had no idea which city I was in or what year it was or nothing. I didn't have a clue on any of those points.

"I somehow knew that I was a race car driver, and I knew Judy was my wife and my best friend. I was confident that she was there somewhere in the building with me, but not in the room at the time.

"I laid there in bed wondering where I was and why I was hurting so bad. I moved over to the edge of the bed and I worked my way out through the two side rails that are on a lot of hospital beds. I got to where I could get the right foot down on the floor and then my left foot on the floor. But when I went to put my weight down, my broken left leg gave way and down on the floor I fell.

"I thought to myself, 'Man, I can't let anyone know this went on. I've got to get back in that bed and figure out where I am.' Then I started thinking, 'Someone I don't know has got me here against my wishes. They've got Judy fooled and they broke my leg to keep me here.'

"Looking back on it today, I can't help but get a chuckle or two out of the deal. But at the time, it was incredibly bad.

"I worked my way out of the bed again and I saw this little dresser by the bed. I decided I'd just hold on to that and slide out because I've got this broken leg. I reached out for the little dresser and discovered it was on wheels. Down I went again.

"I just decided to heck with it at that point. I was laying there on that floor and said to myself, 'They got me here — they can come and pick me up. So I stared hollering for help.

"I found out weeks later that there was closed-circuit TV and the nurses were watching me because the bed had an alarm that went off when I got out of it."

His long-awaited release from Lakeshore came in October of 1988. But while there, Bobby noticed some of his acquaintances — some in much worse condition than he — were getting better, so he reasoned to himself he was getting better as well.

But there came a period where Bobby felt himself not wanting to do anything — no racing, no flying, no fishing, nothing. He continually wished the world would go away, but it wouldn't.

Bobby would watch television but nothing could hold his interest except stock car racing. He could watch a race from start to finish.

It was the only type of program that would keep his mind focused.

He worked hard to recall incidents in his life, such as winning the Daytona 500 with Davey finishing second. For hours, Bobby would sit in front of the TV with remote control in hand; the videotape of the race rolling. But the exercise proved frustrating, often causing him to turn it off in disgust.

Then, at the suggestion of Dr. Stevens, Bobby went back to Pocono International Raceway and stood looking at the area of the track where the crash occurred. Still, the memory of that race didn't come to mind, except for a very small part of that day.

"The only thing that comes to mind about that day was the drivers' meeting before the race. Darrell Waltrip had spun me out the week before at Riverside and that really didn't set very well with me.

"I remember Dick Beaty (NASCAR Winston Cup Director) asking if there were any questions just before the meeting concluded. I stood up and said, 'Hey Dick, what happens if some asshole spins you out?'

"At that point, Michael Waltrip stood up and said, 'I'm not the asshole, I'm just his brother!'

"That's all I remember about that day at Pocono."

On Jan. 31, 1989, Bobby made an appearance at a dinner banquet in his honor at the Charlotte Motor Speedway.

"An Evening With Bobby Allison And Friends" offered Speedway Club members and guests cocktails and dinner along with highlights of Bobby's career, testimonials from speakers and an opportunity to meet Judy.

Squire was the master of ceremonies. Speakers included retired Air Force General Tom Sadler of Butler Aviation, Gossage, Charlotte Observer motorsports writer Tom Higgins, NASCAR Vice President of Administration Jim Hunter and CMS President H.A. "Humpy" Wheeler.

Soon, Bobby slowly entered the large banquet room on the fifth floor of the speedway's Smith Tower. Some applauded, while others simply sat in awe of their hero and friend.

His steps were slow and calculated, limping slightly from the discomfort of steel pins in his leg. His balance was controlled at times by a steady hand on the back of a chair or table. His eyes searched helplessly over some of the faces for clues in hopes of remembering areas of his past that simply wouldn't come forth.

After Bobby found his place at center stage, the keynote speakers told of times past, to the laughs of a full house. Finally, it was time for Bobby to stand before the microphone. But a standing ovation halted his words for at least five minutes.

"I still hurt and I'm out of balance a lot of the time due to the head injury," Bobby said. "But I do whatever it takes to make progress.

"I've been working out five days a week at the Birmingham Police Academy Fitness Training Center, trying to get my strength back. Everyone has come to me and said, 'Hey, you look great.' I wish I felt as great as I look.

"I've been told I won the Daytona 500 last season, but I can't recall that I did. Some things I do remember, but there are many things that I do not."

Bobby thanked those in attendance for their expressions of love and their prayers for his safekeeping. With that, he bid everyone good night, again to a standing ovation.

Before the evening concluded, Bobby was presented an original portrait of himself painted by motorsports artist Sam Bass, while Judy was presented with a piece of crystal from CMS.

On Feb. 2, Bobby returned to Lehigh Valley Medical Center for surgery to remove the four rods placed in his left leg in June. While there, the shunt that was placed in his head for drainage of fluid into the stomach was also removed.

He was scheduled to be released from Lehigh on Feb. 7, but the actual release date was Feb. 17. Doctors felt due to extreme nausea and dizziness, the shunt had to be re-installed.

His release date was just in time to watch the 1989 Daytona 500 on television. Once secure at home, he carefully slipped into his easy chair.

Six months passed.

Bobby continued to improve although at times, it seemed to be at a very slow pace. Medications were prescribed to combat the nausea and dizziness which still existed, even with the shunt.

Over that period of time, Bobby's personality had changed a bit as well, but that was not uncommon. Head injuries often did that to people.

More evident than before was a humbleness. He became more of an emotional person; one whose self-confidence had dwindled.

"I'm somewhat more emotional than I was. I have gone through a period where it was really easy for me to cry, where I laughed at things quickly and easily. Some of these were not having the emotional control I thought I always had.

"Head injuries are hard to forecast for anybody. Different people respond in different fashion or amount. One thing that seems to be a common thing is people in good physical condition normally do the most amount of recovery."

Bobby found himself struggling to do what was once second nature — such as working around airplanes.

Often, he would ride down to his hangar at the airport in Bessemer, unlock the door, look in, close the door back, make sure the door was locked and leave.

Later, he was able to go from looking at planes to actually flying them again. It was a major accomplishment.

Bobby's interest in racing never wavered.

Through conversation with a friend, Don Hackworth, who had been the general manager of Buick Division through the middle 1980s and had remained close, Bobby was introduced to Bob Bilby, an entrepreneur with interests among Detroit's automakers. While in Brooklyn, Mich., for the Winston Cup event on Aug. 20, 1989, Bobby and Bilby met in John LaFere's motorhome in the paddock area at MIS. While there, a deal was struck to form a race team for the 1990 season.

It would be a team with equipment coming from both initial partners. Bobby would lend items from his Hueytown shop while Bilby would offer the Chevrolets he had purchased from Junior Johnson when the Ingles Hollow, N.C., car owner switched his operation to Fords.

Two other partners, Nathan Sims and Frank Plessinger, also entered the fold, adding stability to the team.

The Stavola Brothers, for whom Bobby drove when his crash occurred, elected to return to a one-car team for 1990 thus opening the door for Bobby to hire all his old crew.

Alexander, who had substituted for Bobby at Stavola Racing, was hired as the team's driver.

Initially, the team rented space out of the shops owned by Norman Negre, who's facility was just north of Charlotte near Salisbury, N.C. By May, the team's permanent shop was finished in an industrial park near Charlotte Motor Speedway.

In April, Alexander resigned, saying he hadn't sufficiently recovered from his own head injuries suffered in a crash during a non-NASCAR event in Florida in December of 1989.

Jeff Purvis was hired to run one race and was then replaced by Hut Stricklin.

As the 1992 Winston Cup season began, Bobby found himself

working more and more with Clifford's racing career.

Their youngest son began racing in 1983 and entered various racing divisions, such as the Busch Grand National Series, ARCA, the All-Pro Series and other stock car circuits over the previous eight years.

Older brother Davey had so much confidence in Clifford's ability to turn wrenches on a race car he hired him as his crew chief in ARCA competition in 1984 and 1985, which contributed heavily to Davey's winning the Rookie of the Year honors in '85.

In November, Judy purchased a 1991 Buick Regal from Bobby Allison Motorsports, as the team was switching to Chevrolets. Clifford ran the Buick in the ARCA race in Atlanta in November 1991 and then began to prepare it for the ARCA race at Daytona in February of 1992.

Going into Speed Weeks, Clifford joined car owner Barry Owen for select Busch Series events.

On April 1, 1992, Bobby was informed of the death of his father, Edmond Jacob "Pop" Allison who had battled cancer for eight months. He had been well known throughout the racing community and everyone shared the loss.

On the afternoon of Aug. 12, Bobby, Judy, Clifford and his wife Elisa left for Brooklyn, Mich., for the Busch Series race there.

While in Michigan, the family stayed at a lakefront home on Clark Lake, courtesy of the LaFere family.

Both Bobby and Clifford hoped they would have the time to toss a fishing hook in the water while there. Still, it was a perfect place to relax and enjoy the beauty of the Irish Hills.

That night, Clifford and Elisa went down to the dock and fished as they had done in the past when time permitted.

Once at MIS on Aug. 13, Clifford stood in the garage area, routinely talking with Owen and Reds Kagle about chassis setups and different ways to make the car perform better.

With all preparations complete, Clifford slipped behind the wheel of the newly renovated Chevrolet Lumina that had once been an Oldsmobile Cutlass. He placed a two-way radio plug into each ear and placed the open-faced helmet over his head. With a quick tug of the chin strap, it was secure.

The practice session was going well.

Bobby expressed a last-minute thought or two at the driver's window and received a slight nod of the head from his son.

"We're gaining on 'em Dad," Clifford said with a smile. "We're gonna get 'em."

Bobby smiled and returned to a standing position. As he did, his son backed out of the garage stall and roared through the garage area toward the race track.

He made the first lap and his time was his quickest of the session at that point.

Both Bobby and Owen were standing in the garage area timing Clifford with a stop watch.

Owen said, "He just crashed."

"What?" Bobby said.

"He just crashed," Owen returned in a disappointed tone.

At that moment, the ambulance and safety truck whizzed by, going down pit road. But they were going straight to turn four as opposed to circling the track. That was an early indication to Bobby that something was wrong.

"Is he talking to you?" Bobby asked Owen.

"Clifford, do you read me? . . . Clifford can you hear me?" Owen quickly asked over the two-way radio headset he was wearing.

Bobby walked out of the garage area at a quick pace and once he reached pit road he saw Clifford's car. He was stopped by a NASCAR official.

"They don't want you up there," the official said.

"I'm going to go," Bobby said. "I'm his father and I want to be there."

A couple of minutes passed while the NASCAR official walked with Bobby to the wrecked car.

As Bobby stepped close to the right side of the car, he could see his son's helmet and driver's uniform. His body was slumped to the right and he was not moving.

Gary Nelson, technical director for NASCAR, was halfway through the driver's side window loosening the safety belts when Bobby arrived on the scene.

A safety worker stopped him and told him he couldn't go any closer.

"I will not get in anybody's way," Bobby said.

Allowed to move closer, Bobby walked to the front of the car and looked in through the windshield.

He could see his son was dead.

At that moment, he turned to catch Elisa, who had scaled two chain link fences to get to the race car.

"Is he talking?" Elisa asked.

"No," Bobby replied.

"Is he breathing?" she asked.

"I don't know for sure."

The roof was cut off the car for easier access in extracting Clifford out of the wreckage. Once out of the car, his helmet was removed and he was laid on a stretcher.

The ambulance rolled away at a steady pace. NASCAR official Les Richter and MIS vice president and general manager Gene Haskett were en route to the crash site by way of service road in the infield area when they met Bobby as he walked back to the garage area. He could see great concern on their faces.

"Get in the car," Haskett said to Bobby. "They're taking him to Foote Hospital."

Bobby thought they were referring to the infield hospital. With that, Haskett drafted an employee to drive the car. As they started to leave the vicinity, Bobby saw Tim Reese, a friend of Kagle and Clifford's, walking away. He said to him, "Get in the car with us."

As the driver turned into the Winston Cup garage area, Bobby could see the infield hospital was closed. He noticed the driver had accelerated to a speed that would not allow him to stop there. With that, Bobby concluded they were going to some major hospital nearby.

The destination was W. A. Foote Memorial Hospital in Jackson, Mich., located some 10 miles away.

Upon his arrival, Clifford was immediately taken into the emergency room trauma area.

Bobby, along with friends and other family members, gathered in a small waiting room located just off of the emergency room. It was there Bobby was informed that all efforts had been made to save his son. But the actions of the medical staff were in vain.

The doctor extended the opportunity for Bobby to spend a few moments alone with Clifford.

When Bobby entered the room, he prayed God would give him the necessary strength to say goodbye to his son one last time. As he stood over him, he thought of the love and admiration he felt for Clifford and the closeness they had recently shared. Through many trips around the country, their friendship had grown to its greatest level.

But in the blink of an eye, his son was gone and only memories remained.

Soon, the family returned to Hueytown by private plane.

Arrangements were also made to transport Clifford's body home as well.

"One reason I was spending less and less time there (with his Winston Cup team in Charlotte, N.C.) was because I was really getting a lot of enjoyment out of Clifford and he was helping me to recover.

"I still don't want to give him up. But it (crash) happened. I feel like he got to heaven and that helps, but I really miss him . . . and that smile."

"I felt that just the idea that some success was being achieved helped me not to hurt quite as bad as I did when I woke up in the morning. I woke up looking at doing something or seeing what could be done on that given day. But that deal went away. And that was probably my best excuse for being away from Charlotte. There are other excuses, but I'm sure that's my best excuse.

"I'm not looking at 1993, I'm looking at Monday and Tuesday and Wednesday and Thursday and Friday and Saturday and Sunday. It's a day at a time."

Considering what he's been through it wouldn't be hard to think Allison might feel some bitterness toward the sport which brought so much fame and prosperity to him over the years. But driving race cars has been his first love over any other career choice and there are many positive memories concerning the sport.

"Racing is still a really straightforward activity. Dangerous, certainly. But pick up today's Charlotte news and there will be a column about someone that got killed on one of the highways over the weekend. If you really look through the paper you may see someone killed at a job site somewhere or maybe in his swimming pool or the river.

"I feel so bad about that and hate to even have to justify racing by saying someone could have gotten killed somewhere else. My son could have gotten killed somewhere else. But if somebody could give me a written guarantee that you could live your life in complete happiness and never have to worry about any illness or injury or accidental death, as long as you didn't race, then I would say, OK, we shouldn't race."

Even with all that has happened, Allison manages a smile from time to time and continues to brighten the days of others with his charming wit and sense of humor.

But still, there are days when the 55-year-old native of Miami, Fla., feels great sadness concerning the circumstances around him.

"I went and talked to some key people including one doctor who has really been a help to me," Allison said. *"I asked him why I*

shouldn't just go to 'Two Bit', Miss., and get a cabin and never come to the race track or never see anymore of the heartbreak and failure.

"They convinced me that that's just not how the world is. They say I can't recover any better someplace in hiding than if I get myself back to work. So I'm trying one more time to get myself back to work.

"I go through periods of saying I wish it (son's death) didn't happen or saying I wish things had gone well. Then I say I'm like all human beings and have done enough wrong that I have no argument I shouldn't have to suffer. But why can't my suffering not include other people?

"I'm Catholic and I'm not as good a Catholic as I'd like to be. But I do try hard. I can say that through my faith that I feel I deserve more than what's happened, but I just really hope and pray that it doesn't include other people again."

"But the best way to conclude the story would be to say I've had a career that has had highs as wonderful as winning the Winston Cup championship. Unfortunately, it has had lows as low as losing a son."

"Still, I've been blessed with the ability to do what I've wanted to do in life. And as a result of that, many wonderful friendships have been produced from it.

"Even though I've suffered from physical and mental pain along the way, I consider myself one of the luckiest people in the world."

EPILOGUE

During the months following Clifford's death, Bobby worked more closely with his Winston Cup race team on a day to day basis.

On Sept. 3, 1992, Hut Stricklin, set to drive for Junior Johnson and Associates in 1993, was released as the team's driver just after the completion of the Southern 500 at Darlington (S.C.) Raceway.

Upon his release, Jeff Purvis was hired to replace Stricklin for races held at Richmond, Va., on Sept. 12; North Wilkesboro, N.C., on Sept. 20; Martinsville, Va., on Sept. 28; and North Wilkesboro, N.C., on Oct. 5. His best finish, a 22nd, came at Richmond.

Jimmy Spencer replaced Purvis in the team's Chevrolets at Charlotte Motor Speedway on Oct. 11, where he recorded a strong fourth-place finish. Performances at Rockingham, N.C., Phoenix, Ariz., and Hampton, Ga., produced 11th-, fifth- and fourth-place finishes, respectively, to close out the season.

As of this writing, Bobby continues the search for sponsorship for the 1993 Daytona 500—and beyond.